FIGURES of SPEECH

FIGURES of SPEECH

———

American Writers and the Literary Marketplace,

from Benjamin Franklin to Emily Dickinson

———

R. JACKSON WILSON

The Johns Hopkins University Press

Baltimore

Copyright © 1989 by R. Jackson Wilson
All rights reserved
Printed in the United States of America

Originally published in 1987 as a Borzoi Book by Alfred A.
Knopf, Inc.
Johns Hopkins Paperbacks edition, 1990, published by
arrangement with Alfred A. Knopf, Inc.

The Johns Hopkins University Press
701 West 40th Street, Baltimore, Maryland 21211

Library of Congress Cataloging-in-Publication Data
Wilson, Raymond Jackson.
Figures of speech: American writers and the literary market-
place, from Benjamin Franklin to Emily Dickinson /
R. Jackson Wilson. p.   cm.
"Originally published in 1987 as a Borzoi book"—CIP t.p.
verso.
Includes bibliographical references.
ISBN 0-8018-4003-1
1. American literature—19th century—History and criticism.
2. Authors and publishers—United States—History.   3. Lit-
erature publishing—United States—History.   4. Authors and
readers—United States—History.   5. Books and reading—
United States—History.   6. Franklin, Benjamin, 1706–1790
—Authorship.   I. Title.
PS201.W48   1990   810.9'003—DC20   89-27564   CIP

Page 297 constitutes a continuation of the copyright page.

For Emilia

I will be flesh and blood.
For there was never yet philosopher
That could endure the tooth ache patiently,
However they have writ the style of gods
And made a pish at chance and sufferance.

Much Ado about Nothing, V. i.

CONTENTS

ILLUSTRATIONS

———

PREFACE

Books have a number of characteristic markings that make them appear to be separate and discrete proprietary entities. They are contracted for, copyrighted, and offered up for sale. Titles are attached to them, as to real estate and other property. They are routinely called by their authors' names, in the possessive, as in "Dickens' *Great Expectations*." Their physical casings, their covers and jackets, are like boundary signs, declarations of uniqueness and separation. And all these markings help obscure the fact that every book is very much a social product, the outcome of a complicated process of learning, imitation, borrowing, and outright appropriation. In a proper world, there would be no copyrights. In our improper world, though, there are only prefaces where at least some of the people who participated in the making of a book can be named and given the most glancing and inadequate kind of thanks.

Anyone who works on the history of writers and writing in the nineteenth century owes a particularly large debt to two historians. William Charvat's books and essays, and especially his *Literary Publishing in America, 1790–1850* and *The Profession of Authorship in America, 1800–1870*, are the points of entry to the field. And implicit on every page of this book are some of the ideas of the intellectual that everyone interested in the history of English and American culture must think of as the Master, Raymond Williams. Of his great effort, three books have had a special salience for me: *The Long Revolution, Culture and Society, 1780–1950,* and *Keywords: A Vocabulary of Culture and Society.*

I have worked for many years under the influence of a group of remarkable people who clustered in the late 1950s and early 1960s around two equally remarkable teachers at the University of Wisconsin, Merle Curti and William R. Taylor. David Allmendinger, Paul Bourke, Neil Coughlan, Jim Gilbert, Steve Nissenbaum, and Donald Scott have continued for many years to be the presumed audience for every new notion that strikes me. They have no idea, surely, how many thoughts I have abandoned because I was sure they would not be able to approve. Some have worked more closely with me than others. Certain accidents of personal history have led to Paul Bourke's having had a particularly emphatic influence on this book, even on its details. And Steve Nissenbaum has been a constant source of good will, clarity, and some extraordinarily smart ideas. But it is difficult to imagine having written anything at all without the implicit collaboration of all of these colleagues and their great teachers.

Over the years, I have learned more than I can say from the three most brilliant students I ever have taught, Charles Clyde Bowden, Dan Singal, and Peter Buckley. John Lax and William Pencak were never my students, properly speaking. But they made my intellectual world a good deal brighter than it would otherwise have been. A generation of students at Smith College has sat patiently through my attempts to make sense out of the way that intellectuals in America have gone about their work. The Connecticut Valley has given me the uncommon luxury of spirited exchanges with the likes of Paul Seton, Eric Reeves, Leo Weinstein, John William Ward, Leo Marx, Robert Gross, and Joe Ellis. Bernard Bailyn was generous enough to read and comment on my chapter on Benjamin Franklin. Maynard Mack graciously did the same for the chapter on Washington Irving. I profited as well from the advice of David Nasaw, David Simpson, and Jackson Corley Wilson. Stanley Elkins and Eric McKitrick have been the most faithful supporters and colleagues that anyone could hope for. And my intellectual debts to Paul Pickrel and Ronald MacDonald cannot be repaid for the simple reason that they cannot be measured.

I was helped along considerably by years as a resident fellow at two most excellent institutions, the Charles Warren Center at Harvard University and the National Humanities Center. My gratitude to their directors, Donald Fleming and Charles Blitzer, and to their staffs, is very large indeed. Fred Matthews, William Cooper, and James Henretta were particularly helpful colleagues at the Warren Center. At the National Humanities Center, Phil Berk, Charles Caramello, Morris Eaves, Donald Green, and Charles Royster were constant sources of both good advice and encouragement.

My editor at Knopf, Jane Garrett, has kept faith when a sensible person would not have done so. And my alter-editor, David Follmer, has been equally blind to my shortcomings. The two, laboring along in a setting of corporate dealings that make American publishing houses frequent targets of acquisition and merger, manage to lend credence to my wistful notion that bookmaking might really be something more than a business.

The librarians at Smith College, the National Humanities Center, the Houghton Library at Harvard, and the Rathbun Free Memorial Library of East Haddam, Connecticut, have been extremely helpful.

Finally, I have to thank the woman to whom this book is dedicated. She is, to put it simply, both the finest historian and the nicest person I know.

FIGURES of SPEECH

INTRODUCTION

In the preface to *The Tragic Muse,* Henry James proposed a curious paradox. Writers, he said, are like conjurers, and are successful only when their secrets are kept. When their art really works— "triumphs," he said—artists disappear from the transaction between their creation and their audience. The workings of the artist are dissolved in the work of art, and "all we then—in his triumph—see of the charm-compeller is the back he turns to us as he bends over his work." And so, James concluded, the writer—the real, flesh-and-blood, historically identifiable person—can never be the "hero" of a successful piece of writing. The extent to which the artist *is* revealed is only the measure of his failure: "The privilege of the hero belongs to him only as to the artist deluded, diverted, frustrated or vanquished; when the 'amateur' in him gains, for our admiration or compassion or whatever, all that the expert has to do without."

For the historian—or for anyone else interested in the relationship between art and social experience—this is a cruel judgment indeed, if it is final. It divides the world of texts: there are those that succeed as art, and so conceal their makers; and there are those that fail as art, but might be useful in a documentary way because they reveal something about the people who produced them.

Like so many remarks of Henry James, this one is worth noticing not because it is true (or false, for that matter, since it is the kind of observation that probably cannot be either), but because of the range of things it can remind us of. It reminds us, first, that dividing the world of written texts into triumphs and failures—that central undertaking of nineteenth-century literary "criticism" and "appreciation"—was not a form of inquiry at all, but a rather arbitrary exercise in conferring conspicuous privilege on some pieces of writing and denying it to others. And James' paradox depended exactly on this: that the low "privilege" of heroic self-revelation was not a privilege at all, but something that came only to writers who were "amateurs." For the true artist—his "expert"—the cost of his success was a kind of self-denial, a successful *withholding* of the self from the work, a "doing without."

The paradox presumed an equation in which, for the writer at least, art and experience are not just radically separated, but radically opposed. Whenever a writer's personality or actual experience gains the stage, art withdraws. The expert succeeds only by managing to become invisible to the reader, and to do this means renouncing any expectation of "admiration or compassion or whatever" from the audience. The amateur, on the other hand, may find a measure of this "admiration or compassion or whatever," but only at the cost of *being* an amateur—"deluded, diverted, frustrated or vanquished." The rewards of the amateur are exactly what the expert must do without. The true artist's motivations must be beyond any low considerations, beyond any considerations at all but the literally self-less creation of the triumphant work.

James' distinction between the amateur and the expert should also remind us that he was writing about artistic "triumph" at the peak of a triumph of another kind—the triumph in Europe and America of a vital and dynamic literary marketplace in the setting of capitalism. During the two centuries and more before James began his literary career, the species of goods that was becoming identified and labeled as "Literature" and "Art" had been successfully commoditized. The work of people who had come conventionally to be called "authors by profession" or "men of letters" or just "writers" had become a specialized career. People who had once only read had become the "reading public." And that public has been transformed into a market by an increasingly organized and aggressively entrepreneurial industry of booksellers and publishers.

This particular triumph had made it possible for the "expert" to produce works of art that were also something else—commodities offered for sale in the hope that they would bring profit as well as fame to their authors. James himself was just such an "expert," of course. He knew perfectly well that the "reading public" did not make a very careful distinction between experts and amateurs, but had instead a fickle and undiscriminating tendency to reward artistic failures. This was enough to cause anyone with a refined sense of what the life of the writer was all about to be fretful, to insist perhaps overmuch on the distinction between the true artist and the amateur. And so, curiously enough, for James and the many other nineteenth-century writers and critics who had similar notions, it was the "amateur" who ran the danger of being crass, and the crass man or woman could never hope to be anything but an amateur. The motives of the experts (James chose not to say "professionals") were above reproach because the very nature of true art required them to surrender any hope of "admiration or compassion or whatever."

James' "whatever" did not explicitly include money, of course. But his paradox cannot but remind us also that in the odd logic of the self-conscious and socially precarious "Culture" of the Victorian world, making money was a low motive indeed. And the prevailing conception of the artist, the writer, the person Ralph Waldo Emerson called "the intellectual man," was of someone for whom profit ought to be the least and last thought. One of the oddest facts about the emergence of such conventional notions as Art, Literature, and Culture is that they took form during the very historical period in which it became possible for the men and women who produced the art to make money off their efforts—sometimes lots of money, and money's concomitant, fame. And the more highly developed became the markets for the objects of Culture—the essays and poems and lectures, the paintings and symphonies, the sculptures and the novels, the whole material paraphernalia of the life of the "mind"— the more insistent became the distinction between the works of persons of "genius" driven by the love of truth and beauty, and the sordid productions of hackney artists driven only by the love of profit and the tawdry celebrity that might come with it.

The motives that lead men and women to take up writing as a vocation are no doubt as numerous and as complicated as the motives that impel them to do anything else. It would be absurd— though tempting to a few—to suppose that once the literary marketplace had developed, it corrupted everyone who went near it, and that the *only* motive for writing, in the end, was somehow to extract profit from the public-as-market in the form of money and celebrity. It may be satisfying to strip away the pious masks that writers, artists, and intellectuals so like to put on, to expose the pretension that they write only for lofty purposes, or for no conscious purpose at all (the loftiest possible motive). But such satisfactions are short-lived and do not lead anywhere. Exposing little secrets, merely revealing artists' necessary hypocrisies, is not method, it is only a species of what Thorstein Veblen called "the Higher Gossip."

On the other hand, however, it is equally absurd—though tempting to a great many—to ignore the little secrets and the necessary hypocrisies that make it possible for artists and writers to get along in a world where "creative" works are also commodities. One of the most carefully nurtured practices of intellectuals in the world of capital and commodity has been to insist that they are the critics of its materialism, the exposers of its cruelties and its tawdriness, the custodians of the truly human and humane capacities of men and women, capacities that cannot be reduced to mere commodity. During the first half of the nineteenth century, especially, there took shape a very powerful conception of what it meant to be a writer, one of Emerson's "sons of Genius." It was a mythic conception, and like any good myth it had many versions. Some of the versions can fairly be called "Romantic" or "Transcendentalist." Other versions were genteel, priestly, or reformist, and harped away at the corrosive impacts of capitalist "progress" on traditional forms of landscape, social harmony, or religious faith. But all the versions of the myth had one thing in common: they treated men—and, increasingly, women—of letters as gifted individuals who were inspired by purposes that were at odds with the tendency of the age to reduce life to exchange, community to market, and value to price.

As Karl Marx and Frederick Engels once observed, "Whilst in ordinary life every shopkeeper is well able to distinguish between what somebody professes to be and what he really is, our historians have not yet won even this trivial insight. They take every epoch at its word and believe that everything it says and imagines about itself is true." In a certain sense, this book is a kind of shopkeeper's book. It takes what writers say about themselves as professings. Its initial assumptions are: that it is a little foolish to take any writer entirely on his or her own terms; that "creative" people, like the rest of us, do their work in a very specific historical context or setting; that artistic work, like any other, is molded by the social and economic relations that are part of the setting in which it is done; that the most salient feature of that setting in Europe and America for the past two or three centuries has been capitalism; and that writers' primary connection to that setting has for a long time lain directly through the literary marketplace.

The problem with applying a squinting shopkeeper's eye to writers, artists, and other intellectuals, though, is that the things they profess about themselves are very much part of what they are. Marx and Engels' shopkeeper in "ordinary life" seems to be able to see past profession to reality. But for those who try to understand what a writer "really is," the task is not so simple. What a writer professes may not be exactly accurate, but it definitely is real.

Philosophers and linguists distinguish a kind of speaking and writing, "performative utterance," that brings to pass the very conditions it states because the speaker or writer has the necessary authority to make it so. A minister who says "By the authority vested in me, I now pronounce you . . ." has not said something true but has *made* something be so. A judge who gloomily delivers a sentence that for very curious reasons we call "capital" is not making a prediction about the convicted prisoner's future, a prediction that might turn out to be true or false. The delivering of the sentence is exactly what makes the guilty person into a condemned person. Authors seem to do the same thing. The very word "author" shares its origins with "authority," and authors when they utter are laying claim to a kind of authority that gives their work something of the character of a performative utterance. But the difference is that ministers and judges are exercising an authority that has already been vested in them, while authors are trying to lay claim to authority. In social practice, a pronouncement by an official with the power to make it cannot be false. It may be misguided. It may be morally wretched. The couple may eventually divorce, or the condemned prisoner may escape. But the couple has been married, and the prisoner condemned, no matter what the outcome, so long as the credentials of the minister or the judge are authentic. Authors, on the other hand, are asking their readers to *give* credence to what they are reading, whether it is a poem, a novel, a philosophical essay, a piece of social analysis, or a scientific paper. Only if his countrymen will lend Antony their ears does he have the proper authority to bury Caesar. And whether those ears are lent will depend in large measure on how well Antony speaks. In performative utterance, authority and capacity validate what is said. For authors, what is said validates authorship. For the author, utterance is not *per*formative but formative. Whether a writer is to be allowed to speak in the capacity of an authority depends on how capable is the work itself, how persuasive, how artful, or how successfully it maintains the appearance of passionate reason or disinterested faith. In an important sense, authors do not make books; books make authors.

But in the ordinary world of Marx and Engels' shopkeeper, it is perfectly obvious that books are made by men and women who are only professing to be authors. And they certainly do have an actuality and an experience that is different from what they profess to be in their work. When they profess themselves as authors they inevitably omit, disguise, and deny much or most of that actuality and experience. Like James' expert, they are necessarily withholding much or all of the self, and presenting themselves in their work *only* as its creator, with their backs turned to the audience. And that back is not the back of a person, really, but the back of an author, bent to the task. What they ask to be validated, given credence, and lent authority is not themselves. It is the figure of the author that is presented in the work. And the figure is not autobiographical in any simple sense. It is a figure that exists mainly in the writing itself, defined and limited by what is in the book or poem or essay. It is only a figure of speech.

This figure of the author is not exactly what literary critics refer to as the "persona" of a piece of writing, or a "narrative voice," or "dramatic speaker." It is not the "I" of a first-person narrative, an autobiography, or a lyric poem. It is not the voice that directs itself to a "dear reader," or says that we must now reluctantly take our leave of a charming scene. Such devices are just that—devices—and are part of the writer's kit of tools. The figure of the author that is implicitly present in every piece of writing is the figure that is asking the reader for the authority to employ such devices, to speak in such voices, to adopt this or that persona, to display—or conceal—a particular kind of narrative presence. The difference is an elusive one. But it is important. To study personae, speakers, and voices is a fit undertaking for criticism, and can be done perfectly well with reference only to literary texts taken in and of themselves, without reference to the facts of a writer's life. On the other hand, to study a writer's life is something a biographer might do, and do well, without paying any critical attention to a writer's uses of personae or dramatic speakers. But the ways writers figure themselves, to their publics and to themselves, are ideas that have a dual ground, a footing both in the minds of the people who held them and in the texts in which they are manifested. Authorial figurings belong both to experience and to art. And so to study writers' notions of what it meant to *be* a writer is an undertaking that requires a close attention to biography (but not biography as such) and to texts (but never to texts as such).

This book is an attempt to probe one bit of the long history of the relationship between writers and the literary marketplace, the period between the closing decades of the eighteenth century and the middle of the nineteenth. More exactly, it is a set of five related studies of Americans for whom writing was a principal vocation: Benjamin Franklin, Washington Irving, William Lloyd Garrison, Ralph Waldo Emerson, and Emily Dickinson.

More exactly still, this is a book about the way these five people conceived the activity of writing. It is one thing to write. It is quite another to be a writer, to have writing as a calling and to think of it as the primary and defining fact of a life. For the people who are the subjects of this book, the most obvious and inescapable fact—both of experience and art—was that their main connection to the world around them was the published word. But they happened to live in a world where, it seemed, that connection could be completed—publics reached, audiences met, constituencies aroused—only through the mediation of the market. Their principal creative effort—and the principal creative effort of other writers who were their contemporaries, too—was to elaborate a conception of the writing career in a world of exchange.

An important fashion in literary criticism is one that supposes texts are "self-reflexive." What is meant by this, conventionally, is that literary texts point to themselves, are even "about" themselves. I am interested in a different kind of reflexivity, one in which texts can be understood as being about their authors, and more particularly about their authors' careers as writers. There is probably no more awkward and no more accurate way to put it than this: This is a book about writers who were writing about being writers. They were inventing portrayals or figures of the writer that would enable them to come to terms with the fact that they lived and worked in a world where prose and poetry had become, like everything else, potential commodities.

These writers' portrayals of *the* writer were, of course, works of art, linguistic figments. And if James' paradoxical comment about what it means for a "charm-compeller" to succeed holds, they would be useless as documents. But James' paradox—and the many others like it that have culminated in the gleefully abject propositions of much contemporary critical theory—is not genuine. Art does not succeed only when a charm-compeller manages to remain entirely out of the picture. It is not true, either, that any piece of writing that reveals the artist is a failure. What anything "is" depends entirely on the uses we intend to make of it. Every piece of writing is both a text and a document, a fit subject for either criticism or history. And there is no piece of writing, no matter how "triumphant" it is, that cannot be made to tell something about the person who wrote it. In James' terms, all art does in fact fail, and all artists are to one degree or another amateurs—deluded, diverted, frustrated, and vanquished. The figures of the writer put forward by the people who are the subjects of this book were all works of art. To the extent that they succeeded in their charm-compelling, their figures of speech did conceal and deny much. But—fortunately for the historian—no artist succeeds perfectly in the magical disappearing act that James had in mind.

But if it is possible to read literary texts as documents, and use them to get at a real history, it is equally true that working with the kinds of writing produced by people like those who are discussed here is a very tricky business. It must be pursued with considerable caution, and above all with an awareness that the best clues to the correct track are often the false scents that writers lay down.

One of the principal false scents that has made it difficult to understand American writers in the first half of the nineteenth century is that they produced something like a collective portrait of an idealized "self" that seems to stand quite apart from the material and social realities of the development of industrial capitalism. American writers were much preoccupied with the lives and fates of singular individuals who had profoundly problematic relationships with society at large. Hawthorne's Hester Prynne or Arthur Dimmesdale, the character who is the "I" of *Walden,* Emerson's Poet, the hero of Cooper's Leatherstocking stories, Melville's Ahab or Ishmael, the chanter of *Leaves of Grass,* the "supposed person" who is Dickinson's "voice"—these and the many other "selves" like them were the most characteristic creations of American literature during the period. And they do seem to have much in common. They all transcend the boundaries that define ordinary men and women's lives in the social order. They have a peculiar kind of "innocence" about them—even when they are as possessed as Ahab is with a demonic determination to destroy a great "evil," or are as despairing as the speaker in some of Dickinson's best poetry. They own no property, hold no jobs, have no professions, do not marry (or even seem to have sexual experience). But despite all their "renunciations" (as Emerson called them), such figures also make extraordinarily large, even "imperial," claims for themselves, claims to secret knowledges and insights that set them apart from the world. Typically, the lives of such figures of the transcendent "self" are utterly skew to the world of customary and social experience. They resort to the sea or to solitary ponds, to the forest, to the edges of settlement and the margins of civilization, or they are simply and radically reclusive.

Much intelligent effort has been spent over the years explaining how and why such transcendent "selves" as these should have had so prominent a presence in American literature. Writers in England, it has been suggested, wrote social novels, in which family, property, and institutions set the problems and determined the outcomes; Americans, on the other hand, wrote mostly fantasies and "romances," with unbounded individuals at their centers, individuals with no real connections to family, property, or institutions. On the assumption that literature enfolds some sort of telling truth about the culture or society that "produces" it, historians and critics have suggested that the figure of the radically free individual in American literature was a "reflection" of some important fact about American society: the frontier, say, or social mobility, or the lack of a "feudal past." Or something in the common culture, perhaps—a "democracy" or an "individualism"—was a pervasive attitude in society at large, and only needed to be given "voice" by artists. Or American writing has been treated as a type of Romantic reaction *against* the unpleasing realities of social class, of factories and cities, of a growing and increasingly forced conformity to law and the industrial regime.

But the figure of the free and transcendent individual, the innocently imperial self at odds with the world, was the deliberate creation of two or three generations of writers who knew a good deal
about what they were doing. Every significant example of the transcendent individual was some writer's way of representing the projective figure of the artist, the poet, the man or woman to whom
letters was a calling. And such figures typically subverted property,
scorned profit, and stood militantly apart from any concern with
market relations. The writers who created those figures of speech
understood very well that *their* lives were defined above all by the
marketplace. They did not experience the world as observant individuals who were merely noticing the social and economic realities
around them. They did not merely watch and "respond" to "industrialization" or "the city" or "the frontier." Whatever other social
characteristics they might have had, they were above all else writers,
and it was as writers, primarily, that they tried to make sense out of
things. And as writers they all understood that they might enter the
literary marketplace or not, might succeed or fail in it, might be
excited by it or appalled. But whatever their attitudes and experiences may have been, it was the market, more than anything else,
that established the conceptual problems they set out to solve in their
work. In the most practical terms, their perceptions of the marketplace determined what they would write and what they would not,
in what form and style, and for what kind of supposed audience. But
most of all, the ways they conceived their relationship to the marketplace lay behind the representations of themselves in their works.

The market promised writers what no other system of support
ever had. It held out the grand promise of an audience that was
practically and immediately limitless, and not implicitly restricted by
class or political or religious persuasion, nor lying far ahead, in
"posterity." The literary marketplace seemed also to offer writers a
radical autonomy, a liberating independence from the requirements
of authorities or institutions, a world composed only of the author
and the public, with language itself as the only link between. And it
was this heady fact that lay behind the creation of the figures of
the radically free, transcendent individuals who gave so much definition to American writing in the generations between Franklin and
Dickinson.

But those imperial selves—the Ahabs and the Hesters, "I, Walt,"
the "I" of *Walden,* and the rest—were always as deluded, diverted,

frustrated, or vanquished as they were free. Their very freedom tended, curiously, to make them ineffectual, incapable of any kind of activity that might actually produce beneficial consequences. The principal figures in the American literature of the period—not the writers themselves, but their figures of speech—are constantly being driven away from civilization, into a progressively more toothless and pathetic isolation, like Cooper's Deerslayer-become-Hawkeye-become-the-aged-hunter. When they do exert themselves, the result is often death and disaster, as it is for Ahab. Or, like Ishmael, they are left only with the capacity to tell the tale. They die, like Dimmesdale, at the peak of a career that has brought them the appearance of civic power, but only at the price of their capacity to speak the simple truth. Or they end by being only the "captain of a huckleberry party," as Emerson would eventually say of Thoreau. But what Emerson said of Thoreau he was also saying implicitly of his own representation of the Poet as a man whose repudiation of institutions deprives him of any means of effective action in the world. Whitman's figure of the poet, for all his vigor and determination to "merge," is trapped within a kind of sacrificial voyeurism, and cannot become actively engaged with the "average unending multitude," caught in an esthetic isolation for which auto-eroticism would become the most adequate symbolic representation, and death the only solace. Dickinson's poet-figure makes her own quite imperial claims, to such affairs as "Circumference" and "Possibility." But that same voice speaks even more often of failure, defeat, and solitude. And the last thing anyone could imagine her "supposed person" doing is joining a movement for women's rights or an abolitionist society in the hope of actually accomplishing some instrumental purpose.

This plaintive and surrendering side of the expansive figure of the transcendent individual probably had many sources—European models, say, or some kind of psychic impact of changing family practices and class relations. But it was most immediately related to the perceived realities of the literary marketplace. Writing for the market had its problems as well as its enticements. Most obviously, the market held out the possibility of failure that was as unbounded as its promises of success. The market seemed to place the writer in an unmediated relationship to the public (though in actual practice, publishers and booksellers, journals and reviews, and other institutions did always intervene). This enabled writers to think of success as something that they could earn as a result of their quite solitary efforts. But it also meant that failure could not be laid off on the whimsy of a patron or the bigotry of an institution. Failure had to lie either in the public (the "fickle" public, as writers in the nineteenth century liked to call it) or in the writer. Before the triumph of the literary marketplace, people had written for limited constituencies within a framework of known expectations, under the control of a patron or an institution with definite ideas of what ought to be accomplished. Now, writers for the market contemplated an audience that was unknown, anonymous, and distant—a mere "mass," as people had begun to call it. And this helped to induce fantasies of alienation and solitude as urgent as the contrary, expansive fantasies that were encouraged by the market's offerings of success, profit, and celebrity.

The representations of the writer created by the people who are the subjects of this book were projective idealizations, creations of a writerly "voice" speaking in an imagined capacity, a "supposed person" addressing an equally supposed audience. But the figurings did have their origins in matters of fact, in experience. They were not mere inventions, fantasies, and idealizations. They were the outcomes of existential circumstances, of real-life efforts, hopes, and fears. And for the writers who are the subjects of this book, the circumstances and the efforts, hopes, and fears had primarily to do with their vocational identities as writers.

No one is *only* a writer, of course, and no writer is *only* a creature of the market. Like other people, the writers who are the subjects of this book had complex identities. They were members of social groups and classes, or were on the margins of one class looking anxiously for ways to make a pronounced gain or avoid a pronounced loss of status. Class facts like these did count for much in their lives. They also belonged to families, and their relationships with parents, wives or husbands, and even children helped to determine the ways they thought of themselves as writers. Four of them were men, and one a woman, and they happened to live in a period when the consequences of this "primary" difference were being drastically redefined. They had sexual lives, too. They loved, or lost, or never loved at all. And such matters were sometimes of critical importance to them. They were sometimes active in political movements, or had significant institutional commitments and professional credentials: Benjamin Franklin became a revolutionary patriot and a Founding Father; Washington Irving toyed with being a lawyer and a businessman; William Lloyd Garrison began his career as a journalist and arch Federalist; Emerson began as a Unitarian minister; Dickinson was "at home," but it happened to be the home of a man of means, and a very active Whig lawyer.

All of these things—class, family, sex and sexuality, political and institutional engagement or disengagement—were important and integral to the lives of these writers, as they would be to the life of any other writer who could have been one of my subjects. But it was primarily as writers that they contended with the other aspects of their experience. If they had class anxieties or ambitions, they tried to resolve the anxieties and satisfy the ambitions as writers. If what mattered most to them at some juncture of their experience was that they loved or lost, they made an effort to translate this, too, into terms that they could manage to make part of their representations of themselves as people whose calling was language. For Benjamin Franklin, an active career in public life was a reward for his work as a writer, and being a Founding Father was not just something to do, it was also something to write about. Irving's trivial and unsatisfying taste of life as a lawyer and merchant became an implicit subject matter of his art. Garrison's abolitionist commitment can be directly traced to the way he had tried to devise a satisfactory figuring of himself as an author by profession. Emerson's notion of what it meant to be a minister was the material out of which he tried to generate a countervailing conception of the Poet. And for Emily Dickinson, being a woman and being "at home" were not just biographical conditions. They were also the necessary conditions of her effort to devise a satisfactory figure of the "supposed person" who could stand behind the various voices of her poems.

This book is a study of five very different people who had extremely idiosyncratic lives. They worked in different genres, came from differing backgrounds, and each one worked out his or her relationship to the literary marketplace in quite personal ways. But for each of them, in the final analysis, the main problem *was* that relationship and the main creative outcome was their representation of the writer. The particular circumstances and experiences that gave each of their lives a unique character were very real and very important. But they made it their business to translate circumstance and experience into prose and poetry. They all understood their own lives—at the critical and determining junctures—as being writers' lives. And each of them tried to translate that understanding into a representation of the writer, a figure of often heroic proportions, attempting to discover and address a public in a society where only commodity seemed to matter, but in a culture where what mattered most was that art and literature be understood as undertakings that dealt only with "ideal" or "spiritual" things like truth and beauty.

To readers who are familiar with books about American culture or literature, my cast of characters might seem a little odd. It may be that explaining the reasoning behind my choices will go some distance toward explaining what this book is all about, what its arguments are, and the limits of what it sets out to do.

To begin with, the category of "American writers," as it has been conventionalized by literary critics and intellectual historians over the past half-century, often does not include people like Franklin or Garrison. They are more often cast as political figures or reformers or something of the sort, and the term "writers" is reserved for people who produced poetry or novels or some other kind of "creative" work—what is sometimes called "literature." One of the principal assumptions behind this book, however, is that it ought to be possible to develop a way of studying people for whom writing of *any* sort is a principal vocation. When Franklin said that writing had been a "chief means of my advancement," he was acknowledging the simple truth that he was, first and last, a writer—no matter whatever other careers his writing led him into along the way. Garrison, who is usually thought of simply as an abolitionist, began with an intense ambition to succeed by, as he put it, "turning *author."* The paths Garrison took and the choices he made (including abolitionism) were very much the outcomes of these beginnings. For some purposes, it is no doubt useful to group writers by genre, to study novelists or poets or writers of autobiographies, for example. It may even be instructive, depending on the nature of the inquiry, to work with a very general concept like "literature" (which might or might not take in most of Franklin's writing, and which would almost certainly exclude most of Garrison's). But genre, like any category of inquiry, can mask as well as reveal. And what genre usually masks is nothing less than history: the fact that a poet, a novelist, a journalist, and a philosopher who share a common historical context may have more important things in common than, say, a lyric poet of the sixteenth century in England and another lyric poet who worked in the United States in the twentieth century. On this kind of assumption, I have made my choices of subjects in a way that tries to ignore the question of genre.

What this has meant in practical terms, however, is that I have tried to choose one practitioner for each of the principal kinds of writing that Americans in large numbers were doing during the period. I have written one chapter on Franklin as the author of an autobiography; another on Irving, whose work was mainly fiction; a third on Garrison, a journalist and reformer; a fourth on Emerson, who was primarily an essayist and (loosely speaking) a philosopher; and a fifth on Dickinson, a poet. And I have supposed, for reasons that I hope will come clear, that it did not matter much *which* poet or writer of fiction or essayist I chose. The same points I make about the five writers I selected could be made with equal force about others. Melville or Hawthorne would have done as well for my purposes as Irving or Emerson. Whitman could easily be substituted for Dickinson (instead of being made the subject of a brief epilogue). The same kinds of arguments, more or less, could be made about Edgar Allan Poe or Henry David Thoreau that are made in the chapters on Franklin, Garrison, or Emerson.

A second reason that my selection of writers might seem somewhat curious to readers habituated to certain conventions is that it links writers whose work was done in the 1820s and after with others whose careers took shape well before that. Emerson and Dickinson belonged to the period that is often singled out as the American Renaissance, the age of "classic" American literature, of *Moby Dick, The Scarlet Letter,* and *Walden.* And it has long been an article of faith that the writers of this period were redefining American "culture" in ways that set them off firmly from the period that came before. The argument that is implicit in my joining Franklin and Irving on one side, with Emerson and Dickinson on the other, is that the existence of the marketplace set inescapable problems for writers from at least the 1770s on. These problems, I am suggesting, went much deeper than any generational concern to promote a particular kind of national literature or culture.

Another kind of reader, though, might find my selection of writers altogether *too* predictable. One of the effects of the intensive academic study of American writing has been the shaping of a restrictive canon of works that are deemed somehow to be more than writing, and more even than "literature." A limited number of authors are placed firmly at the center of the conventional canon: Emerson, Hawthorne, Whitman, Melville, and Thoreau almost always find a secure place among the authors whose work supposedly gives voice to an *American* "experience" or "character" or "culture." A few other writers are clustered about this center, and debate smolders on about whether they belong in the canon, or are eccentric or "minor" writers: Poe, Dickinson, Irving, jostle for a place. (More precisely, their academic partisans jostle.) And readers who are impatient with this old and prestigious way of going about things may look askance at my choice of subjects, and even complain that I am continuing the practice of "privileging" certain texts and writers.

In recent years, scholars have attempted to dismantle the American canon in two ways. The first is to argue that some writer who has been excluded—Harriet Beecher Stowe, for example—is really "as good as" a Hawthorne or a Melville, and so belongs in the canon. And it may be that if enough people present enough new candidates for privilege, the traditional canon will cease to have much practical effect. But this way of "decanonizing" American writing is slow and depends on precarious judgments that are finally no more than literary-critical assessments of how "fine" a writer's work is. A second, and probably better, way of trying to break down conventions that privilege this text or that is to find new grounds on which to claim an honorific status for particular works. The most common method in academic culture today is to suggest that one writer or another is important because he or she gave voice to the experience of a particular group—women, perhaps, or workers or blacks. This attempt to create what amounts to a plurality of canons is surely refreshing. But in the end a number of parallel canons may not be any better than one. There is no more reason to suppose that a given writer was the voice of a discrete social group than there once was to suppose that another writer was the voice of all America.

A third, and perhaps more effective, way of getting at the problem of textual "privilege" is not to claim privilege for work that has always been denied it, but to deny it to work that has always had it. The mindless way of doing this would be simply to proclaim a kind of populism of reading, to argue that for the historian all texts are equal, all are documents, and no document is any "better" than any other. In the end, this kind of populist strategy is likely to persuade only the already persuaded. A more promising approach is to challenge the kinds of grounds on which writers have conventionally been elevated to importance. And, for American writers, this means above all challenging the very idea that there is anything like a national "experience" or "character" or "culture" to which any writer *could* have given voice. And one way of doing this is to suggest that familiar conceptual entities like the imperial self or the transcendent individual were not the literary byproduct of a national character, but were instead a function of practical matters that had a peculiar and immediate relevance for men and women who were making careers as writers in a market society.

It will be immediately obvious to anyone who is even a little familiar with the writers I have chosen that there is another kind of apparent anomaly in my selection. One of them, Dickinson, seems to have been able to defy the literary marketplace altogether, scorning publication as the "Auction of the Mind of Man." But another argument I am proposing is that the writers who affected scorn for the market—Poe, say, or Melville or Thoreau—were no less concerned with it than the most ardently entrepreneurial writer. In fact, the few poems in which Dickinson expressed her own fragile belief that the true poet did not deign to publish relied on notions that many other writers (who *did* publish, when they could) had already made into clichés. Indeed, since the middle of the eighteenth century, probably the most commonly expressed view of the market among writers on both sides of the Atlantic was that it was a foul thing, holding out nothing to the true artist but a temptation to compromise the promptings of genius in order to win the favor of the "multitudes." And such views were voiced as often by writers who were assiduously pursuing their publishing careers as by those who hesitated at the borders of the enterprise, complaining about the death of traditional patronage, or dreaming that they might write as amateurs. A Goldsmith, a Wordsworth, or a Coleridge was just as likely as Emily Dickinson to revile the marketplace. And the fact that she did finally decide not to publish much poetry only makes her the more interesting as a study in the social and political economy of authorship.

*Engraving of 1777 by Augustin de Saint Aubin, after a drawing
by Charles Nicolas Cochin. The legend says simply that Franklin
was born in Boston in New England, January 17, 1706.*

I

—

BENJAMIN FRANKLIN

In the winter of 1776–77, Benjamin Franklin sat for a portrait. It was a rush job, only a drawing to be used for an engraving to be put on sale later in the year. Its purposes were political. Franklin was in France as commissioner for the rebellious American Colonies. And the engraving, like the Franklin medallions that appeared in France at about the same time, was part of a publicity campaign to cultivate French support for the cause of American independence.[1]

Like any good publicist—and he was surely one of the world's best—Franklin arranged things carefully. The artist, Charles Nicolas Cochin, was an experienced man of sixty-one, politically uncontroversial, by and large unimaginative, and thoroughly professional: in short, exactly the sort of man needed for the task. The sitter was seventy, the agent of a government born in the extreme controversies of revolution and war, a man of tireless imagination, and thoroughly professional: in short, perfectly suited to his role. He chose his clothes carefully. He wore a plain brown coat of the kind French aristocrats liked to associate with the "Quaker" faith Franklin let

---

[1] A charming and nicely detailed discussion of the Cochin drawing and the resulting engraving is in Charles Coleman Sellers' *Franklin in Portraiture* (New Haven, 1962), 227–30. On Franklin in France, see Alfred Owen Aldridge, *Benjamin Franklin and His French Contemporaries* (New York, 1957).

them suppose he held to. At his neck was a simple bit of marvelously white linen. But his master stroke was a large, limp cap of marten fur. It was exactly the detail that might most effectively foster a public image of Franklin as the simple man of virtue from the New World. He wore it for the portrait despite the fact that the first purchase he had made in France, a few weeks before, was wigs—of the smaller French fashion, to replace the larger and heavier English wigs he had worn in London. And he let some long strands of gray hair fall from under the fur cap, to emphasize the fact that he might not wear a wig even if he were hatless. (During much of the winter and spring, he took to wearing the fur hat even at receptions indoors, as though it were part of him and not just a garment; later, when the French alliance had been successfully made, he stopped using the hat altogether.)

The plain suit and simple linen scarf, and particularly that fur hat, were just the things to wear for a man whose collected works had been republished in France in 1773 with a little poem on the frontis-piece that said he was the man who *"Fait fleurir les Arts en des Climats sauvages."* But more than "Climats sauvages" were involved. Franklin's simple costume was not merely the costume of an American. Aggressively simple clothes were becoming the fashion for intellectuals in France, and wearing them was subtle testimony to his reputation as a learned man. Even the fur hat had been adopted a decade earlier by Jean-Jacques Rousseau. Franklin understood his problem very well. He had to convince the French not only that he was a figure of New World innocence and simplicity, but also that he was a man of profound learning, an authentic philosopher. In a portrait made ten years earlier, by the British painter David Martin, Franklin had posed in an ornate blue coat, with elaborate braid and gold buttons. He had worn a full-scale English wig. And he had been very much the philosopher, deeply absorbed in his books and writing, working intently under a bust of no less distinguished a colleague and model than Isaac Newton. Now, for the French, Franklin had put off the gentleman's bright colors, the braid and buttons and the wig. But he decided, for the second and almost the last time in his life, to use one prop that did effectively suggest his philosophical achievements: his glasses, the bifocals he himself had invented, and that had been such an important feature of the Martin portrait of the complete philosopher.[2]

---

[2] Sellers' account of the Martin portrait is in *Franklin in Portraiture*, 328–40.

The David Martin portrait of Franklin, 1766. The bust is of Newton.
No titles or writing is legible on the books or papers.

The result was a masterpiece—of posing if not of art. The picture held in balance two potentially contradictory assertions of personality. It was the portrait of an American, a plain man of simple virtues, in touch with wilderness, a naif. But it was also the portrait of a philosopher and savant, and this sagacious man also knew how to frame his mouth in a way that suggested shrewdness and perhaps even irony. A noted *abbé* was astonished by Franklin's appearance, and caught the contrasting elements exactly when he noticed the "simple and singular costume of this grave personage." Franklin had mastered the art of looking both "simple" and like a "grave personage," both a man of "Climats sauvages" and a venerable man of the world, both Bonhomme Richard and the learned Doctor Franklin. He was innocence and irony together, Candide and Voltaire in one deft stroke.

Even the simplest portrait is a contrived affair—usually the product of the artist's efforts more than the subject's. But Franklin's 1777 effort went far beyond the ordinary limits of poses and props. It managed ingeniously not merely to suggest but to insist on certain definite messages. Its most immediate content was of course political. But the politics of revolution and war shaded over into larger ideological claims about the relationships among knowledge, virtue, and natural innocence. And to these ideological messages was joined another claim—the most elusive but perhaps the most insistent of all—that here was a truly extraordinary man, not a typical American at all, nor even just a man of earnest virtue and learning, but a man of remarkable vision and insight, a celebrity worthy of the boast that saluted him everywhere in France, that he had ripped the lightning from the sky and the scepter from the tyrant.

In 1771, about halfway between the time of David Martin's philosopher portrait and Cochin's fur hat drawing, Franklin went to work on another portrait of himself, a manuscript that eventually became known as his autobiography. He described growing up in Boston, being an apprentice in his brother's newspaper office, then running away to make a new start. He told of how he had gone first to New York, looking for work as a printer. There was no work there, so he headed on south, for Philadelphia. Here Franklin paused in his narrative to take a quick inventory: "near 300 miles from home, a Boy of but 17, without the least Recommendation to or Knowledge of any Person in the Place, and with very little Money in my Pocket." Then he began to be "more particular" in his description of his trip. He was setting the stage for what is probably the most artful paragraph in his autobiography, a sketch of himself that would become nearly a folk image for generations of readers. He wrote with care and economy, and with a fine eye for detail, of the seventeen-year-old boy's first morning in Philadelphia. He has only a Dutch dollar and about a shilling in copper coins, and he gives the copper away. He is hungry. The trip down from New York has been a hard one. He has spent a miserable and wet night on an old boat in a storm. Another boat on which he traveled, just the night before, was lost for a time in the darkness. He has had a fever. He knows no one, and even his companions on the boat are headed farther down the Delaware. He has committed a serious crime by violating his indenture to his brother, so now he is incognito. For the moment, he has only the somewhat ragged working clothes on his back, plus a spare shirt and stockings stuffed incompletely into his pockets. He has some difficulty getting food because he does not know the names and prices of bread in this strange place. He tries to ask for "bisket," and gets nowhere; then for a "threepenny Loaf," with the same result. Finally, he asks the baker for three pennies' worth of anything, and is surprised at being given "three great Puffy Rolls." He tucks one under each arm and starts munching on the third while he walks up the streets away from the Delaware River. He can eat only one of the rolls, so he turns back toward the Delaware, where he drinks from the river. Then he gives the other two rolls away, to a woman he had been on the boat with, as though to divest himself of every remaining bit of surplus. He wanders into a Quaker meeting. He looks from face to face, but no one speaks, and he falls into a sleep so deep that he has to be roused when the meeting is ended.[3]

The story may be true, even in its details—just as it is true that Franklin really owned a fur hat in 1777. But, true or not, it is a piece of writing as cunning and effective as his decision to wear that hat for the Cochin drawing. In one paragraph, Franklin created a classic picture of a lad poised between a past he has escaped and a future he has not yet begun to have. He is caught in midair, without resources and hindrances, simultaneously lost and free, hungry and broke but content with bread and water, alert and watchful but able to sleep innocently in that silent meetinghouse. He is on his own, without family, property, or job. He is pure possibility.

But Franklin's skill was even greater. He managed to build into his sketch another, quite different figure, a sage and celebrated old man, who was, after all, managing the whole scene. He began his paragraph by intrusively pointing out the contrast between the boy he was about to describe and the man he had become. "I have been the more particular in this Description of my Journey, and shall be so of my first Entry into that City, that you may in your Mind compare such unlikely Beginnings with the Figure I have since made there." He ended the paragraph with a wry sentence about the meetinghouse: "This was therefore the first House I was in or slept in, in Philadelphia"—a quick reminder that he would not only sleep in but eventually own a number of others. And at almost exactly the mid-

---

[3] Benjamin Franklin, *The Autobiography of Benjamin Franklin*, ed. R. Jackson Wilson (New York, 1981), 24–9. Another version of Franklin's first hours in Philadelphia (for which Franklin may have been an oral source) was published in England during the Revolution. See Alfred Owen Aldridge, "The First Published Memoir of Franklin," *William and Mary Quarterly* 27 (1967): 624–8.

point of the paragraph, he inserted another even more pointed reminder of the man that boy would become. "Thus I went up Market
Street as far as fourth Street, passing by the Door of Mr. Read, my
future Wife's Father, when she standing at the Door saw me, and
thought I made as I certainly did a most awkward ridiculous
Appearance."[4]

The effect of these three sentences is the same as the effect of
wearing his bifocals in the 1777 drawing. The risk that earnest and
innocent youth might be taken as permanent awkwardness and rus-
ticity is offset by an insistence on "the Figure I have since made."
The gratuitous agreement with Miss Read's later report that the boy
looked "ridiculous"—"I certainly did"—is an equally emphatic reminder that the man writing this paragraph is a man of fame, reputation, and learning. The boy may be perfectly naive, but the writer
visibly hovers over him, wearing a sophisticated look that blends
affection with canny assessment. Here, as in Cochin's drawing,
Franklin's vision is bifocal. Here, too, he is Voltaire to his own
Candide, refusing to be taken as either, insisting on being taken as
both.

The technique Franklin put to work in this famous paragraph was
one he used over and over in the book he called his "History." It was
a writing stratagem that enabled him to generate a figure of himself
that was simultaneously that of an earnest young tradesman and a
wily old celebrity. He was writing a book that could be read in two
distinct ways, by two different kinds of readers. An innocent
reader—Franklin obviously had in mind aspiring young men of the
type he had once been—could read it deadpan, as an improving and
inspiring set of lessons on life. Thousands of young men would
eventually read it that way. But Franklin could expect a more so-

---

[4] The problem of Franklin's varying voices is taken up in one of the most intelligent modern
commentaries on the autobiography, Robert M. Sayre, *The Examined Self: Benjamin Franklin,
Henry Adams, Henry James* (New Haven, 1964), 13–33. Sayre's argument, in essence, is that
Franklin found three different voices, or manners, in the autobiography, but found them
sequentially: In the section written in England in 1771, Franklin assumed the role of the
"retired country gentleman giving a private account of his unusual and adventurous history";
in the second part, done in France in 1784, he assumed a manner he had adopted for the salons
of Mmes. Helvetius and Brillon—the ingenuous "Philosophical Quaker"; Franklin's third
voice, taken up in Philadelphia in 1788 when he began his last work on the book, was that of
the revolutionary patriot, civic projector, and mild Anglophobe.

It is more profitable, and nearer the truth of the matter, to read the autobiography as a book
in which Franklin does speak with distinct voices, not sequentially but at once, and not at all
in the confused or uncertain way Sayre suggests, but with the control of a skilled prose artist.

phisticated reader to have quite a different sense of him and his book. In the early pages, gently and without insisting overmuch on the point, he made it very clear that he had mastered the essential books of the eighteenth century. In the course of arguing that modern Romance languages should be learned before Latin, he unobtrusively made it clear that he was, linguistically, a very learned gentleman. He even toyed with improvements on some lines of Alexander Pope. The reader who absorbed the import of such passages would neither admire a tradesman's struggle for success, nor mock the pious moralism of a provincial burgher. Such a reader would see beyond the surface of things. In fact, if Franklin could expect a cultivated reader to admire anything, it would be neither his youthful character nor his middle-aged achievements; it would be his mature capacity to control scenes and passages in which irony was gently superimposed on earnestness, to the damage of neither. For such a reader, this was the awareness that would rescue Franklin from the main nightmare of the self-made man: that he might appear ridiculous to people of refinement and cultivated taste. Franklin was the very model of the bourgeois-become-gentleman. But he knew he spoke prose, and an artful prose it was, for those who could read it.[5]

It is a bit indiscreet to attribute artful stratagems to the writer of a personal history. Autobiographies are normally meant to be taken as faithful reportings, with no textual space for a cunning narrator. And Franklin's is seemingly one of the most plain and honest of autobiographies. It was written in straightforward English prose. There is

---

[5] Some interesting remarks on the assumption of a double audience—an assumption inherited from the sixteenth century by both visual artists and writers—are in Ronald Paulson, *Emblem and Expression: Meaning in English Art of the Eighteenth Century* (London, 1957), 58 ff., and *Popular and Polite Art in the Age of Hogarth and Fielding* (South Bend, Ind., 1979), 10–23. See also the challenging and fundamental essay of E. P. Thompson, "Patrician Society, Plebeian Culture," *Journal of Social History* 7 (1974): 396–404.

What I am suggesting, however, is not that Franklin was addressing two kinds of readers that ought to be thought of as plebeian and patrician, but that he was writing for two different kinds of bourgeois readers, one of them aspiring and naive, the other well-off, educated, and penetrating. If it is true that a culture that could be called middle-class was taking shape in the eighteenth century, then it was finding a place *between* the plebeian and the patrician, the bucolic and the urbane, the "heretical subculture" of the poor and the skeptical high culture of aristocrats. The arts and literature of the middle class emerged with wary frontiers on both older cultures. Toward the ruder irreverences of the plebeian world, the culture of the bourgeoisie turned a resolute face of "improvement" and "success." To the elegant irreverence of aristocrats, the arts of the middle class responded with a variety of strategies, ranging from denunciations of "vanities" and "frivolities," through claims of superior sagacity, to a genial good humor that bespoke enlightened self-confidence.

no pretension in either its content or its language. Readers may have admired Franklin; they may have chuckled with him; or they may have become indignant at his moralizing and apparent small-mindedness. But whatever Franklin's huge audiences have felt about his book, they have almost always agreed on one point: that the man they have met in the book *is* Franklin, plain and unadorned. The man seems to be so fully and honestly in his book that generations of readers have responded to the story as if it *were* the man.[6]

In ordinary men and woman, plainspokenness may be a mere habit. But in a writer it is something else. It is a device designed to disarm and invite the reader onto the author's ground. Franklin's autobiography, especially in the part he wrote in England about his youth in Boston, Philadelphia, and London, is a very seductive book. It involves the reader so gently, so imperceptibly, in the story that it is difficult to see the writer at work. Even the beginning, with its return address ("Twyford, at the Bishop of St. Asaph's 1771"), its conventional salutation ("Dear Son"), and its stiff opening sentence ("I have ever had a Pleasure in obtaining any little Anecdotes of my Ancestors"), was a bit of framing whose obvious purpose was to create the impression that the reader was looking over Franklin's shoulder, eavesdropping on a man writing, not a writer. Franklin's most stunning artistic achievement in his autobiography was, in fact, to generate an atmosphere of artlessness. And this, in turn, has led most of his readers to make an almost perfect confusion between the tale and its teller.[7]

But Franklin was above all a teller, a writer. He did many things, but he almost never did anything without writing about it. He invented a new kind of stove—then wrote about it. He devised electrical experiments that may have been the most important scientific work of the century—then wrote about them. He wrote early and often: poems, broadsides, essays, letters, almanacs, speeches,

[6] During the past twenty years, a number of scholars have begun to insist that Franklin was, after all, a literary artist, and that his autobiography needs to be read as a work of art and not as a record of the man himself. One of the first readers to emphasize this distinction was David Levin, in "The Autobiography of Benjamin Franklin, Puritan Experimenter in Life and Art," *Yale Review* 53 (1963): 258–75. Sayre, *The Examined Self,* makes the same kind of point, as do John William Ward, "Who Was Benjamin Franklin?" *American Quarterly* 32 (1963): 541–53; Daniel B. Shea, *Spiritual Autobiography in Early America* (Princeton, 1968), 234–48; John F. Lynen, *The Design of the Present: Essays on Time and Form in American Literature* (New Haven, 1969), 144–5; and John Griffith, "The Rhetoric of Franklin's 'Autobiography,' " *Criticism* 13 (1971): 77–94.

[7] *Autobiography,* 1.

projects and by-laws, metaphysical essays, parodies, epitaphs, and even prayers. By the time he set to work on his autobiography, he was in fact a very famous author. A fourth edition of his *Experiments and Observations on Electricity* had just been published in England. The next year, he would be made a foreign associate of the Académie des Sciences. Two years later, in 1773, the French edition of his various writings was published. He had already been called by David Hume the first man of letters America had produced. In August 1772, he boasted that "Learned and ingenious foreigners that come to England, almost all make a point of visiting me." And he understood perfectly well that "a principal Means" behind all this fame was his ability as a prose writer.[8]

Franklin knew the popular rhyme "The man of words and not of deeds/Is like a garden full of weeds." But for him, language and action were so inextricably blended that he could frame a hilarious alternative: "A man of deeds and not of words/Is like a garden full of . . ." He was a writer with more than enough wit and skill to write for two audiences at once, to write a sketch that skillfully juxtaposed youth and age, innocence and irony. He had more than enough talent and experience to write a whole book with such method. The autobiography was not a series of barely connected spurts of prose, each with its own logic. A governing set of authorial purposes and writing techniques gave the whole book a definite shape, consistency, and subtlety.[9]

Franklin began his autobiography in England during a time of "leisure" in 1771. His ambition to make a place for himself in English politics and to take up the life of an English country gentleman had been thwarted. The American "cause" was not yet an appealing alternative. He was sixty-five and at a loose end, resting at the

---

[8] Still the standard source for biographical information on Franklin is Carl Van Doren, *Benjamin Franklin* (New York, 1938). The boast about learned foreigners is in Leonard Labaree et al., eds., *The Papers of Benjamin Franklin*, vol. 1 (New Haven, 1959–), 9:259. These volumes will be cited as *Papers*. Franklin's judgment about "a principal Means" is in *Autobiography*, 15.
[9] The two couplets were in a letter from Franklin to his sister, Jane Mecom, September 16, 1758. The second was immediately followed by a coy disclaimer (he had "forgot the Rhime," but was sure it was something that did not smell like perfume). Franklin was using the second formulation to mock those who insisted on the letter of religion, and took no account of good deeds. But only a man with a very rich idea of the relationship between belief and action could have framed such a marvelously coarse jingle. Cf. Henry F. May, *The Enlightenment in America* (New York, 1976), 126–7.

Decemé et Gravé *par F.N. Martinet*

Il a ravi le feu des Cieux :
Il fait fleurir les Arts en des Climats sauvages.
L'Amérique le place à la tête des Sages
La Grèce l'auroit mis au nombre de ses Dieux.

Frontispiece to the 1773 French edition of Franklin's works. Engraving after a mezzotint made off a 1762 portrait by Mason Chamberlain. The poem printed below the figure reads:

> He has torn fire from the skies
>> He made the Arts flourish in savage climes
> America puts him at the head of all Sages
>> Greece would have numbered him among her Gods

country house of a friend. Franklin was never to finish the book. But he was never to stop writing it, either. He wrote about two dozen large manuscript pages in 1771, then dropped the project. He took it up again after the Revolution, when he was at leisure in Passy, just outside Paris, and got off a few more pages. Another long burst of writing, about equal to the first, began back in Philadelphia in 1788. After a short interruption, he returned to the task in the fall of the next year but he managed only a few more pages before he died the following April, at eighty-three.[10]

Franklin never got his manuscript ready to become a book. It did not even have a title, though it is certain that Franklin would not have called it an autobiography. (He did eventually make some revisions, but preferred to keep writing, grumbling when his would-be publisher asked him both to finish the book and to take a more active part in Pennsylvania politics. How, he asked, could a man simultaneously enlarge his life and complete a memoir of it?) In the end, the book was not published in full in English until almost thirty years after he died, and then in a confused and heavily edited fashion. Two hundred years later, it is still being republished with four awkwardly separated "Parts"—the decision of the book's many editors, not Franklin. The story stops in 1757, when Franklin still had more than thirty years to live. It is the life of a Founding Father, but it halts without warning almost two decades before the beginning of the American Revolution. The narrative is full of what seem to be the garrulous interruptions and digressions of an old man. The long first Part was framed as a "letter" to his son and his "posterity"; when Franklin began the second Part, he had permanently broken with the son, who was a Loyalist, and so he addressed the rest of his book to "the Publick." The first Part was written in England by a reasonably loyal subject of George III; the rest was done in France and America by a triumphant revolutionary. All of this, combined with Franklin's advancing years, could have generated a book that is fragmentary and confused, a book that hardly could be expected to have much coherence or consistency, let alone a subtle form and plan. Indeed, the autobiography seems to fall into two unrelated halves. In Parts one and two—roughly the first half of the manuscript—the subject is the efforts of a boy and young man to become virtuous and to

[10] A useful account of the writing of the autobiography is in James A. Sappenfield, *A Sweet Instruction: Franklin's Journalism as a Literary Apprenticeship* (Carbondale, Ill., 1973), 178–82.

succeed in the world; the focus is on the self; struggle and change are mainly inward. The second half—Parts three and four—is mostly about public life; there is no more inner struggle, the man is more or less the same at fifty as he was at twenty-five. He grows older, of course, and richer, but no wiser. He now moves among the temptations of the world with a sure confidence that his character has been safely fashioned. He has been formed, and can now set about to reform some of the world around him. He has learned to be a good man; now he can get on with the business of becoming a great one.

These differences between the two halves of Franklin's story were not a result of age or of the lapses of time between the writing of the different parts of the book. Nor do they mean that the book did not have a plan. On the contrary, the shift in focus between the two halves was quite central to the plan of the book. Franklin chose a conventional ground plan for his memoirs, one that was fully antic- ipated in the first half of his manuscript and executed in the unfin- ished second half. The transition from private to public, from being good to doing good, actually occurs at the end of the first Part, where Franklin begins to talk about the Junto, his club of ambitious young men who would meet to discuss business, self-improvement, and civic reforms. The last paragraph he wrote in England in 1771 was about his work on the creation of a subscription library, and it begins with the telling words, "And now I set on foot my first Project of a public Nature."[11]

No eighteenth-century reader, British or American, would have been uncomfortable with an autobiography that began in youthful uncertainty, then passed to an inventory of emblematic accomplish- ments. There was already a rich fund of both fictional "lives" and autobiographies with exactly this schematic division. It was the pat- tern in the most famous fictional lives, John Bunyan's *The Pilgrim's Progress* and Daniel Defoe's *Robinson Crusoe*—though Defoe turned the pattern to much more complex and sophisticated purposes than most other writers. It was the customary shape of spiritual autobi- ographies not only among Puritans in America and England but among religious writers of all persuasions. Edward Gibbon, who was writing version after version of his own memoirs at about the same time Franklin was at work on his, also used it—changing the turning point in each of his six drafts, but still employing the pattern of preparation and false starts, followed by decisive change, followed again by achievement and retrospective evaluation. Franklin's manuscript may have been unfinished, but he conceived his book as a whole, within which he could deploy to good effect the ironic figure of the shrewd old philosopher observing, assessing, and sometimes smiling over the earnest youth and the middle-aged burgher.[12]

Franklin's picture of what a spiritual life ought to look like was probably taken from those two literary monuments of the age, *The Pilgrim's Progress* and *Robinson Crusoe,* the first published twenty-six years before he was born, the second thirteen years after. And here lay the sources of a potential difficulty. Defoe and Bunyan both wrote about the soul, and their primary audience was an audience of devout believers. They both had wanted to show how the Christian's struggle toward faith can finally triumph, not just over ordinary temptation but over despair—the supreme threat to the soul in both books. In Bunyan and Defoe, as in their greatest predecessor, Augustine, the stakes are infinitely high. What is at risk is not merely material advantage or reputation, nor even bare survival, but eternal life. This lent automatic drama to their stories, at least for those who believed. For the Christian pilgrim, the reward was infinite, and this made the dangers monstrous, the situation desperate beyond measure.[13]

Because of this, Bunyan and Defoe (and many other writers like them) were able to employ an uninhibited rhetoric of lamentation and exultation. Dread and deliverance are on every page. Bunyan framed his story as a dream that begins in a fearsome "Denn" in

[12] Franklin discusses Defoe and Bunyan in *Autobiography*, 13, 25–6. The first commentator to insist on Bunyan as an important model for the autobiography was Charles Sanford, in "An American Pilgrim's Progress," *American Quarterly* 6 (Winter 1954): 297–310. For a general context for Bunyan, see Paul Delany, *British Autobiography in the Seventeenth Century* (London, 1969). The uses of Bunyan's model in British writing is taken up in John Morris, *Versions of the Self: Studies in English Autobiography from John Bunyan to John Stuart Mill* (New York, 1966), 89–104. Crusoe is examined as a figure whose primary significance is as an emblem of economic change in Ian Watt, *The Rise of the Novel: Studies in Defoe, Richardson, and Fielding* (London, 1957). Two arguments that Crusoe's significance is not primarily economic but religious are Martin J. Greif, "The Conversion of Robinson Crusoe," *Studies in English Literature* 6 (1966): 551–74, and J. Paul Hunter, *The Reluctant Pilgrim* (Baltimore, 1966). By far the most intelligent writing on Gibbon's autobiography is in Patricia Meyer Spacks' fine *Imagining a Self: Autobiography and Novel in Eighteenth-Century England* (Cambridge, Mass., 1976).

[13] Augustine's *Confessions* is discussed in contrast to Franklin's autobiography in Sayre, *The Examined Self,* 7–12.

the midst of a "Wilderness." And within four sentences, the subject of the dream, the pilgrim Christian, is utterly out of hand:[14]

> And behold I saw a man clothed with rags, standing in a certain place, with his face from his own house, a book in his hand, and a great burden upon his back. I looked, and saw him open the book and read therein. And as he read, he wept and trembled. And not being able longer to contain, he spake out with a lamentable cry, saying *what shall I do?*

Defoe used the same kind of unrestrained language, even when his social and psychological purposes were much less straightforward than Bunyan's. When Crusoe is washed up, half-drowned, onto his island, he exults in a salvation that is infinitely more than the salvation of the body:[15]

> I was now landed, and safe on shore, and began to look up and thank God that my life was saved, in a case wherein there was, some minutes before, scarce any room to hope. I believe it is impossible to express to the life what the ecstasies and transports of the soul are when it is so saved, as I may say, out of the very grave. . . . I walked about on the shore, lifting up my hands, and my whole being, wrapt up in the contemplation of my deliverance, making a thousand gestures and motions which I cannot describe.

Franklin was also writing about a spiritual pilgrimage. And he was working within the conventional design proper to such books. But he never allowed his young character to despair, or to utter a "lamentable cry." He relinquished the emotional and rhetorical lat-

---

[14] Bunyan's opening dream sequence is in *The Pilgrim's Progress from This World to That Which Is To Come* (Oxford, 1980), 1.

[15] Crusoe's exultation at his "salvation" is in *The Life and Strange Adventures of Robinson Crusoe,* (New York, 1975), 39. Shea, *Spiritual Lives,* makes an interesting effort to define Franklin's autobiographical writing by reference to distinctions between American "Puritan" and "Quaker" models. But as a caution against such excessive precision, G. A. Starr makes the case, in *Defoe and Spiritual Autobiography* (Princeton, 1965), that "spiritual" autobiography was a practice across the entire spectrum of English Protestantism. Still, Starr's argument that "spiritual autobiography was the common property of English Protestantism, not the private domain of enthusiasts" might need to be broadened: intensely felt *experience*—as distinguished from certain writing habits—was hardly confined to dissenting groups ordinarily described as "enthusiastic." Indeed, the kinds of intensity and acuteness that might lead people to write spiritual lives were hardly confined to experiences normally referred to as "religious."

itude of "Denns," shipwrecks, or cannibals. There is no way at all to know what the emotional life of the actual Benjamin Franklin was like, either in youth or in middle age. In real life, he may even have "brake out," or made indescribable gestures. But in his autobiographical version of himself, he almost never loses his temper, and if he does, the outcome is harmless. His love for Miss Read, as he told it at least, is a quietly moderated affair with as much in it of prudence as passion. His description of his grief over his second son's death is muted and controlled. His problem was to find a way to tell such a story without being mired in a slough of tedium and triviality.[16]

Franklin clearly wanted his readers to find drama and moment in his memoirs. When he had little time left to write, and knew it, he chose to continue to work on his autobiography rather than to write an alternative book on The Art of Virtue, a book that would not have been a story at all, but a lecture on morality and discipline. He chose, emphatically, personal narrative as his last art form. This choice posed an intricate problem: to find a way to forgo the linguistic privileges of lamentation and exultation, to surrender the traditional narrative issue of the eternal fate of the soul, and still to write a life that would seem dramatic and in some way even momentous. In his storyteller's world of people doing quite ordinary things, where was the heroic test to be? In a life that seemed to have no higher aim than routine self-discipline, wealth, and civic Projects, what were the heroic odds? Franklin wrote in apparent deadpan seriousness about such events as getting his first silver spoon and china bowl. (His wife, not he, he carefully remembered, had bought them.) But what literary skill could turn this into an event of spiritual consequence? What hazard to the human spirit lay in a silver spoon and china bowl? Or buying beer on credit? Or overeating? Instead of an Island of Despair, Franklin had the safe, rectilinear streets of Philadelphia; instead of the terrors of enslavement, death, and damnation, he had workaday getting and spending; instead of wild verbal transports, he had a language that was constrained and modest. There was a terrific disparity between the conventions of the spiritual life and the story Franklin was telling. But this very disparity was exactly what generated possibilities of irony. He could intervene

[16] *Autobiography*, 126. Richard Bushman, in "On the Uses of Psychology: Conflict and Conciliation in Benjamin Franklin," *History and Theory* 5 (1966): 225–40, tries to bring some theories of ego-psychology to bear on Franklin's ways of avoiding conflict and conciliating adversaries. But Bushman is not as aware as one ought to be of the difference between a "personality" and a deliberately constructed, quasi-fictive character in an autobiography.

at will in his story, smiling over the "ridiculous" element in his early strivings—not too severely, of course, and just often enough to remind the reader that there was a sophisticated author behind the naive narrative, an author more than able to make his own wry assessments of his youthful hero.[17]

Such a tactic could even lead Franklin to hint that he might be making a parody of the very idea of spiritual pilgrimages. He could certainly have counted on a sophisticated audience ready to appreciate a winking burlesque of pious conceptions of self-improvement. And Franklin was a skilled and experienced parodist. He had always had to struggle to control a sometimes embarrassing propensity for "Satyr." (After the Revolution, a telling myth grew up that he was not allowed to write the Declaration of Independence because everyone was afraid he would bury a joke somewhere in it.)

When Franklin told the story of his running away from Boston, he described himself as a reasonable facsimile of Bunyan's pilgrim: He, too, is clothed in rags, he has turned "his face from his own house," and he has some obvious questions about *"what shall I do?"* But Franklin's presentation of his situation was as comic as it was fearful. He did not give himself a "great burden upon his back," but made a point of saying that his trunk was coming round by sea. His confusion about what to *do* turns out to be mainly a confusion about the prices of Philadelphia bread. And instead of "braking out in lamentation," as Crusoe did, he falls asleep in a Quaker meeting. The terrible insecurity that might have threatened to overcome a teen-aged runaway in a strange city dissolves into a temporary puzzlement, followed by a nap.

Defoe had Robinson Crusoe engage in intense bouts of self-examination. In truth, Crusoe's story is much more about what goes on in his head and heart than about his practical problems on the Island of Despair. At one of his lowest moments, for example, he is terrified by fantasies of cannibals. Finding a cave that might shelter him, he looks in and sees two beastlike eyes staring back at him. His fervid imagination convinces him that it might be the Devil himself. But then he heroically catches hold of himself, and reasons "that he that was afraid to see the Devil, was not fit to live twenty Years in an Island all alone; and that I durst to believe there was nothing in this

[17] *Autobiography,* 101.

Cave that was more frightful than my self." Crusoe's main achievement, after all, is not the "Inventions" that enable him to survive, but instead his willingness at last to investigate the inward cave where something lurks as frightful as his self.[18]

Franklin's truest subject was also self-examination. But when it came time to tell the story of his own exploration of his self, he did it in a way that sophisticated readers would quickly see veered toward parody. Franklin introduced the subject—his famous "Project for arriving at moral Perfection"—just after writing with some wit and a little anger about a Presbyterian preacher whose sermons he had heard "now and again" in Philadelphia. The sermon he claimed to remember across half a century was on a passage from Paul's letter to the Philippians: "Finally, Brethren, whatsoever things are true, honest, just, pure, lovely, or of good report, if there be any virtue, or any praise, think on these things." Paul's letter had much in common with Franklin's "Project." Paul asked the Philippians to strive to make their "conversation" "becoming"; to avoid strife through humility; to "Let your moderation be known unto all men"; to learn to live for the future, "forgetting those things which are behind, and reaching forth unto those things that are before." And Paul's goal was also perfection—through Christ, of course, "who shall change our vile body, that it may be fashioned like unto his, according to the working whereby he is able even to subdue all things unto himself."

The Presbyterian minister's failing, as Franklin told it, was that he could only interpret Paul's injunctions to mean reading Scripture, attending church, and, above all, "Paying a due respect to God's Ministers." And so, Franklin concluded, he stopped going to church at all. With this, he said, he was going to "leave" the religious question without apologies.[19]

But as soon as he "left" the subject, Franklin sprang his own version of Paul's hope for subduing all things. The words he chose would eventually take a place among his most cherished and most derided. "It was about this time that I conceived the bold and arduous Project of arriving at moral Perfection. I wished to live without commiting any Fault at any time; I would conquer all that either Natural Inclination, Custom, or Company might lead me into." The words are soldierly and militant: "bold . . . arduous . . . conquer."

[18] An excellent discussion of Crusoe's terror of the cave is in Spacks, *Imagining a Self*, 34.

[19] *Autobiography*, 102–11.

A few sentences further on, he will be "guarding," only to be "surprized" (and he meant surprised in a military sense: taken unaware, or ambushed).

This sort of vocabulary was quite appropriate to Philippians. Of all Paul's letters, it was the one written in the most desperate straits. He was in prison, facing the possibility of death. He was telling his beleaguered followers, the members of the first European congregation he had established, that they must have great courage, for they will seek their salvation "in fear and trembling." Paul was looking for "any means" for attaining salvation. He was certain that he was not "already perfect." The only thing he had learned for certain was to forget the past and to "reach forth. . . . I press toward the mark."

The latent connection between the minister's sermon on Paul's letter and Franklin's description of his own "Project" would have been obvious to any scripturally literate and watchful reader. Naive readers could trust Franklin's flat statement that he had "left" the subject of religion. They could forget all about Paul and read on, relaxing into Franklin's modest homemade plan, enjoying the notion that a man could improve his character the way he might weed a garden. But those sophisticated readers that Franklin certainly wanted would have seen at once that an intricate and perhaps amusing scheme was afoot. They might even have suspected that a connection was signaled by the obtrusive absence of any transition between Franklin's complaints about the Presbyterian minister and his announcement of his own "Project."

Franklin had none of Paul's conviction that vile bodies could be made perfect only by Christ's own fashioning. Given its proper scriptural framing, there is gentle comedy in Franklin's description of the way he laid out little columns under the names of the virtues he decided to cultivate, and made little marks to keep account of how often he had failed each day. (Could he have been conscious as he wrote that the word "mark"—hardly a common scriptural word—appeared twice in the King James Version of Philippians, and the noun "account" once?) Paul's letter was probably the most sectarian of his writings. Franklin's boast was that his Scheme had "no Mark of any . . . particular Sect." Paul's most urgent social rule for the Philippians was, "Look not every man on his own things, but every man also on the things of others." Franklin's message was that a man who does not look first on his own things is not fitted to look on the things of others. The Christological centerpiece of Paul's letter was that Christ "humbled himself . . . wherefore God also hath highly exalted him." Franklin included humility among the virtues he wanted to cultivate, with the hilarious gloss "Imitate Jesus and Socrates." Then he ended by saying that pride was the most difficult of the passions to "subdue": "Disguise it, struggle with it, beat it down, stifle it, mortify it as much as one pleases, it is still alive. . . . For even if you should conceive that I had compleatly overcome it, I should probably be proud of my Humility."[20]

Franklin's "Project" was remote from the kind of "fear and trembling" so important to Paul, to Bunyan and Defoe, and to dozens of other writers of English and American spiritual autobiographies. Franklin's subject was the same as theirs: the "arduous" pilgrimage of the man or woman bent on the bold conquest of besetting sins. The difference is that Franklin wrote about his "Project" from an ironic distance, occasionally even casting doubt on the idea of moral striving and pilgrimage. He did this over and over again in the autobiography. He told of pulling a drowning man from stormy waters, and finding that the man had a copy of *The Pilgrim's Progress* in his pocket. But the man turns out to be no pilgrim at all, only a drunken Dutchman. (Still, Franklin was careful to add, that copy of Bunyan's book was beautifully printed.) He twice mentioned that he, like young Robinson Crusoe, threatened to run away to sea, over his father's objections. But all he told about was running away on a boat that made a calm inland passage down through Long Island Sound; his nearest approach to shipwreck was having to spend a wet night in a leaky boat hold. One of the favored devices of conventional spiritual lives was the illness that brings a man face to face with death and provokes a conversion. Franklin described such an illness, "when I had just passed my 21st year." But he ended in irony, not a new awareness of eternity: "My Distemper was a Pleurisy, which very nearly carried me off: I suffered a good deal, gave up the Point in my own mind, and was rather disappointed when I found my Self recovering; regretting in some degree that I must some time or other have all that disagreeable Work to do over again."[21]

Paul told the Philippians about his own profound faults—that he had been a Pharisee and a persecutor of the church of Christ. Frank-

---

[20] Ibid.,115–16. A neat comparison of Franklin on the subject of pride with a similar remark in the autobiography of Jonathan Boucher is in Griffith, "The Rhetoric of Franklin's 'Autobiography,' " 87.
[21] Franklin, *Autobiography, 25.*

lin, too, littered his book with frettings about his own "errata." But they turn out always to be certain harmless little mistakes. The one he chose to give most attention to was merely that he lent out a small sum of money that did not really belong to him. He was inviting some of his readers, surely, to smile at a tradesman's quest for Perfection, and to smile a little, too, at the literary and scriptural models of spiritual questing.

Franklin's writing strategy fed on doubt about how "serious" he was being, not just in the pages about his "Project," but throughout the autobiography. Indeed, this was one of his main purposes: to keep alive a certain confusion about whether he was in earnest after all. For example, just after describing his plan of daily moral accounting, Franklin told one of his finest anecdotes. It concerns a man who wants a smith to grind an ax head for him until it is bright and shiny. The smith agrees to hold the ax against the wheel if his customer will do the turning. After a long grinding, the tired customer inspects the ax and declares himself satisfied. The smith, enjoying the game, objects that the ax is still only "speckled." "Yes, says the Man; but—*I think I like a speckled Ax best.*" This anecdote has charmed many sympathetic readers into thinking that Franklin was admitting that since perfection is impossible, a person ought to be happy with modest gains, with being morally speckled. Such a possibility ought surely to have preserved Franklin from the angry commentaries that have cried humbug on his little "Project." The problem is that as soon as he finished the anecdote of the speckled ax, he disavowed it. It was, he said, a form of thinking that only "pretended to be Reason." The truth is, he concluded, that the only thing anyone can do is to keep grinding, always, never becoming reconciled to any speckles at all. The effect of telling the seductive story of the ax, then quickly disowning it, is to create for inquisitive readers a highly ambiguous moral outcome. The implicit rhetorical victory certainly goes to the anecdote, even though the author flatly repudiated it. But Franklin was not through with ambiguity yet. He immediately passed to a listing of the promptings of his own weakness:[22]

---

[22] Ibid., 111–12. Even the most sensitive readers usually misconstrue the speckled ax anecdote. Sayre, in *The Examined Self,* concludes that the anecdote deflates the entire Project, making it not irony or parody, but something approaching farce. Shea, in *Spiritual Autobiography in Early*

Something that pretended to be Reason was every now and then suggesting to me, that such extream Nicety as I exacted of my self might be a kind of Foppery in Morals, which if it were known would make me ridiculous; that a perfect Character might be attended with the Inconvenience of being envied and hated; and that a benevolent Man should allow a few Faults in himself, to keep his Friends in Countenance.

Again, as with the speckled ax, there is a pronounced disparity between Franklin's overt position on the matter of perfection, and the way he couches these "suggestions." The promptings of weakness are rejected even before being listed, but the rhetorical weight—and wit—is all on their side. Franklin's governing strategy was to write a book with just such a bifocal moral vision, a book that could be read at least two ways, by two different kinds of readers.

When Franklin sat for the Cochin drawing in 1777, he did something that went beyond the devices of the fur hat and the bifocals, beyond the political tactics of an American commissioner. He allowed Cochin to pose him three-quarters (much easier for the artist than a face-on portrait). But he did not look in the direction his head was aimed. Instead he turned his eyes sharply to his right, looking toward the viewer. The result was that his right eye did not look through his bifocals at all. It was no easy task, for these were not half-glasses, and they were not worn loosely, down on the nose. They were large and close-fitting. He could not have looked over them, and it took some effort (and certainly forethought) to look out from behind them. The effect was remarkable. The plainest message the glasses gave was that he needed them to see, both up close and at a distance. But here he was, lancing a canny right eye out of the picture, as though he had perfectly clear vision in it, a keenness of sight that could have dispensed entirely with glasses—even bifocals. The picture insisted, in fact, that he had no less than three ways of focusing on the world, each one adequate for some purpose: two through his glasses, which he needed for everyday kinds of seeing; and a third *around* them—a very special way of seeing or being seen.

America, does not go quite so far, but does take the speckled ax story at face value, even suggesting that it contains a sort of key to Franklin's moral system.

In his autobiography, too, Franklin managed to suggest a form of social vision that went beyond both the hopeful foreseeing of earnest youth and the ironic hindsight of venerable sagacity. He managed, that is, to fortify his life story with a systematic social analysis and commentary. During the two centuries since Franklin wrote his History, writers like Max Weber have treated him as the model of the petit bourgeois spirit—as a man, that is, whose purposes are only steady work and accumulation. Others, like D. H. Lawrence, have ridiculed him as a man who wanted only to build a constricting little "paddock" for experience, inside which he might comfortably jog round and round, avoiding every risk to the spirit. But Franklin lived and wrote in a very particular social setting, and much of his effort was to suggest a penetrating analysis of that setting which would make his life seem heroic—not just earnest, and not merely the subject of his own saving ironies, but authentically bold and arduous.[23]

Franklin was too good a writer to have made such a social analysis openly. For one thing, to be open about it would have made the figure either of the earnest youth or the ironic savant difficult to sustain. For another, it would have entangled him in disputatious prose that would have weighed heavily on his narrative. Finally, his most engrained habit as a journalist, almanac-maker, and publicist was to fold argument unobtrusively into his writing, to persuade by humor, parable, and other forms of insinuation, rather than frontally. And so his social commentary—what might be called the ideology of his autobiography—is threaded through his book, surfacing only intermittently, and then in an indirect and even coded fashion.

The outlines of Franklin's social commentary are as simple and as unsurprising as they are unstated and elusive. His picture of his world centered on the fact that individuals who lacked power were dependent on those who had it. By hint, by indirection, and by parable, he gradually built a description of eighteenth-century society as a complicated web of relationships of power in which he, and others like him, were caught, subject to the arbitrary whims of other

[23] The debate on whether the "real" Benjamin Franklin was a wise and good man, a witty man, a Bounderby figure, or a mere confidence man—a debate that seems at last to be exhausted and was never very sensible anyhow—can be followed for all it is worth in Charles Sanford, ed., *Benjamin Franklin and the American Character* (Boston, 1955).

people. In such a world, a young man's efforts at self-control were more than half-comic attempts to acquire better habits that might lead to china bowls and silver spoons. The struggle—after all—was against the whole world, against a social order saturated with rank, authority, and patronage. And in such a world, any attempt to gain a measure of autonomy for the self could be understood as a real spiritual adventure, of which economic success or security was only a minor and even trivial component.

Early in his memoirs, Franklin gave a compressed history of his ancestral family. The Franklins, he claimed, had lived since "time immemorial" in a house at Ecton, on a thirty-acre freehold, with a smith's business. The family was part of the free-born yeomanry. But not all of its members, by any means, enjoyed this status. In every generation, as far back as the record went, the eldest son had inherited the house, the land, and the smithy. Such a family was a miniature patronage system, with entitlements guaranteed and favors anxiously sought. As for himself and his direct line of descent, Franklin observed pointedly that he was the youngest son of a youngest son of a youngest son, and so on for five generations. He and every man in his direct line had always occupied the lowest rung on the ladder of arbitrary entitlement, suckling always at the hind teat of privilege.

Franklin said he was offering this bit of family history only as an "anecdote." But it begins to take on weight when he describes how his father and uncle, the two youngest sons in their generation, had broken with the family past. They had inherited no property. They had become dissenters, while their older brothers remained in the Church of England. And, most momentously, they had left home to go to New England. This cutting loose from the past, with its customary forms of property and religion, was what Franklin eventually celebrated in the epitaph he wrote for his father: that he had raised his family "without an Estate or any gainful Employment."[24]

But even if Josiah Franklin had inherited nothing and worked for no man, still the lines of authority and patronage persisted. Franklin's father was in effect his first patron, deciding first that young Benjamin should go to grammar school and study for the ministry, then chang-

[24] *Autobiography*, 4–7, 11.

ing his mind and deciding to make the boy a tradesman. It was Josiah
Franklin who signed the paper apprenticing Benjamin to his brother
James. It was to his father that Benjamin appealed, without success,
for help in setting up as a printer in Philadelphia. And if family
functioned as a kind of patronage system, then apprenticeship was
another institutionalized nexus of authority and obligation, power and
dependence. The world Franklin pictured himself growing up in was
a world where men who have power or money or position can
dispense or withhold it for good reason or bad, or for no reason at all.
In such a world, words like "bold," "arduous," and "conquer" might
after all fit a young man's attempts to break free. Franklin defined his
own initial ambitions in simple terms: to become his own master in
his own house and shop. But such a simple ambition could take on
heroic proportions in a society dominated by arbitrary power. He
described, with little obvious passion and with no comment, how he
had been beaten as an apprentice—and it did not help that the man
doing the beating was his own brother. He told about being publicly
humiliated by his next master, cruelly betrayed by the governor of
Pennsylvania, and forced even to abandon his trade of printing to
apprentice himself to a charitable merchant. Against such men and
such powers, he has no resources outside the self. In real life, of course,
he may have used every avenue of advancement, every trick of the
patronage system. But in the autobiography, he arranges the contest
as one between a young man alone and an entrenched and ominous
system of social predation.

One of Franklin's favorite, and most artful, writing devices was to
use charming anecdotes of no apparent consequence to the unsus-
pecting reader but full of meaning for those who could penetrate
them. And he used such an anecdote, early in the autobiography, to
establish the main argument of his social commentary. He had described growing up in Boston, being apprenticed in his brother's
newspaper office, then running away to Philadelphia to make a new
start. He goes to work for that "odd fish" of Philadelphia printing,
Samuel Keimer. Then the governor of Pennsylvania takes a sudden
interest in him, and even offers to lend him a hundred pounds to buy
printing equipment in England so he can set himself up in compe-
tition with Keimer. He remembered being a little overwhelmed. Sir

William Keith had been, after all, a knight, and governor of a great province: "How could I think his generous Offers insincere? I believ'd him one of the Best men in the World."[25]

The moment was one that any writer loves. There was no doubting where the story would lead next; all Franklin had to do was to write it, to tell how he had gone to England, trusting Keith's promises, only to find that he had been betrayed. There had been no hundred pounds—not even any of the letters of introduction Keith promised to send on the ship. And so Franklin wound up alone in London, and had to make his own way.

But Franklin did not seize the moment. His marvelous storytelling skill seemingly deserted him, for a while at least. For several pages, he had carefully set the stage for his trip to London and Keith's betrayal. But instead of driving on with his narrative, he decided to pause, to insert a comic but irrelevant account of the way he broke his vegetarian diet on his runaway trip from Boston to Philadelphia. Then, after this anecdote, he spent several more pages tidying up his life story, making a sort of interim statement of accounts. There was a quick characterization of his relationship with Keimer (which really belonged back a few pages with a memorable description of Keimer's personality). Then he wrote a short paragraph on his suspended courtship of Deborah Read. Next came a list of the friends he had had in Philadelphia at the time, with a couple of pages of anecdotes about them. Only then, finally, did he get back to his story and tell how he had sailed for England, still counting on Keith's generous patronage, but with the smell of betrayal already in the Atlantic winds.

Franklin's intrusion of the anecdote about his abandonment of a strict vegetarian diet was an awkward interruption. He wrote no transition from the sentences explaining his scheme to go to London with Keith's promised backing. He simply injected a paragraph beginning, "I believe I have omitted mentioning that on my first Voyage from Boston . . ." (He had his manuscript with him, and could easily have checked. He was writing, as was his custom, on paper ruled down the center. He wrote on the left side, and kept the right half free for corrections or insertions. He could have gone back—as he sometimes did—and put this paragraph where it belonged: in his story of his first trip from Boston to Philadelphia.)

[25] Ibid., 31–41.

After this clumsy start, Franklin told one of those little stories that are so treasured by those who admire him as a homespun sage:[26]

> being becalm'd off Block Island, our People set about catching Cod and hawl'd up a great many. Hitherto, I had stuck to my Resolution of not eating animal Food; . . . I consider'd . . . the taking every Fish as a kind of unprovok'd Murder, since none of them had or ever could do us any Injury that might justify the Slaughter. All this seem'd very reasonable. But I had formerly been a great lover of Fish, and when this came hot out of the Frying Pan, it smelt admirably well. I balanc'd some time between Principle and Inclination: till I recollected, that when the Fish were opened, I saw small Fish taken out of their Stomachs: Then thought I, if you eat one another, I don't see why we mayn't eat you. So I din'd upon Cod very heartily and continu'd to eat with other people, returning only now and then occasionally to a vegetable Diet. So convenient a thing it is to be a *reasonable Creature,* since it enables one to find or make a Reason for every thing one has a mind to do.

The moment is one of Franklin's best; the autobiography would be a poorer book without it, and there surely is no reason to wonder why he wanted to include it somewhere. Nor is there any profit in wondering whether he remembered the incident on the day when he was writing these particular pages. The order in which he recalled things and the order in which he wrote them were probably very different; we can know something about the second, but nothing much about the first. The puzzle, instead, is why Franklin chose to plant the anecdote precisely where he did in his narrative, chronologically out of place, and with no obvious connection with what he had just written or with what he was about to write.

One simple solution would be to conclude that Franklin was only being hasty or careless. This might explain why he put the passage where he did in a draft, but it would not explain why he decided to leave it there when he later made revisions in the manuscript—especially when he had that invitingly empty right-hand side of his pages to work in. Franklin was a very inventive and careful writer. He would not have been blind to the fact that introducing the fish-eating story where he did would create a small but aggravating problem: A few pages earlier, he had already told about eating a dinner of ox cheek on that same trip down from Boston to Philadelphia, and he had mentioned this much more serious breach of dietary principles without even pausing to comment.

The story of the codfish was clearly not just about a boy's decision to abandon a vegetarian diet. Nor was it merely a cute philosophical reflection on the way "Reason" can mediate between inclination and principle, though on the surface, it does work in a nicely ironic way between those two extremes. It is a commentary on questions lying somewhere between an individual's personal decisions and the abstract philosophical grounds on which moral choices ought to be made. This was Franklin's favorite writing terrain, the social. The anecdote raised two problems, one involving power and the capacity to do "injury," the second concerning Franklin's own relationship to the others on the ship, those he called "our People." In his "reasoning," these two social issues are closely related. First, is it all right to kill fish? Second, will he lurk off alone in some corner of the ship while the others fall to fishing, cooking, and eating? Or will he be able to join them in their slaughtering and feasting? The appealing but utterly silly answer to the first question is that it is all right to injure those who injure others. And this, in turn, makes it all right for the runaway, alone and traveling under an assumed name and a false cover story, to take a place as a member of the toiling and celebrating "People." The problem turns out to have little to do with one boy's diet, and probably even less to do with reason, inclination, and principle. It concerns, instead, the paramount social questions of power and community and self.

No matter how out of place the anecdote is chronologically, Franklin put it exactly where it belonged conceptually. In the end, it was not so much an anecdote as it was a parable. And, rightly understood, the parable brings the mounting issues of his situation as a young man in Philadelphia into the sharpest kind of focus. He had just been describing his dependence on Keimer—that "odd fish." He and Governor Keith have been assiduously cultivating each other. The young man's purpose is to break free of his status as Keimer's journeyman, to become Keith's client and Keimer's competitor. Keith has more sinister purposes. If he does what he promises, it will injure Keimer; if he does not, it will injure Franklin; either way, he will achieve the essential purpose of "aristocrats" everywhere: to be able to inflict pain or give pleasure gratuitously, or for reasons known only to themselves.

Franklin was describing a young man caught up in the social net of dependence and injury, that predatory chain in which big fish like Keith devour careless little fish like the "poor ignorant Boy" he called himself. What made the young Franklin vulnerable was his "inclination" to enter the chain of social predation, conspiring with Keith to injure Keimer. (In fact, immediately after the codfish story, Franklin described with relish the way he had symbolically brought the gluttonous Keimer down by first convincing him to go on a strict vegetable diet, then agreeing to join him in a feast of roast pork: "He invited me and two Women Friends to dine with him, but it being brought too soon upon table, he could not resist the Temptation, and ate it all up before we came.") Principle might have suggested trying to avoid the nets of power and dependence altogether, even at the cost of being some kind of lonesome outcast from "our People." But reason, conveniently enough, suggested another answer: Try to earn a place at the head of the chain, as one of the terminal predators who can decide, reasonably, when and what to eat, but who do not need to fear being eaten. And since a boy cannot suddenly leap out of his dependence, it made sense to look for the protective company of others. And this, in turn, led Franklin with perfect logic directly from the codfish tale through his account of Keimer and the roast pig to his first courtship of Miss Read, and then on to an affectionate discussion of his Philadelphia friendships. Breaking out of the chain of dependence would not be easy, but one effective strategy for a young man might be to try to move in a school of similarly placed men, and with someone like Deborah Read Franklin as an unobtrusive "helpmate."[27]

So what appears at first sight to be a hasty writer's lapse turns out to be an ingenious writer's trick, and a trick that gave Franklin the point of departure for a moral analysis not only of his situation as a young Philadelphia printer, and not only of his climb to wealth, power, and fame, but of the social context that defined both his dilemma and his escape from it. As anecdote, the fish story may interrupt the narrative, but as parable, it helps to organize that narrative into a deft commentary on eighteenth-century social relations. It makes Keimer and Keith into something more than curious indi-

[27] Ibid., 42–50.

viduals (which they also are, of course). In light of the parable, they become representative social types. And what they represent is an organized mesh of relationships of patronage and clientele, which threatened always to determine individual experience not according to effort and desert but through whimsy, cynicism, and someone else's superior capacity for doing damage.

The codfish anecdote was not an isolated prose gesture. It was only one of a number of moments in his manuscript in which Franklin made eating a social metaphor. The contest between his own ambition and the structures of power was what gave significance to such apparently trivial choices as decisions about what to eat, when, and with whom. He carefully pictured himself as an apprentice, with a "repast" of a slice of bread, a handful of raisins, and a glass of water. But what he had in mind was that by eating this, instead of taking his meals at his master's table, he had gained a measure of independence. He could then use that independence to read, to improve his mind—and, even more, his pen, which would eventually be a "principal Means of my Advancement." He told of buying some gingerbread from a woman in New Jersey while he was a runaway. He is tattered, but because he has developed his "conversation" she later gives him a whole dinner of ox cheek. When he wrote about the moment of his most intense solitude, on that first day in Philadelphia, he described eating the simplest meal of all, bread, and then washing it down with the simplest drink, water from the Delaware. Then, as he went on with his story, a kindly man points him toward a job, and gives him breakfast in the bargain. Those who give the food might be generous. Or they might be deceivers only pretending to disburse largess. When Governor Keith first meets Franklin at Keimer's shop, at least as the old autobiographer decided to tell it, he offers to treat Franklin at the tavern to some "excellent Madeira." The only secure meal is one eaten alone, and as rudimentary as possible—or perhaps occasionally shared, like the one he remembered having with a landlady in London: "half an anchovy each, on a very little strip of bread and butter, and half a pint of ale between us." The first sign of luxury Franklin chose to reveal in his own household was that silver spoon and china porridge bowl. When he described his first trip back home to Boston, to ask his father for help, he drew a very pointed scene in his brother's printing shop. He wants to make some sort of display to show that he has achieved

success. He lets the men see his watch. But then he caps the performance with a symbolic act of largess: He treats his brother's men to
drinks. What he bargained about with his brother before, he now
dispenses. A little later, he used the roast-pig incident to signal his
triumph over Keimer; in the emblematic world Franklin was con-
structing, there could be no surer sign that Keimer was a doomed
victim of "natural inclination."[28]

There is an explicit connection between temperance in food and
drink and Franklin's practical hopes of success: He wanted to be
clearheaded. But food and drink mean much more in the autobiography. They were Franklin's signals to the reader that his struggle is
not against his brother or Keimer or Keith or even his own father. It
is against a social system that threatened to snare an unwary pilgrim
in a net of power and dependence, patronage and clientele. There is
no reason to doubt that all these incidents of eating and drinking
actually happened, or that food and drink were as ubiquitous signs of
social relations in Franklin's actual experience as they seem to be in
human cultures in general. Franklin ate hundreds of meals, and
treated dozens of men to dinners or to some "excellent Madeira."
But autobiography does not usually notice what the members of a
society take implicitly for granted. Like any autobiographer, Franklin chose to tell some things and to be silent about others, and such
choices always make a point. When he wrote about his father, for
example, he characterized the man briefly and deftly. But he chose to
tell only one extended anecdote, and that was about eating:[29]

> At his Table he lik'd to have as often as he could, some sensible
> Friend or Neighbour, to converse with, and always took care
> to start some ingenious or useful Topic for Discourse, which
> might tend to improve the Minds of his Children. By this
> means he turn'd our Attention to what was good, just, and
> prudent in the Conduct of Life; and little or no Notice was ever
> taken of what related to the Victuals on the Table, whether it
> was well or ill drest, in or out of season, of good or bad flavour,
> preferable or inferior to this or that other thing of the kind; so
> that I was bro't up in such a perfect Inattention to those Matters
> as to be quite Indifferent to what kind of food was set before

[28] Ibid., 17–18, 27, 29–30, 34, 35, 43, 57.
[29] Ibid., 10–11.

me; and so unobservant of it, that to this Day, if I am ask'd I can scarce tell, a few Hours after Dinner, what I din'd upon. This has been a Convenience to me in travelling, where my Companions have been sometimes very unhappy for want of a suitable Gratification of their more delicate because better instructed Tastes and Appetites.

(The only direct biographical fact Franklin chose to give about his mother was a remark that seems, curiously, both boastful and plaintive: that she had "suckled all her 10 Children.")

Taken at face value, the passage about his father's table protocols is a fine example of Franklin's most familiar writing routines. He took a homely detail and showed how, in the course of a long life, an apparently trivial Invention could produce a great deal of Convenience. But taken as a parable, the anecdote poses a much more serious opposition: between a delicate palate and whatever is good, just, and prudent in life—almost as though a person with an eye to food is apt to be blind to justice. And this opposition has nothing at all to do with Convenience. With uncharacteristic insistence, Franklin struck four times at the obvious point about the food: "whether it was well or ill drest, in or out of season, of good or bad flavour, preferable or inferior to this or that other thing of the kind." The sentence does not build on this repetition; it just hammers, as if the food were not food at all, but something more. And what that something was soon becomes clear: He claims a kind of superiority to those "Companions" along the road who were spoiled by their "more delicate because better instructed Tastes and Appetites."

The second half of Franklin's autobiography is the story of a man who seems to have won his private war against authority, patronage, and class. And there is no clearer indication of this than the fact that the middle-aged protagonist no longer frets about what he eats or drinks. Instead, Franklin begins to pay attention to what he dispenses to other people. As one of two negotiators making a treaty with a group of Native Americans, he concludes the deliberations with a customary gift of rum. The result is just what he expects: "They were all drunk, Men and Women, quarrelling and fighting. Their dark-colour'd Bodies, half naked, seen only by the gloomy Light of the Bonfire, running after and beating one another with Firebrands, accompanied by their horrid Yellings, form'd a Scene the most resembling our Ideas of Hell that could well be imagin'd." The next

day, the band sent an elder to make a sheepish apology, saying that
the "great Spirit" must have meant rum for the Indians to get drunk
with. When he recalled the incident, Franklin observed heavily that
"indeed if it be the Design of Providence to extirpate these Savages
in order to make room for the Cultivators of the Earth, it seems not
improbable that Rum may be the appointed Means."[30]

A bit further on, commenting on his efforts to assist the haughty
General Edward Braddock in his campaign against the French, Franklin used a similar writing strategy. He attempts to persuade Braddock that his formal order of march will open his troops to
ambush—exactly what is going to happen. Braddock's arrogant answer is that while the "Savages" might be able to succeed against
mere colonials, they have no chance against the "King's regular and
disciplined Troops, Sir." The import of the exchange is plain enough:
Franklin pictured himself as the earnest provincial, and Braddock as
the arrogant agent of power. But Franklin added to this picture a
telltale invocation of food. He listed, in loving detail, the parcels he
had dispensed to each of Braddock's regular officers. The list took
sixteen lines to write out, and it dwelt caressingly on each item: the
hams and the raisins, the six pounds of good Muscovado sugar, the
chocolate, the Gloucester cheese, the "2 Doz. old Madeira Wine,"
and the rest of the items that made up each parcel. If the king's
officers were going to march into a disastrous and humiliating defeat, they were going to be superbly fed, as befitted men with "better
instructed Tastes and Appetites."[31]

There was nothing very original about Franklin's commentary on
patronage and power. His essential argument was a fairly routine
restatement of a theme worked out in a sizable body of British and
American attacks on abuses of privilege and corruptions of power.
But Franklin worked bare ideology into a personal narrative that was
charming, readable, and unpretentious. And this enabled him to
revise some traditional premises of spiritual biography and autobiography. One of the initial assumptions of narrative models of the
Christian life, from Augustine onward, had been that the world is a
place of sin, fatally and irremediably. In such a world, the Christian
pilgrimage involved a terrific solitude. The Christian might move

[30] Ibid., 153–4.
[31] Ibid., 176–7.

toward some limited form of community—like Augustine's monastic retreat, or the small band of fellow pilgrims that gathered around Bunyan's Christian, or Crusoe's curious friendship with Friday. But these were communities of withdrawal, islands of temporary fellowship in a lost world.

For Franklin's hero, the outcome is different. He knows evil, not as the inescapable principle of the world but as a social fact. To be sure, evil is everywhere and deeply rooted—otherwise the struggle against it might indeed become comic or ridiculous. Experience threatens always to bind men to patronage and power, just as the need to eat threatens to make them prisoners of "Appetite." But if a man can master himself, he may escape the nets of power. The young hero of this drama may use methods as trivial and homely as making little black marks in a moral account book. But there is nothing trivial or homely about the independence he is after. Gaining autonomy in a world where everything—custom, company, and natural inclination—conspires against it is a bold conquest indeed.

Franklin was not just "secularizing" inherited notions of the Christian career. The goal his young hero turns his eyes to is no less "spiritual" than Augustine's or Bunyan's. It might not fit traditional Christian notions of damnation or eternal life. But its final concern is with character and spirit—not with material gains and losses. Franklin's autobiography is full of men and women he thinks have won the moral struggle but are still poor and powerless—including his own father. The story is also crowded with men (though not women) who have wealth and position, but have utterly lost the struggle to master the self. What mattered to Franklin was not a substitution of secular for religious goals. His concern was to devise a program of moral perfection that large numbers of people might actually work at with a measure of success, not because the spiritual end was modest but because the means were workable. And such people might then confront the world, not as isolated pilgrims, nor huddling together in withdrawn communities, but on something like equal terms. Franklin believed (at least the figure that looked out from his autobiography with the same clear eye that peered from behind the spectacles in the Cochin drawing believed) that virtue might actually prevail, and in history, not eternity.

If virtue was to win out, it would not be the result of the accumulated efforts of solitary men sitting alone at night reviewing their "Conduct" during the day. It would be because men gathered and organized for the purpose. One of the deepest impulses, both of the hero of the autobiography and of Franklin in real life, was for membership. He was a tireless Mason. He formed the famous Junto in Philadelphia to bring young men together to work at self-improvement and public projects. He helped organize libraries and militia companies, fire companies and philosophical societies. As soon as he finished describing his "Project for arriving at moral Perfection," he observed with some force that it was not aimed at himself only, but had always been connected in his mind with another *"great and extensive project."* This somewhat mysterious remark came at the end of the section of the book we know as the second Part, which he wrote in Paris in 1784. When he began to write again in Philadelphia, four years later, he immediately returned to the subject, and explained what the extensive project was. He hoped to create a grand "united Party for Virtue, by forming the Virtuous and good Men of all Nations into a regular Body." He grumbled that the "narrow circumstances" of his youth and the "multifarious Occupations" of his later life had prevented him from realizing this dream of a "Society of the *Free and Easy."* But, he insisted, he never stopped believing it was a "practicable Scheme."[32]

Just after he discussed this "Scheme"—the essential public extension of his Project to gain moral perfection for himself—Franklin turned to a capsule history of his main writing and publishing ventures: the *Gazette* and Poor Richard's Almanack. Typically, he made this change of subject abruptly. But there are important connections between the "united Party for Virtue" and the terms in which he describes his writing enterprises. As Franklin pictures them, both the almanac and the newspaper were aimed at giving moral "Instruction." And both had proved to be "practicable." Poor Richard "came to be in such Demand that I reaped considerable Profit from it, vending annually near ten Thousand." The preface to the last almanac, sometimes reprinted as "Father Abraham's Speech" and sometimes as "The Way to Wealth," was the most spectacular success of Franklin's lifetime, both in America and in Europe. He boasted that "The Piece being universally approved was copied in all the Newspapers of the Continent, reprinted in Britain on a Broadside to be stuck up in Houses, two Translations were made of it in French, and great Numbers bought by the Clergy and Gentry to

---

[32] Ibid., 114, 117–20.

distribute gratis among their poor Parishioners and Tenants." And he held up the *Gazette* as an example to young printers, not only that they might profit from it, but also that they might be able to succeed in offering moral instruction.[33]

Both Franklin's idea for a "united Party for Virtue" and his belief that it was "practicable" were drawn from this experience as an author, printer, and bookseller. During his long career, he had had three different notions of what it meant to be a writer. Two of them were explicit, traditional, and could be taken for granted; the third was newer and more problematic. The first was that writing—and the reading that prepared a man to write—was a direct means of getting and keeping advantage in the system of patronage. Franklin tells with relaxed ease of the governor of New York who is willing to meet a poor boy just because the lad owns many books, or about the woman who gives him a dinner just because he has improved his "Conversation." He describes secretly slipping his first essays under the door of his brother-master's newspaper office, in the hope that if they are printed he can reveal himself and gain a redefinition of his apprenticeship. He explains, without self-consciousness, that a pamphlet he wrote favoring a new issue of paper money eventually won him the contract for printing the money itself—"another advantage of my being able to write." His bitter experience with Governor Keith was an extended study in the precarious but typical relationship between a faithless patron and a talented young writer. This writer, the young man using his skills as a way of attracting attention and support from others better placed in the social scheme, is the autobiographical figure of naive youth, ready to work at his prose and his "Conversation," and confident that the system of power will reward him.[34]

Later, when he was able to retire from his printing business, Franklin began to emphasize a second, equally traditional motive for writing. Now he was a gentleman of leisure, and could think of writing as an amateur's undertaking, free of direct instrumental implications. He could even suggest that his own escape into leisured amateurism was mirrored in the experience of the Colonies as a whole. When he proposed the founding of a learned society of like-minded gentlemen, he did it in these terms: "The first Drudgery of Settling new Colonies, which confines the Attention of People to mere Ne-

[33] Ibid., 120–3.
[34] Ibid., 21, 27, 38, 82.

cessities, is now pretty well over; and there are many in every Province in Circumstances that set them at Ease, and afford Leisure to cultivate the finer Arts, and improve the common Stock in Knowledge."[35] It was on these assumptions about the writer's calling that Franklin produced such different pieces of work as the marvelously scandalous "Speech of Polly Baker" and his accounts of his electrical experiments. For the gentleman of cultivated leisure, there was no fundamental difference between tossing off an anonymous bagatelle and publishing a scientific experiment. Both were exercises in the "finer Arts," and either might conceivably add to the common stock of knowledge. In the autobiography, this was the conception of the writer's career that found its voice in the sophisticated ironies of the wily old sage about the efforts of the young man to survive the "Drudgery" of attending to his own "mere Necessities."

Franklin's third notion of the relationship of the writer to his work and his readers was not tied either to patronage or to leisured amateurism. This was the idea of writing for "the Publick," turning out prose for sale—not for patrons or politicians who might reward the author, and not as a display of talented wealth, but as a commodity for the market. Franklin never made this motive explicit (and by the time he set to work on the autobiography it was probably more habit than idea, though no less strong). In fact, whenever he declared a motive for writing, it was never simply to earn money from sales. He insisted in the autobiography that the real purpose of Poor Richard was to improve the manners and morals of the people. He took pride in the fact that "The Way to Wealth" was distributed in France "gratis." He comforted himself with the thought that the *Gazette,* however profitable it may have been, was full of "Instruction." But writing for the market was one of the most central and important facts of his life. No serious writer in America, and few in England, enjoyed anything like Franklin's success at reaching large audiences.

No American before Tom Paine had so many readers. And no American before Washington Irving came even close to earning the kind of money Franklin did from his work. By the time he was able to retire from active participation in his firm in 1748, his annual income from it was a very handsome £2,000. Of this, only about one-fifth came from printing jobs, public and private. Three-fifths

[35] "Proposals for Promoting Useful Knowledge among the British Plantations in America," *Papers,* 2:380.

came from the *Gazette,* in which Franklin's own prose had always played an important part. The other one-fifth came from the almanac, which he chose to continue writing long after he became a silent partner in the firm. More than anything else—at least during the period of his life covered in the autobiography—Benjamin Franklin was a writer by profession. He had ambitions, and used his prose to attract the patronage that might help satisfy them. Then he had leisure, and wrote as though it were an act of noblesse oblige. But writing things for a public to buy was one of the most consistent practices of his life. It was probably this, more than anything, that had made his writing the "chief Means of my Advancement." In the autobiography, the figure of the writer who had been able to use the market to gain freedom from both patronage and "Necessity" stands behind both earnest youth and ironic age, making Franklin's intermittent and coded judgments on the nature of power, dependence, and patronage, judgments that transcend both the earnestness of the boy and the ironies of the old man.[36]

In all this, Franklin seemed casual, even innocent. But, as he well knew, he was actually entering one of the most serious and sophisticated debates of his age. He was carefully homespun, as always. But he was engaging questions that every major British writer had fretted over for two generations. The debate turned on the consequences of a popular idea that Britain was making a fateful passage from what Adam Smith termed a "crude" to a "civilized" state. As

[36] An extremely useful and detailed discussion of the business of the firm of Franklin and Hall is in Lawrence D. Wroth, "Benjamin Franklin: the Printer at Work," *Journal of the Franklin Institute* 239 (1942): 105–32. It is difficult to judge just how "provincial" Philadelphia or New England was in the eighteenth century. London got its first daily newspaper, *The Courant,* only in 1702. *The Spectator* was normally printed in a run of only 3,000 copies, and a popular weekly paper of the 1730s was printed in editions that usually ran under 10,000 copies. See J. H. Plumb, "The Public, Literature and the Arts in the 18th Century," in Paul Fritz and David Williams, eds., *The Triumph of Culture: 18th Century Perspectives* (Toronto, 1971), 27–48. Later, in the 1760s, Samuel Johnson estimated that the *Gentleman's Magazine* sold about 10,000 copies of each issue—though this was probably much too generous an estimate. At the beginning of the 1760s, the London *Public Advertiser* was printed in runs of only about 2,000, probably about the same number that Franklin printed of the *Gazette* in the 1740s. A very popular political book, like Burke's *Thoughts on the Cause of the Present Discontents,* was lucky to sell as many as 3,000 copies, about a third as many as Poor Richard at its annual peak. The main difference between London and Philadelphia probably lay not in the number of any book or pamphlet that could be sold, but in the number that were published. In the 1760s, about a hundred political pamphlets were being issued in London every month. John Brewer, *Party Ideology and Popular Politics at the Accession of George III* (Cambridge, 1971), 141–8. See also two very careful essays, Terry Belanger, "Publishers and Writers in Eighteenth-Century England," and W. A. Speck, "Politicians, Peers, and Publication by Subscription, 1700–1750," both in Isabel Rivers, ed., *Books and Their Readers in Eighteenth-Century England* (New York, 1982), 5–25, 47–68.

Smith formulated it, the specialization of labor was the key to rapid economic development and the astonishing increase in the wealth of the nation. The discovery was gratifying, but it brought with it a serious problem. The division of labor resulted in a dramatic stupefaction of the mass of men. In a crude society, most men knew more or less the same things, and all men understood implicitly the way the world worked. Between the states of knowledge of the simplest men and the most sophisticated there was not much of a gap. But in a civilized world, the specialization of work bound most men—not just laborers, nor even artisans, but manufacturers and entrepreneurs as well—to an awareness narrowed to their task and their "interest." And men driven by interest were in fact driven by greed, which excited "passion," which in its turn distorted perception and language. And so, the outcome of the discovery of economic progress was the parallel discovery of an epistemological crisis, in which most men lost any capacity to take an objective, "enlarged," or "liberal" view of social questions. As Franklin formulated the problem, "few in Public Affairs act from a meer View of the Good of their Country, whatever they may pretend," or "from a Principle of Benevolence." In such a world, the nature and interest of society at large became a mystery. If it were to be understood at all, it would be only by a few men who were somehow freed from the subjectivities of "interest" and the riot of "passion."[37]

Smith himself relied, lamely, on "the few, who, being attached to no particular occupation themselves, have leisure and inclination to examine the occupations of other people." But leisure and inclination were weak hopes, indeed. Everyone who took up the question, from whatever ideological perspective, agreed that the newly emerging "civilized" world of commerce and manufactures was much more complicated than the old "crude" world of bucolic subsistence. Franklin could see that in America, growth and development had liberated people from the need to attend always to rude necessities, and had created a new leisure class that could undertake intellectual work. The problem, as much in the Colonies as in London or Scotland, was

[37] Franklin, *Autobiography*, 118. The British discussion of the problem of knowledge in a society characterized by complexity, diversity, and specialization of callings and interests is brilliantly discussed in John Barrell, *English Literature in History, 1730–1780: An Equal, Wide Survey* (London, 1983). The remarks of Smith, Mandeville, and Ferguson discussed here and in the next few pages are in, respectively, *An Inquiry into the Nature and Causes of the Wealth of Nations* (1776), and *An Essay on the History of Civil Society* (1778), as cited in Barrell's introductory chapter, "Artificers and Gentlemen," 17–50.

that this same process seemed to have created a society much more difficult to comprehend than the old.

Was any group still fitted by training, experience, and social position to grasp the new world whole, understand it in the round? Was anyone free enough of interest and passion to be able to take an objective view of things? The favored eighteenth-century metaphors for society were a machine, a hive, a landscape, and a play. The epistemological crisis turned on a fear that *everyone* was in the social hive with a specialized function, and no one could gain the wisdom of the beekeeper; that all people were cogs and wheels in the social machine, all blind to its overall design; that everyone stood at a particular point in the landscape, unable to gain a privileged view that would reveal the genial harmonies of the entire vista; that each person had a part to play, and could finally only deliver the lines, with no grasp of the flow of the action. Samuel Johnson counted the costs of specialization with characteristic bluntness: "Any action or posture long continued, will distort and disfigure the limbs; so the mind likewise is crippled and contracted by perpetual application to the same set of ideas." He may have been more blunt than some of his contemporaries. But his concern with the "contracting" effects of the division of labor were only typical of a widespread fear that no one, in the end, could claim a proper vantage point on human affairs.[38]

The solutions to the epistemological puzzle were various, and each one was full of trouble. Almost no one hoped for much in the way of divine revelation into the workings of a commercial economy or a constitutional polity. It was difficult to continue to rely simply on the leisured few, for part of the problem was that "civilization" gave rise to so much technical mystery that only deep study could penetrate its workings. And the "few" had traditionally been brought up to everything but deep study; when Defoe worried that a "scholastic education" might become a "clog" to the gentleman's "natural parts," he spoke to the most ingrained habits of the gentry and aristocracy. As for technical matters, isolating Robinson Crusoe on his island was the only thing that justified his learning practical skills that Defoe thought in normal circumstances were much "beneath a gentleman." It had once been possible to suppose that the mere ownership of land was enough to make someone "independent" of the particular "interest" that tainted all callings. But it had become

[38] Samuel Johnson, *The Rambler*, November 12 and February 26, 1751.

abundantly clear that land in an economy of commerce and credit was a commodity like any other, and that the landed gentry were just one more interest, pursuing special needs, seeking particular advantage, and fully vulnerable to the taint of factional "jargon." By the 1770s, it was plain that owning the land produced no more insight into the true nature of the land*scape* than a land agent or a tax gatherer might have.

Another possible solution was to let those trained in the learned professions be the sources of the "liberal" understanding that had once been supposed to belong, more or less innately, to landed gentlemen. This was the kind of proposal William Blackstone made in his *Commentaries,* which was published in Philadelphia in 1771. It had become clear, he thought, that "gentlemen" were no longer putting their sons in the Inns of Chancery and Court for training in the law. At the same time, the universities where the gentry and nobility were trained taught only Roman law, and nothing of the grand English Constitution. This was Blackstone's version of the epistemological dilemma. Professional lawyers understood only the cant and jargon of daily practice; gentlemen and nobles learned, at most, only a few vague principles derived from "Mediterranean latitudes." As a remedy Blackstone proposed that law be made a "science," and taught in the universities. But he was conscious of the delicate danger of infecting a son of the gentry or nobility with too *much* knowledge of a specialized discipline. So the "academical expounder" of the law "should consider his course as a general map of the law, marking out the shape of the country: . . . it is not his business to describe minutely the subordinate limits, or to fix the longitude and latitude of every inconsiderable hamlet."[39]

One obvious difficulty with such schemes lay in the fact that men of learning had always been the dutiful servants of gentlemen, not their superiors in real wisdom. Another was that learning itself, like the land, threatened always to become an interest. Johnson saw it: "There are few," he said, "among men of the more liberal professions whose minds do not carry the brand of their calling." Adam Ferguson saw it even more clearly. Men given to scholarship and speculation "at a distance from the objects of useful knowledge, untouched by the motives that animate an active and a vigorous mind, could produce only the jargon of a technical language." And

[39] *Commentaries on the Laws of England,* 2 vols. (Philadelphia, 1771), 1:35.

for Ferguson's readers, the message was clear. "Jargon" was not just a trap of pedantry. It was an unmistakable sign of interest. "Reason itself," as Ferguson put it, "becomes a profession . . . thinking itself, in this age of separations, may become a peculiar craft."

Franklin's idea for a Society of the Free and Easy was designed to meet just this epistemological problem. He was captivated by the idea of a large and "regular Body" whose members—all much like him, of course—would have the "leisure necessary to contemplate other men's occupations." But they would not have lived "at a distance from the objects of useful knowledge." Indeed, they would typically be men whose leisure had been won through a mastery of practical affairs. They would have been disciplined morally through intensive self-examination. Most important of all, they would not be acting alone. No single person could be expected to carry the burden of objectivity. But acting together they could hope for a measure of transcendence over their particular and private points of view. They would be a "Party." But they would not be like all the other parties that were so central to the political life of both the Colonies and England. They would be defending an "interest," to be sure. But the "interest" would be the common good, consensually understood by men of affairs well acquainted with what Ferguson called "the motives that animate active and vigorous minds." Such men might be able to escape from the epistemological trap described by writers like Ferguson and Bernard Mandeville, whose *Fable of the Bees* was a favorite of Franklin's: that even the best-intentioned people "primarily consider'd that their own and their Country's Interest was united, and did not act from a Principle of Benevolence."

Priests could no longer pretend to a real grasp of Franklin's "Principle of Benevolence." Gentlemen had failed in it. Scholars were lost in technical jargon. But a growing class of leisured, disciplined, and "ingenious" men—one of Franklin's favorite terms—just might bring it off. They understood machinery; they had been in the hive and done their work; they had made their way through whole landscapes of effort; they had learned their parts and played them well. Together, they might transcend interest, subdue passion, renounce cant, and come to a fluent and usable sense of what Franklin called "the Good of Mankind." As a project, the idea was vague and even utopian. As an ideological gesture, it shaded toward mere piousness. But it solved very real problems for Franklin. In its terms, he was able to define, simultaneously, both the kind of constituency of which he might hope to be a part and the kind of audience he most wanted to address—neither earnest youths nor sophisticated and otiose gentlemen, but a large and growing audience of men capable of distinguishing, finally, between the requirements of their own "Interest" and the "Principle of Benevolence."

Franklin's writing career came at a critical juncture in the history of the literary marketplace. It was already becoming possible for a young man, or even a young woman, to think of writing as a career from which a living, and even a fortune, might be earned—and without the traditional machinery of patronage, subscriptions, or sinecures. One of Franklin's young friends, James Ralph, went to England and managed to have a career, sometimes successful, sometimes merely notorious, as an author by profession. By the middle of the eighteenth century, there was already a huge English and American market for "popular" literature—cheap magazines, broadsides and ballads, and the like. And a growing number of English writers had begun to try to make careers selling lengthier and more "serious" work. Franklin began the autobiography as a book whose audience would be at least as much British as American. And when he presented his reasons for continuing it, after the Revolution, he prudently introduced into his text an encouraging letter from an Englishman who had been his London publisher and who was still active in the English book world. He was preparing his book for the most advanced literary marketplace in the world.[40]

But there were still important limits to the writer's market. During the middle third of the eighteenth century, the decades when Franklin had become a successful author, the buying audience for cheap books, magazines, and newspapers was already growing rapidly. But the publishing institutions that were to turn that potential audience into a thriving market for serious writing existed only in the most rudimentary form. The most important English authors still published their work in ways that would practically disappear soon after the end of the century. Though he earned a great deal from his work, Pope was his own publisher—as Franklin was. Samuel Johnson occasionally resorted to subscriptions—as Franklin did. And in the latter part of his career Johnson had to depend heavily on royal

[40] *Autobiography*, 52–3, 61, 201.

patronage—just as Franklin depended somewhat on his appointment as assistant postmaster for the Colonies.[41]

The practical limitations of the literary marketplace helped sustain ideas of authorship and audience that pictured writers and readers as something other than anonymous sellers and buyers with nothing more in common than the fact that one produced words as a commodity and the other bought them as a mere "good." When Franklin began writing his autobiography, authors and booksellers still did not aim serious writing at a scattered and shapeless mass public. For Franklin, the subscribers to the *Gazette* had been named individuals; most of them lived in Philadelphia and quite a few were friends, collaborators, or acquaintances. The same thing had been true, though less so, of many of the purchasers of his almanac. One of the men who encouraged him to finish his autobiography, the American Quaker Abel James, could speak of the "millions" of young men who might read the autobiography; and there was a certain plausibility to such a guess, especially for a writer who had already gained such an astonishing audience. But Franklin was still habituated, as most writers were, to thinking of his readers in limited and concrete terms—a scientific or philosophical elite, a group of subscribers, like-minded tradesmen or fellow members of a party or a Junto. In fact, he still thought of readers as a potential constituency for action. They were not a market of mere purchasers, unknown and unknowable, of mixed and unrelated persuasions, but a collection of men who might be moved to Projects, in their own lives and in "Public Affairs." There was a clear parallel between the Junto—and its grander version, the "united Party for Virtue"—and the reading audience Franklin thought he might be addressing.

In the nineteenth century, new generations of writers in Britain and America would begin, and with considerable anxiety, to learn to think of their readers in different terms, as a distant public with which they might, after all, have no nexus other than the word, sold and bought. Partly because of this, they would begin to magnify distinctions

---

[41] Michael Foss, *The Age of Patronage: The Arts in England, 1650–1750* (Ithaca, N.Y., 1971), 162–87; Bertrand H. Bronson, "The Writer," in James L. Clifford, ed., *Man Versus Society in Eighteenth-Century Britain: Six Points of View* (Cambridge, 1968), 112–32; Alexandre Beljame, *Men of Letters and the English Public in the Eighteenth Century, 1660–1744: Dryden, Addison, Pope* (London, 1948), 317–86; Maynard Mack's superb *Alexander Pope: A Life* (New Haven, 1985); J. D. Fleeman, "The Revenue of a Writer: Samuel Johnson's Literary Earnings," in *Studies in the Book Trade in Honour of Graham Pollard* (Oxford, 1975), 211–30. I am in debt to Donald Greene for several useful conversations on Johnson.

between language and experience, words and actions, ideas and things, the scholar or "Poet" and the man of affairs. Franklin could see only a part of that new horizon. He could think of the "millions" who might read his book. He could even imagine an audience among "the virtuous of all nations." But for him, the important thing about those millions was exactly that they might not only become virtuous, but also be united together for doing good, in a Party that might actually operate in history. For Franklin, it was a smooth step from remembering that he had told a couple of friends about his idea for the united Party to thinking that it might be made to happen through personal contacts, in the same way that the Masons, or the Junto—or even the Revolution—had been made to happen. And for a writer with such a conception of his audience, there was no ground for compelling distinctions between idea and action, men of words and men of deeds, the "finer Arts" and "useful Knowledge."

At about the time Franklin began writing his autobiography, a fictive farmer from Tarrytown, New York, fell asleep. At about the time Franklin stopped writing his book, Rip Van Winkle woke up—to a popular fame that would eventually be almost as great as Franklin's. Rip Van Winkle was not just a simple farmer, a victim of "Drudgery" and "Necessity." He was also a man who loved ideas. In fact, he hardly farmed at all, but preferred to idle at the village tavern, talking with his "fellow-sages and philosophers." Together, they formed what Washington Irving called "a kind of Junto." When Rip finally wakes from his twenty-year sleep, the Junto is gone. His village has become a bustling Yankee town, and the tavern a hotel. He has no friends left. But he does become a celebrity. He sits all day near the hotel, telling his curious autobiography to anyone who will listen—mostly to children and to people who are just passing through town.

The remaking of Tarrytown, and Rip's own transformation from a member of the men's daily Junto into a storyteller to children and strangers, was much more than an adaptation of a ubiquitous folk-tale. It was Washington Irving's meditation on a revolution in what it meant for a young man or woman to think of becoming an "author by profession." At the beginning of his story, Rip Van Winkle is very like his fellow villagers. He is part of their economy and society in the same fluent way that Franklin pictured himself as part of the Philadelphia world. At the end of his remarkable career,

Rip is a man who is distinguished not by wealth or accomplishment, but because he has known a grave mystery that is beyond the reach of the people who listen to his tale. Franklin, unlike Irving, still thought of himself at the end as a man who could even seize lightning from the skies without having to surrender a familiar sense of identity with his Junto or the "good and virtuous of all Nations."

As a writer, Franklin anticipated the nineteenth century in some important ways. He was the first American to gain both wealth and celebrity from his writing, working outside the ministry and not depending primarily on either private wealth or public sinecure. In this, he forecast the careers of a number of the most important writers of the next century, from Irving to Emerson, Hawthorne, and Melville. But Franklin was also very much a man of eighteenth-century Boston, Philadelphia, and London, a man whose perception of the literary marketplace was not yet the vision of a mere *market,* but still of a kind of *place,* which might even contain people who could be addressed not just as readers but also as potential collaborators or constituents. For Franklin, writing about the virtues of individuals and the vices of society did not point—as it would later—toward solitude and Nature, or the transcending mysteries of wilderness and sea, or toward some idiosyncratic radicalism. In principle, at least, being a writer led toward active participation in existing social and political institutions, or to making new institutions where old ones did not translate individual virtue into public consequences. And this was so not just because Franklin began from eighteenth-century philosophical premises, nor only because his society was objectively so different from, say, Emerson's or Whitman's. What was going to change in the half-century after Franklin's death was not only philosophical principles or social facts, but also the understanding of what it meant to be a writer, trying to address a mass of strangers about such matters as principle and reality, and deciding, too, whether to do so explicitly for rewards measured out in the market. As it turned out, the redefinition of the profession of authorship, and of the implied relationship of writers to their work and their publics, had a great deal to do with what would come to be counted as either philosophy or fact.

Irving at twenty-two, a painting by John Wesley Jarvis

II

WASHINGTON IRVING

Washington Irving was an unusually amiable and gentle man, according to most of the people who knew him. But amiability and gentleness did not make him a passive subject when he sat for portraits. In fact, he exercised an unusual command over the men who drew or painted him. A portrait is the outcome of a complicated dialogue between subject and artist. The artist brings those skills and habits that constitute style—including powerful conventions about "expression" and stance, clothes, props, and background. But the subject has a field of action, too, a margin within which to present the self. The subject proposes himself to the artist. In a word, he poses. And if he is skilled enough at looking his look, he may impose himself on the portrait. If he lacks skill, or if the artist gets control of the situation, the pose may be disposed of, and the disappointed subject will feel that somehow his "likeness" has not been caught.

Out of such silent contests between artists and their subjects come portraits that lie somewhere between representation and caricature. The question in any particular case is, who was most in control? Washington Irving managed to exert a marked degree of control over his portraits, and so to project surprisingly consistent likenesses. Whether he was twenty-two or seventy, whether the medium was crayon, pencil, or oil, whether the artist was American,

Irving at thirty-seven,
a painting by Charles R. Leslie

Irving at thirty-seven, from
a painting by Gilbert Stuart Newton

English, or German, Irving always came out the same. The conventions of portraiture must be taken into account, of course: the preoccupation with youth, the insinuations of sensuality or of brooding genius that made half the men of the early nineteenth century look a bit Byronic or Napoleonic. But (even after such conventions have been allowed for) Irving managed to impose a striking, almost a stubborn, self-representation on whoever sketched or painted him.

He started with small things. He almost always cocked his head, sometimes a little and sometimes drastically (except in the earliest drawing, done in 1805 by John Vanderlyn in Paris, which was, uniquely, a profile). So doing, Irving then lifted one eyebrow a bit—usually his left. And he looked disarmingly and directly at the artist, not off to the side or at some object in his hands or into a middle distance. The effect was to call attention to his eyes, which always— orb, socket, and brow taken together—came out much larger than life. These efforts could only be amplified by the artists' usual cosmetic work, and the outcome was that Irving looked determinedly younger than his years. At forty, he looked twenty; at seventy, he looked forty-

*Irving at forty, from a drawing by
Karl Christian Vogel von Vogelstein*

*"The Author of the Sketch Book," a lithograph from
about 1821. A depiction of "Geoffrey Crayon" for
which Irving no doubt posed, and liked a great deal.*

five. When Irving had himself sketched in company with Daniel
Webster and William Cullen Bryant in 1842, he managed somehow
to come across to the artist as at least half a generation younger than
the other two men. Webster, who was almost exactly Irving's age,
looked not only older but much more grim, almost sullen. And poor
Bryant, who was actually eleven years younger than either of the
others, was bowed and melancholy beside the cheerful, half-smiling
Irving. The other two men look away. Irving, head tilted a little,
looks directly at the artist—and so at us.

This projection of ungrudging youth was so powerful that it even
controlled the perceptions of artists who worked only from others'
pictures of Irving. In a hilarious composite portrait of Irving and his
"literary contemporaries," which the artist obviously took from
portraits of quite mature men—a sort of Famous Authors deck of
playing cards, with all the cards on the table—Irving not only up-
stages all the other writers and gains the focal center, he also looks
much younger and infinitely fresher. The other men of letters are
bent and a little pathetic, all staring off in one direction or another.

Irving at forty-five,
from a portrait by David Wilkie

Irving in his sixties, a daguerreotype
conventionally attributed to Mathew Brady,
from about 1849

And there, in their antique midst, is Irving, bland and unfurrowed, gently forthright and indomitably amiable.

Something more was at stake than bland youth, though, something else in the portraits that made Irving look consistently arch, coy, even a bit elfin. (If any fattish man of seventy ever could look elfin, it was Irving.) The cocked head and lifted eyebrow were almost always complemented by an incipient smile. But the smile was always on the point of becoming something else, a knowing and aristocratic smirk, perhaps, or even a leer. All in all, what Irving was working at was the image of a young dandy, fashionably decked out and accoutered, keenly observing and about to be amused, but finally holding back and being merely detached and innocent.

When it came time, in 1849, to have a daguerreotype made, Irving stuck to his pose. His head was tilted, his left brow lifted, and his hair brushed carelessly forward in the old insouciant, dandified way. But the result was a bit ludicrous. He was past sixty; and the photographer did not have the same cosmetic capabilities that a painter could bring to bear. So the daguerreotype exposed the pose. Irving's features—

Irving, at about seventy, with his dog, Ginger

his "real" face, if anyone has such a thing—were too heavy, too tired, lined, and pouched, to serve as a medium for the personality he was still trying to project. Taken by itself, the daguerreotype is merely self-contradictory. But when it is put in place in the sequence of Irving portraits, a sequence that makes his own purposes unmistakably clear, the daguerreotype may suggest more than contradiction; it may say something about just how urgent were the contrivances Irving brought to all his sittings. It might even suggest that he brought the same habits of contrivance to his work and his life.

There is nothing unusual about contrivance, of course. The little tricks that Irving used in his portraits would not be interesting if they were not echoed in a range of similarly contrived posings in his experience at large. He was a man of postures and stances, always uncertain about just who or what he was, but with a rich inventory of people he might want to be.

William Cullen Bryant, Daniel Webster,
and Irving, 1852

The look of the youthful dandy in Irving's portraits, for example, was repeated and reinforced in his "real" behavior. During his middle twenties, when he was supposedly embarking on a career as a lawyer, Irving was a member of a sort of club of New York dandies. The club had various names: the Nine Worthies, the Ancient Club of New York, The Ancient and Honorable Order, or (Irving's own favorite) the Lads of Kilkenny. Its members were all professional men and businessmen in their middle twenties or early thirties, bachelors, well-off and well-read. For several years, beginning in 1806 when Irving was twenty-three, the Lads of Kilkenny met in taverns and in the members' rooms, always intent on what Irving called "high jollity." The style they cultivated was that same compound of bland youth and aristocratic sophistication that Irving was able to project so consistently into his portraits. They drank champagne when they could, porter when they could not. They talked a good deal of "maidens." They wrote satirical pieces for a little periodical they called *Salmagundi; Or, The Whim-Whams and Opinions of Launcelot Langstaff, Esq., and Others* (1807–8). But most of all, they

"Washington Irving and His Literary Friends,"
a composite painting, 1863

simply acted like innocent blades, behaving as though they still lived in a traditional society in which men in their twenties and even thirties were considered "youths" until they married, and were obliged (or privileged) to consort together and to devise their own sometimes raucous forms of entertainment.[1]

The Lads spent much of their time at a mansion on the Passaic just above Newark that belonged to one of their number, Gouverneur Kemble. They named it "Cockloft Hall." (It was a measure of the innocence of their dandyhood that they probably were not making a

---

[1] There is a good account of these goings-on in the best modern biography of Irving, Stanley T. Williams' *The Life of Washington Irving*, 2 vols. (New York, 1935), 1:75. Williams will be cited hereafter as *STW*; he is a source of much sound information on Irving's life, though a bit on the literal side in matters of interpretation, and too disposed to take Irving at his word. The Lads are discussed in some detail as well in Pierre M. Irving, *The Life and Letters of Washington Irving*, 4 vols. (New York, 1863–64), 1:454. This classic nineteenth-century life and letters is the basis for almost all modern biographical work on Irving, and amounts almost to an edition of Irving family papers. It is cited hereafter as *PMI*. See also George S. Hellman, *Washington Irving, Esquire, Ambassador at Large from the New World to the Old* (New York, 1935), 66, and *Salmagundi; Or, The Whim-Whams and Opinions of Launcelot Langstaff, Esq., and Others* (New York, 1807–08). "Whim-wham" was a slang expression for, roughly, a whimsical notion.

phallic joke—any more than they were when they created the fictive
figure of Launcelot Langstaff.) At Cockloft Hall, the Lads would
sport. Irving's brother Peter (eleven years older than he) long remembered "the procession in the Chinese saloon, in which we made
poor Dick McCall a knight, and dubbed him by some fatality on the
seat of honor instead of the shoulder." He also remembered how the
Lads "sported on the lawn until fatigued, and sometimes fell sociably
into a general nap in the drawing-room in the dusk of the evening."
This sporting on the lawn regularly included games of leapfrog.[2]

Irving was one of the younger members of the Lads of Kilkenny,
and there was nothing particularly odd about his being part of their
madcapping. But a decade later, now in his mid-thirties, Irving was
at it again—this time in London, where he was still trying to decide
on some kind of career for himself. In 1817 and 1818, Irving and
the painter Charles R. Leslie formed the nucleus of a new group
that Irving again dubbed "the Lads." These new Lads' sports were
about the same as those of the New York group: dining, drinking,
snobbish banter, excursions into the country, where they pranced
and played at blindman's buff. The members were a bit different,
though. This second group of Lads was composed not of lawyers,
doctors, and businessmen, but of writers and artists. And they were
decidedly older than the Lads of Kilkenny had been; most, like
Irving, were in their mid-thirties and forties. Like the Lads of Kilkenny, these older London Lads had their pet nicknames. Gilbert
Stuart Newton, the nephew of Gilbert Stuart and one of Irving's
portraitists, went under the *nom des jeux* of "the Childe"—after

---

[2] Gouverneur Kemble to Irving, 1824; Peter Irving to Irving, 1832; in *PMI*, 1:166–7. The
question of whether the Lads intended anything remotely "dirty" by such words as "Cockloft" and "Langstaff" is an interesting one, and impossible to settle. But in general Irving
displayed a remarkable modesty and even lack of sensitivity to any explicitly sexual humor. He
could even be quite priggish. For example, in Marseilles in 1804 he was shocked by the
costumes of female dancers in a ballet: "a flesh colored habit fitted exactly to their shapes so
that it really looked like their skin. . . . I felt my American blood mounting in my cheeks on
their account, and would have been happy to have given them another petticoat or a thicker
robe." The stage, he muttered into his journal, should "improve the heart," but instead is
"degraded by performances devoted to sensuality and libertinism." Nathalia Wright, ed.,
Washington Irving, Journals and Notebooks, Volume 1, 1803–1806 (Madison, 1969), 82, 89n, 477–8.
Cf. *STW*, 1:48–9, 55.

Irving, writing only for himself and in his own diary, rigorously censored every bit of rough
language, even when he was only quoting someone else: "Kean asked, How long, sir, am I to
act with that d----d Jesuitical bug--r, Young?" Walter A. Reichart, ed., *Washington Irving,
Journals and Notebooks, Volume 3, 1819–1827* (Madison, 1970), 236–7, 252; Hellman, *Washington
Irving*, 161–4. Surely no man who wrote "d----d" in his own diary would publicly joke with
"Langstaff."

Byron's Childe Harold. William Willes, an Irish landscape artist, was known as Father Luke. Another member, who apparently needed no nickname to distinguish him, was Peter Powell, an animated near-midget in his fifties.[3]

\The Lads of Kilkenny had been a reasonably appropriate affair for Irving to have been involved in, by the standards of the day. But the London Lads were something else again. They were markedly over-age in grade, pressing their bachelor "youth" much further down the track than the norms of either New York or London would routinely have allowed. There was something odd about a thirty-five-year-old Irving chasing a laughing Leslie through a London rainstorm, both shouting, Irving losing his shoe in a full gutter, Leslie finding it and running away from Irving (who once more gave merry chase), and Leslie later leaving the slipper carefully filled with water on the stoop of Irving's lodging house.[4]

But for Irving, such antic friendships were very important. His bachelor intimacy with Leslie in London was one of the most trea-sured facts of his life there. And the Lads of Kilkenny he remembered always, often, and warmly. These Lads, the friends of his twenties, were still his friends in his forties and fifties—despite the many years he spent in Europe. He saw them seldom, but Henry Brevoort, James Kirk Paulding, and several of the others were his most assid-uously serviced correspondents all through Irving's middle age. In letters to Brevoort, Paulding, or Kemble written a dozen years after the fact, Irving would lovingly recall their "jollities." When they married, one by one, he wrote seriocomic letters of complaint about his "old cronies snugly nestled down with good wives and fine children"—like so many Brom Boneses to his Ichabod. He was, Irving would say, "doomed" to bachelorhood; but he still looked forward to the day when the Lads, made single again by age like so many Rip Van Winkles, might "form a knot of queer, rum old bachelors, at some future day to meet at the corner of Wall Street or walk the sunny side of Broadway and kill time together." Of all the Lads of Kilkenny—except perhaps for his brother Peter, who also

[3] An excellent discussion of the London Lads is in Ben Harris McClary, ed., *Washington Irving and the House of Murray: Geoffrey Crayon Charms the British* (Knoxville, 1969), 14–15. See also W. P. Frith, *Autobiography* (London, 1887); Charles R. Leslie, *Autobiographical Recollections* (London, 1860); and *The Letters of John Constable, R.A., to C. R. Leslie, R.A., 1826–27* (London, 1931), 65–6.

[4] Leslie, *Autobiographical Recollections,* 63; Washington Irving, *Notes While Preparing the Sketch Book &c., 1817,* ed. Stanley T. Williams (New Haven, 1927), 80–2.

never married—Irving had the most difficult time letting go of his sportive "youth." And the Lads of London were, for him, a reconstitution of scenes and habits that had belonged with more propriety to the preceding decade of his life.[5]

Irving's half-joking hope that the Lads might someday be reunited as "rum old bachelors" points to another, seemingly contradictory pose that he and some of his friends assumed: the aged relic. In their twenties, the Lads of Kilkenny were already "old cronies" to Irving. He would sit with one or another of them and while away an afternoon with "segars," musing crustily on the declining times. And this was also the literary persona that came easiest to Irving in his early writing. His first published pieces were a series of letters (1802–03) in the New York *Morning Chronicle* (a newspaper his brother Peter owned) over the name of "Jonathan Oldstyle, Gent." As his names and his rank unsubtly suggested, Oldstyle was elderly, rustic, but well-bred. He was also a cranky, sometimes vulgar, and occasionally merry man, full of complaints about the low state of society, particularly in the theater. His deepest faith was that "Nothing is more intolerable . . . than innovation." He was a vestige of an older, better, pre-Revolutionary order of things.[6]

In their *Salmagundi* skits, Irving and the other Lads—now including brother William, who was almost forty—adopted a similar voice. Many of their "whim-whams and opinions" were on the Oldstyle theme of decline. Their manner was crotchety, avuncular, and didactic. And one of the most interesting of the *Salmagundi* pieces, most likely Irving's writing, was a study of "The Little Man in Black." The Little Man was another aged bachelor, a scholar "far gone in whimsy." Because of his curious and obsessive scholarship, he had become completely alienated from the Hudson village of his

[5] Irving to Paulding, May 27, 1820, in Ralph M. Aderman et al., eds., *Washington Irving: Letters, Volume I, 1802–1823* (Boston, 1978), 585. This admirably careful work will be cited here as *Letters*. Irving to Brevoort, August 15, 1820, in *The Letters of Washington Irving to Henry Brevoort*, George S. Hellman, ed., 2 vols. (New York, 1915), 2:133–5 (cited hereafter as *ItoB*). A very useful summary of notions about youth in "preindustrial" Europe is in John R. Gillis, *Youth and History: Tradition and Change in European Age Relations, 1770 to the Present* (New York, 1974), ch. 1.
[6] "Letters of Jonathan Oldstyle, Gent.," New York *Morning Chronicle*, 1802–03. The best discussion of Oldstyle is in William L. Hedges, *Washington Irving: An American Study* (Baltimore, 1965).

birth, and had wandered into the City, where he shuffled idly about, muttering to himself in an "outlandish tongue."[7]

The outlandish tongue was, of course, Dutch. And "The Little Man in Black" was a preliminary study for Irving's next authorial stand-in, Diedrich Knickerbocker, the narrator of *A History of New York, from the Beginning of the World to the End of the Dutch Dynasty* (1809). Like the Little Man, Knickerbocker had wandered into New York from an outlying village. He kept a good deal to his own room, "always covered with scraps of paper and old mouldy books." And when his confusions finally overcame him, Knickerbocker skulked away up the Valley. Irving, who began the history with his brother Peter but finished it alone, introduced Knickerbocker to the world in a newspaper "Notice."[8]

DISTRESSING: Left his lodging some time since, and has not been heard of, a small elderly gentleman, dressed in an old black coat and cocked hat, by the name of Knickerbocker. There are some reasons for believing he is not in his right mind.

This ruse was designed to promote sales of the *History*. And two subsequent notices had the same quite obvious purpose. But the conventional literary and commercial functions of the Knickerbocker figure concealed another, more personal and slightly less conventional use. Knickerbocker, as an authorial surrogate, was a nearly terminal case of amateurism. He was so careless of any reputation or income his book might bring him that he left it inadvertently behind in his room when he wandered off toward Albany. The *History* was published only because the landlord thought it might raise enough money to settle the old man's unpaid bill. And so the paired poses of the youthful dandy and the aged relic had something important in common. They were both devices through which Irving could present himself to the world as a distinct amateur. They were gentle evasions of a series of ominous and impending entanglements. Marriage, career, property, even writing for profit—things of that sort were of no real moment to such unyielding amateurs as a Lad or a Knickerbocker. Washington Irving actively yearned for the money

---

[7] *Salmagundi*, letter no. 15; Hedges, *Washington Irving*, 8–9, 56; see also Ralph M. Aderman, "*Salmagundi* and the Outlander Tradition," *Wisconsin Studies in Literature* 1 (1964): 62–8.
[8] *A History of New York, from the Beginning of the World to the End of the Dutch Dynasty* (New York, 1809). The newspaper notices were bound into the third and subsequent editions.

he hoped the *History* would bring in. But, like most anyone else, he was perfectly capable of thinking of himself as a man with no more at stake in life or art than the most casual of lads or the most careless of relics—a man who just might forget a manuscript in his room at "The Independent Columbian Hotel—Mulberry Street."[9]

Irving's third and most famous authorial contrivance was the figure of Geoffrey Crayon, nominal maker of *The Sketch Book* (1819–20). Crayon was an ageless figure, older than a Lad, younger than a Little Man. But, like them, he was a footloose bachelor, who announced in *The Sketch Book's* epigraph:

> I have no wife nor children, good or bad, to provide for. A mere spectator of other men's fortunes and adventure, and how they play their "parts."

The sauntering bachelor, a man of means bent on nothing much but travel or amusement, was just as conventional a figure as the aged man. He was also a marketing device, a way of appealing to readers quite accustomed to accept the "veracity" of such writers' stand-ins. But conventions do not impose themselves on writers, or on anyone else for that matter. Nor do marketing strategies. They are chosen, either deliberately or for reasons that lie on the outer margins of consciousness. And the membrane that separates "life" and "letters" is permeable in both directions: Nothing prevents a literary "convention" from infiltrating experience. So it was with Irving. Crayon's public "Account of Himself" mirrored important elements in Irving's private view of his own life and work.[10]

By the time he finished *The Sketch Book*, Irving had almost completed a grueling task. He had become a committed writer, an "author by profession," hesitant and doubtful, but still determined to make a go of the career. Crayon, by contrast, was a militant amateur. He was a dabbler and scribbler, whose "sketches" were

---

[9] In the first edition, Irving left Knickerbocker wandering aimlessly up the Hudson, a sad and lonely figure. In the second American edition, published in 1812, he devised a softer, happier ending for Knickerbocker. This new ending anticipated a few of the elements of the resolution of the story of Rip Van Winkle. See note 45.

[10] The motto appeared at the front of every edition. *The Sketch Book of Geoffrey Crayon, Gent.* (New York, 1819–20). Unless otherwise noted, all subsequent quotations are from this edition. A fine modern edition with copious apparatus is Haskell Springer, ed., *Washington Irving, The Sketch Book of Geoffrey Crayon, Gent.* (Boston, 1978).

supposed to be the inconsequential and unprofiting gestures of a meandering gentleman, published in the faint but refined hope that they might "amuse." Crayon sketched himself in self-deprecating terms. "I have wandered," he said. His studies had been made with a "sauntering gaze." He had merely "strolled" through Europe in an "idle humor," following his own "vagrant inclination." He had a few "hints" toward some "sketches," and now was casually "disposed to get up a few for the entertainment of my friends."[11]

As proclamations of modest purposes, such self-diminishing remarks were stock strategies. Indeed, almost any fictive author like Crayon had to pretend either that he had found his manuscript in a bottle at the seashore, stumbled on it in an old attic or among the papers of a dead friend, or (if he admitted actually writing it) didn't care a whit for the outcome. Irving pressed the point. He carried such gestures over from Crayon into his own assessments of what he had done. In a separate "Advertisement" for the American edition of *The Sketch Book*—a sort of supra-preface written in a voice somewhere between Crayon's and Irving's own—he assumed the same embarrassed tone. The first sketches (the American edition was published in separate numbers, each containing several sketches) were "experiments," he said. If they should "please" he might follow with others. But he would have to contend with "an unsettled abode" and, above all, with the "fluctuations" of his thoughts. (He had already more or less finished the entire book, in fact.) And, in any case, the sketches were hardly "finished compositions." All he hoped for was to gain a "secure and cherished, though humble, corner in the good opinions and kind feelings of his countrymen." A similar Advertisement to the English edition described the sketches as "desultory papers."[12]

All this was meant to be taken as a kind of joke, of course, a joke that both author and reader were in on. But it had a more serious point. The amateur's determined modesty found its way into Irving's much more private and probably serious estimates of the book. In the spring of 1819, when he sent the manuscript of the first number from London to his brother Ebenezer in New York, Irving sent along a letter saying, apologetically, that "My talents are merely literary." (To neither Irving nor his brother was the occasion "merely literary"; when Ebenezer read the sketches aloud to a group of

[11] "The Author's Account of Himself," *The Sketch Book.*
[12] "Advertisement," *The Sketch Book;* "Advertisement," *The Sketch Book of Geoffrey Crayon, Gent.* (London, 1820).

friends and they applauded, he wept aloud.) At the same crucial moment, Irving wrote his friend Brevoort, asking him to take charge of such matters as copyright and arranging terms with a printer. But this letter, too, was full of Crayonesque amateurism. He had, Irving told his friend, "attempted no lofty theme nor sought to look wise and learned. . . . My writings may appear therefore light and trifling. . . . I seek only to blow a flute of accompaniment in the national concert, and leave others to play the fiddle and French horn." In these letters to both Brevoort and Ebenezer, Irving refused to commit himself to anything. To Ebenezer, he said that he might continue the book "from time to time"; to Brevoort, that he expected to produce new numbers "occasionally."[13]

Even when the stories were powerful, and seem to have been written in a real burst of creative energy and effort, Irving dismissed them as Crayon's "trifles." When he finally sent Ebenezer No. VI, containing "Rip Van Winkle," Irving wrote that the story might "please" because of its descriptions of American scenes. But "It is a random thing. . . . The story is a mere whimsical band to connect descriptions of scenery, customs, manners, &c." And even after *The Sketch Book* had succeeded beyond his own fondest imaginings, Irving still refused to take either it or himself very seriously. His use of the term "desultory" in the English Advertisement was a public echo of a very carefully drafted private letter to Walter Scott, in which Irving wrote that "My whole course of life has been desultory." He could not take up any "sophisticated labor," he told Scott, because he was only a curious kind of "gipsy."[14]

Irving's repertoire of public and private poses—the youthful Lad, the aged relic, the leisured amateur—might well have satisfied any audience he had in mind: his readers, his family, his friends, even himself. But he was a tireless man. He contrived yet another picture of himself. He worked out a full-fledged account of his life as a romantic artist, driven to writing by grief. This version of his experience was not publicly revealed in his lifetime. Indeed, Irving

[13] Irving to Ebenezer Irving, March 3, 1819, *Letters*, 530; to Brevoort, *ItoB*, 2:86–91; see also *STW*, 1:173.
[14] Irving to Ebenezer Irving, December 29, 1819; to Scott, November 20, 1819, *Letters*, 570, 573. The letter to Scott was later printed by Irving in the third and subsequent editions of *The Sketch Book*, producing an almost complete blurring of any line between his own public and private evaluations of himself and his work.

confided it to a manuscript that he kept in a locked box, marked "Private Mems.," until his death. But the story was not exactly a secret one, either. Irving began to work out the first hints toward it in his notebook around 1817, when he was working on *The Sketch Book*. Then, around 1823 or 1824, he began courting a young American girl in Dresden. Apparently the girl's mother fretted at the twin facts that he had never married and was a professional writer. So he drafted (and may have sent) a long letter to the mother, containing a story that ingeniously tied the two problems together so they could be explained away at one swoop. It was the draft of this letter that he locked away in the "Private Mems." box. But he repeated the story orally during later years, and it eventually became a central theme for most of his biographers and iconographers.[15]

On its surface, this new version of himself seemed to contradict the Lad-Knickerbocker-Crayon effect. All those poses entailed a relationship to life and to work that was detached and spectatorial. Now Irving revealed that far from being detached, he had been too much engaged with life, and that his emotional investment in his work was, if anything, too heavy. The central fact of his life, he now decided, was his desperate grief for Matilda Hoffman, a daughter of the man whom Irving had served in New York as a clerk while reading for the bar. Matilda was only fifteen when Irving, about twenty-three, fell in love with her. And, for the rest of his life, she was an extraordinarily delicate memory. She was "shy from her natural timidity . . . just growing up, there was a softness and delicacy in her form and look, a countenance of that eloquent expression, yet that mantling modesty—I thought I had never beheld anything so lovely." Matilda—at least in memory—was full of "sweetness . . . intuitive rectitude . . . native delicacy . . . exquisite propriety." She had every possible virtue but one: She had a certain lack of resistance to colds and consumption. In her seventeenth year and Irving's twenty-fifth, she died.

In middle age, Irving invested a substantial emotional capital in his memory of Matilda Hoffman:

Her dying struggles were painful & protracted. For three days and nights I did not leave the house and scarcely slept. I was by

---

[15] This manuscript fragment is among the Irving papers at Yale University. It is apparently a draft of a letter of April–May 1823, to Mrs. Amelia Foster, and is in *Letters*, 737–45. It is cited hereafter as Autobiographical Fragment. The next several paragraphs are based on it.

her when she died. . . . I was the last one she looked upon. . . .
I cannot tell you what a horrid state of mind I was in for a long
time—I seemed to care for nothing—the world was a blank to
me. . . . There was a dismal horror continually in my mind that
made me fear to be alone.

The mode Irving was trying to establish was run-of-the-mill
Gothic: gloomy, sleepless, steeped in horror. His immediate purpose
was to justify his life to a prospective mother-in-law. (Though a
suspicious reader might wonder whether the real purpose of the letter
might not have been to frighten mother and daughter alike away from
any idea of a marriage.) The letter was, in effect, an argument in self-
justification. The first step in the argument was to show how his
"despondency" had been the product of a "catastrophe." The second
step was to show how his art was the product of despair, a justifiable
search for release from grief. He had been, as he explained matters, in
the midst of writing Knickerbocker's *History* when Matilda died. The
work had not been going well, and he was even a little "disheartened"
by his lack of progress. But then, after her death, he had taken up
writing with a new determination and with a new knowledge that only
art could ease his pain. He had finished the *History*.

Still, according to Irving's "memory" of those years, the pain
would not yield. So he suspended his respectable career as a budding
lawyer and traveled to Europe in 1815. (In fact, fully six years
elapsed between the publication of the *History* and 1815.) But there
he confronted a new form of grief. The English branch of the family
hardware firm went bankrupt, and he had the bad luck to be in
Liverpool, where he could preside over the process. Here was a
second source of "bitterness and humiliation," a new "horrible
ordeal"—not quite so wrenching as the loss of Matilda, but an
adequate occasion for another rush of Gothic self-description.

I felt cast down—abased—I had lost my caste—I shut myself up
from society—and would see no one. For months I studied
German day and night by way of driving off horrid thoughts.
The idea suddenly came to return to my pen, not so much for
support, but to raise myself from the degradation into which I
considered myself fallen. I took my resolution—threw myself a
stranger into London, shut myself up and went to work. . . . In
this way I produced the Sketch Book—You know its success.

There is no way to know what the would-be mother-in-law made of the admission that not only was Irving given to gloomy withdrawals, solitary study of German, and writing stories; there had been financial trouble in his family to boot. But the artfulness of his letter is perfectly apparent. He conjoined two catastrophes, one having to do with love, the other with money. He brought the same vocabulary of "degradation" and "horrid thoughts" to his tale of each. Then he managed to relate each catastrophe to his art, and to end on a note of "success"—though not for himself: for his book.

In this letter, Irving was working from a preliminary set of notes he had set down in 1817 in his writer's notebook—the notebook he later marked "Notes while preparing the Sketch Book." There, among other brief ideas for descriptive settings, he wrote out a longer scene of lamentation. It neatly joined together the elements of his "agony": Matilda's surpassing spiritual elevation, his grief at losing her, and his "humiliating" cares for "worldly" things. The setting was a vacant cathedral. The narrator hears a soft voice singing "Angels Ever Bright and Fair." His heart "melts." He gasps. "The recollection of Matilda!" She so "pure, spiritual and seraphic." She, the very source and origin of "virtue and piety . . . innocent . . . gentle . . . tenderness . . . melody. . . romance." Then the narrator (who is obviously not to be mistaken for Crayon) realizes just how deeply separated from Matilda's spirituality is his own enforced worldliness. He is "desolate—humiliated—grovelling—a miserable worm upon earth." Why? Because he has had "jarring collisions with the world . . . heartless pleasures . . . sordid pursuits . . . gross associations . . . rude struggles." His life has been "depraved . . . deadened . . . worldly . . . crushed to earth. . . harried . . . bare . . . withered up and blighted."[16]

Very little of this kind of mood found its way into *The Sketch Book,* which was by and large controlled by the voice and manner of Crayon, not the desperately grief-stricken romantic. There were, to be sure, a number of sketches in which death was a prominent event. And there were others in which some picturesque scene or moment became suddenly surreal and Gothic, as though an agonized recognition lay always just below the amiable surface of things. But the significance of the cathedral scene of 1817, and of the fully developed romantic autobiography Irving worked out a few years later, did not

---

[16] Irving, *Notes While Preparing the Sketch Book,* 63–4.

lie in Irving's published art. This tale belonged more to the private arts of self-perception and self-projection (and self-deception, too, perhaps). Of those arts he was a diligent and skillful practitioner.

The seeming contradiction between the romantic artist's agony and the varied forms of dispassion and detachment that characterized Irving's other public and private guises does not go very deep. The author driven to art by grief is only another type of amateur. Such a writer works, as Irving put it, "not so much for support." He writes for motives that are not just private, but secret, and hardly to be satisfied by any profit or fame that may be the incidental by-products of his work. This notion was just as conventional as the Oldstyle bachelor or the dandy—though it was somewhat newer and fresher. But, again, convention is not the question—at least not the only question. Irving was still choosing his conventions from among a range of options at his disposal. And his choices all had one thing in common, one element that united their apparent diversity and even contradictions: the idea that the writer must be an amateur. All of Irving's contrivances, public and private, helped him avoid presenting himself to the world in a serious light, either as an author or as a person. In the guise of a Lad or Knickerbocker or Crayon or the driven romantic, Irving could be an amateur at both life and art. And this meant that he could be a gentleman and not just an aggressive entrepreneur of letters.

With any masked figure, our first impulse is to want to strip away disguise and imposture, to get to the actual person behind or within the pose. But this impulse creates its own problems. It can mask the fact that poses may be both as interesting and as important as the real truths they seem to be hiding from view. And, in any case, notions like "actual" and "real" are themselves problematic. Postures, guises, personas, stances—all the contrivances of personality—are not simple masks for some other kind of reality, lying in wait to be uncovered; they belong intimately to the personalities they supposedly hide. Irving's various guises fitted perfectly William James' dictum that if anyone wears a mask long enough, the face will grow to fit it. Whatever may have been the inert facts of his curriculum vitae, Irving did experience the world *as* a Lad of London, and also *as* a Crayonesque saunterer. He was, really, something of a "rum old bachelor"; and he was equally a grieving romantic artist. His contrivances insinuated themselves into his existential choices as well as his art. They were much more than public artifices; they were intimate and even urgent. Indeed, the very meaning of the term "Washington Irving"—what is proper to the noun—has to include every one of his myths and illusions, masks and guises. Like most lives, Irving's was lived out along a dialectical frontier between fact and contrivance, action and metaphor. It would be a waste of time to try to decide whether the poses or the inert facts they were crafted to deal with are finally more suggestive about him or about the more general problem of the man of letters in the nineteenth century.

The last undisguised moment of experience may be the first, the occasion of birth. And even this moment is pregnant with circumstance that even the most innocent flesh is heir to, and that already begins to define the self socially. Washington Irving entered the world burdened with a number of arbitrary identifications. He was a child of the year of Independence, and the son of a patriot who thrust on him the name of the commanding general of the revolutionary armies. He was also the son of a small-time hardware merchant, an immigrant who had worked his way from British common seaman to American tradesman. This William Irving was a devout Presbyterian, who delighted in family devotions and piously hoped that at least one of his five sons would be a preacher. William Irving was also a man whose most ambitious social pretensions were to a type of petit bourgeois life. He was a hardware merchant who lived in the best house on his New York street, to be sure. But it was a mean street, and the house was worth no more than about two thousand very inflated New York dollars at the time Washington Irving was born. When one family out of six in New York had at least one slave, the Irvings had none—and this not out of any ideological conviction. Washington was also the last of eleven children (three of whom died in infancy); his eldest brother, William, was seventeen years older. And this made the younger boy something of a pet of his older brothers—especially after their business began to prosper beyond their father's maddest expectations. In effect, Washington Irving was to live the first half of his life as a client of his brothers' patronage.

These circumstances of birth and parentage touch quite directly on at least two of Irving's mature self-images. He actually was, within his family, a kind of "Lad," pampered and invited to be irresponsible. On the other hand, the pretensions to gentility of Jonathan Oldstyle, Gent., and Geoffrey Crayon, Gent.—like the dandyism of the Lads—was a clear repudiation of both the social status and the class culture of his father. Like many another bourgeois gentilhomme, Irving tried to soften his break with the family's past by cultivating the idea that he had a noble lineage, complete with a family arms that he used to seal letters. In fact, much of Irving's adult life amounted to a kind of systematic contest with such familial realities. His father's patriotism was answered by Irving's spending much of his middle life in England. Also, he became a relaxed Episcopalian with none of his father's Presbyterian piety. And his father's concern with business always seemed a bit "sordid" to Irving, who much preferred to think of himself as the genteel dabbler. (In old age, Irving recovered himself a little: He could say that he did not like to "bore" himself with literary conversation, and preferred to talk about "stocks and railroads and some mode of screwing and jewing the world out of more interest than my money is entitled to.") As for his status as the pet and client of his brothers' patronage, Irving spent the most difficult period of his life puzzling over how to escape it, how to exert his "independence" from the family that had so carefully protracted his dependent, amateur standing.[17]

This manifold of correspondences between family circumstance and Irving's mature life suggests an enticingly simple possibility: that most of what he eventually became was somehow implicit in the facts of his childhood. But this tempting prospect is spoiled by two things. The first is practical: Irving's childhood is accessible only through his own unreliable and shifting memories of it. Second, and more important, Irving's adult personality was shaped not only by childhood circumstance but by two periods of his early adulthood, the second an extension of the first. The first occurred during his twenties, from about 1806 to 1815, while he was in New York; the second occupied much of his thirties, from 1815 into the 1820s. Together, these two periods constitute an enormously protracted period of vocational confusion. But this confusion was not only one of vocation, not just a matter of whether to be a lawyer or a professional writer, or even just a dilettante. The question of vocation

---

[17] The best account of the Irving family is in *STW*, chs. 1–2. The "screwing and jewing" remark is quoted in Edward Wagenknecht, *Washington Irving: Moderation Displayed* (New York, 1962), 71, and was made originally in a family letter.

spilled over into other urgent issues of sex, marriage, social class, and even nationality. At any point during this span of almost twenty years, nothing less than Irving's whole personality was at stake. And it was in these years, not in his childhood alone, that the complicated puzzle of Washington Irving was actually pieced together.

Irving began to read law at fifteen—not an unusually young age for the time. For the next eighteen years, until he was thirty-three, several mutually reinforcing circumstances kept him in what amounted to a state of prolonged juniority. For one thing, his legal apprenticeship was slow and uncertain. He did not pass the bar until 1806, some eight years after he had begun to study. His progress was, in one important way, spectacular. He first entered the offices of an undistinguished practitioner. Then he moved on to Brockholst Livingston, who was about to be appointed to the state supreme court. From Livingston, Irving passed to Josiah Ogden Hoffman, whose reputation as a lawyer and a politician had placed him just next to Aaron Burr and Alexander Hamilton in the city's professional rankings. But this progress in masters had a paradoxical effect. Irving's relationship to Hoffman became very much that of client to patron. He was an intimate of the Hoffman household, a traveling companion to the family, and a gossipy friend to Mrs. Hoffman and her two daughters—one of whom was the future sainted memory, Matilda. Irving's autobiographical formula for all this, when he looked back on it, was that Hoffman "took a fancy to me . . . and made me almost an *inmate* of his house."[18]

Another circumstance that artificially prolonged Irving's juniority and dependence was his health—or his supposed lack of it. During his teens, his family came to the conclusion that he was "frail." There may have been some reason for this. At least Chancellor Kent, on a trip upstate that he took with the Hoffmans and their young "inmate," heard Irving cough through the night and concluded that Irving was "not long for this world." (The chancellor may have changed his mind a few days later, when Irving leaped into a cold stream to wrestle down a wounded deer, with considerable vigor and obvious relish.) Whatever the medical facts may have been, Irving's brothers decided definitely that he was too weak to work. They interrupted his studies in 1804 to send him to Europe for two years, to recuperate. According

[18] Autobiographical Fragment; *PMI* 1:164 ff.; Hellman, *Washington Irving,* 65 ff.

to family tradition, Irving had to be helped aboard ship, and the captain took one look at him and said, "There is a chap that will go overboard before we cross." Still, a few weeks later, Irving was writing home that he had enjoyed the voyage enormously, had become expert at climbing the spars, and had even dared his way out along the main topsail yard. He hit the ground running in France, and kept up a very fast pace, with no ill effects, for months at a time. His "frailty" was probably no more than an excuse for his brothers to offer, and him to accept, their open patronage.[19]

A third element in the equation that made it possible for Irving to put off maturity was the fact that, shortly after he passed the bar, he was relieved of any necessity to earn a living as a lawyer. He was made a one-fifth partner in his brothers' now-flourishing business, a partner with no duties to speak of. He did go to Washington a couple of times to help lobby against the Republicans' restrictive trade policies. But it was clear to him and to his brothers that he was a kept man. As he put it in his autobiographical fragment, "My brothers . . . wished me to cultivate my general talents and devote myself to literature. Indeed, they were all indulgence to me."[20]

His own lack of interest in the law, his supposed frailty, his brothers' willingness to support him, the Hoffmans' great "fancy" for him—all conspired to tempt him to languish in an extended "youth." For nine full years after he passed the bar in 1806, his life had no vocational shape and no independent character. He continued to live at home with his parents until about 1811, and even after that for extended periods. He spent his intervals in Washington more in society than in work, and his letters home to his brothers had almost nothing to do with business. He summered on the farms of friends. He cavorted with the Lads of Kilkenny. He toyed at writing. And in such a setting, conventional modesty flowered into self-deprecation. When he sat in Hoffman's offices, just before his examination for the bar, he could only write quaintly about his "inveterate enemies" on the bookshelves, "the ponderous fathers of the law." After he had passed, and was writing to Judge Hoffman to ask for a patronage position in a new state administration, Irving spoke mockingly and apologetically of himself: "I would humbly put up my feeble voice. . . . There will, doubtless, be numerous applicants of superior

[19] *Notebooks and Journals of Washington Irving*, 1:14–16; *STW*, 1:42; Irving to William Irving, July 1, 1804, *Letters*, 11–14.
[20] Autobiographical Fragment.

claims. . . . I can plead no services that I have rendered. . . . I know there are few offices to which I am eligible, either from age or information." If he occasionally played out a lawyer's coordinate role as a party man—as he did when he helped organize Federalist votes in 1807—Irving had it both ways: He did the thing, then mocked it. "I drank beer with the multitude . . . and I shook hands with the mob—whom my heart abhorreth. . . . My patriotism all at once blazed forth and I determined to save my country! Oh! . . . I have been in such holes and corners—such filthy nooks and filthy corners, sweet offices and oyster cellars!" The habit of deprecating both the law and his own talent for it deepened, until finally, by 1813, Irving had completed one of his principal myths about himself, that he was simply and temperamentally unsuited to the career, to "the dry studies . . . the dry technical rubbish, and dull routine of a lawyer's office."[21]

Of course, this sort of self-deprecation was common stock. But in Irving it was more. It ratified the kind of dandified amateurism he was simultaneously acting out in the "jollities" of the Lads of Kilkenny. And more importantly, it fitted perfectly with his actual condition as a nearly complete dependent on his brothers and on Judge Hoffman. What might have begun as clever irony deepened into style. What might have started as mere wit became an estimate of the self. Verbal ploy deepened into self-perception, until Irving could conclude, quite seriously, that he had fallen permanently into "idle habits, idle associates and fashionable dissipation."[22]

If it had not been for his brothers' and Hoffman's patronage, Irving might have had a career in the law. Many young men did, young men for whom the fathers of the law were just as ponderous and the routine of the law office just as dull. As it was, however, Irving simply could not see the law as a path to an independent life. It was hopelessly entangled in the web of dependence that threatened to hold him always in "idle habits." A more likely path to autonomy lay in what he slightingly called his "fatal propensity" to literature. Among other motives, he wrote for money, and from the beginning. He and his young colleagues earned $100 each for the *Salmagundi* skits—and wondered with some bitterness why they did not get more from the printer-seller. Irving and his brother Peter trans-

---

[21] Irving to Hoffman, February 2, 1807; to Mary Fairlie, May 2, 1807, *Letters*, 223, 231–2; Irving, *Biography of Captain James Lawrence* (New York, 1813).
[22] Autobiographical Fragment.

lated a French book of travels—for the money. And the two of them began the Knickerbocker *History* in 1808 with the same purpose in mind. To whip Washington into action, Peter wrote him that the book would have to be finished soon, for "my pocket calls aloud." When the book was finally completed, it sold well enough to earn Irving $2,000 in the first year, and another $1,000 the second. A revision, published in 1812, brought him $1,200.[23]

The sums were not nearly as magnificent as his earnings from *The Sketch Book* would be. But they were enough to have paid for his father's house several times over. And they were certainly enough to have convinced any young man that it might be possible to make a living out of writing. The amateur status that Irving continued to cling to for years after the *History* was not just a reflection of the realities of the situation. The profession of authorship was precarious, to be sure. But for a New Yorker of Irving's class and experience it would have been a live choice. The immediate success of the *History* might have pointed him toward a possible escape from dependence, and a workable assertion of maturity and autonomy. But Irving did not seize the occasion. He clearly needed, or wanted, more years of preparation. Part of the problem had to do with social class: The imperatives of gentility and of writing for the market still seemed to pull in opposing directions. His hesitation may have been confirmed by the simple generosity of his patrons. And a congeries of "psychological" impediments may have been in the way. But whatever held him back, Washington Irving did understand clearly enough that only something profound and compelling, some wrench that must change his whole life, could explain a decision to take himself in hand, forsake careless youth, and begin a career as a professional. His own grasp of the process was limited and confused. But the issues it raised stayed with him, and they set the moral agenda that his best stories would address—however indirectly or even unconsciously. The stresses of the career decision he so earnestly postponed also lay behind the curious—and false—autobiography he invented after he went to Europe in 1815.

Irving's tale of his love for Matilda Hoffman and his inconsolable grief at her passing was one of his attempts to make sense out of a turning in his life from idleness to authorship. It is not a true tale, but

[23] Peter Irving to Irving, April 30, 1808, *PMI*, 1:214; *STW*, 1:122.

still it is a telling one. In memory, he managed to join his lost love to his vocational dilemmas. In life, Matilda represented the possibility of a serious commitment to the law. According to Irving's account of things, Judge Hoffman would not let him marry Matilda until Irving became a real lawyer, and a candidate for a partnership. And so he set to work with a will, as he remembered it, determined to overcome his own "insuperable repugnance." At the same time, however, he worked away at the *History,* in the hope that *its* success might bring the Judge around to his side. If he could succeed as a writer, then he might be entitled to a patronage appointment in government. Very inventively, Irving managed to load both of his early career choices onto his recollected love for Matilda.[24]

When Irving devised this account of things, Matilda was long dead, and he knew how the story came out. He could, in memory, use his grief as the reason he had abandoned the law and finished the stalled *History.* This neatly transformed the *History* from a project aimed toward profit or preferment into a lover's desperate act, with no consequences outside itself. Matilda served him better in death than she had in life: as a justification for becoming *neither* a lawyer nor a professional writer. As Irving told it, he could finish the *History* only when it was transformed into a romantic, compensatory gesture. And this way of discussing his work was completed when he described *The Sketch Book* as just another compensatory gesture, a response to his second great grief over the bankruptcy of the Irvings' English branch. Taken as an intellectual exercise, the story worked; and the fact that it is not true makes it a revelation indeed.

There is no solid evidence that Washington Irving ever loved Matilda Hoffman, ever declared himself to her, or ever proposed himself to Judge Hoffman as either a son-in-law or a future partner. When Matilda died, he did (as he said) go to the country. But he went to the country every summer anyway. His letters and journal entries, between the time of her death and the cathedral scene of lamentation in his 1817 notebook, contain very little mention of her. Before many months had passed after her death, he was back in his patterns of innocent "dissipation." The letters he wrote to Mrs. Hoffman during the months after Matilda's death do not refer to any betrothal. He did mention the "heart-aching" distress of Matilda's dying, and he did suggest some lines for her gravestone. But these

[24] Autobiographical Fragment.

remarks were nothing more than he might have written to any friend whose daughter had died. And his letters to Mrs. Hoffman about Matilda were no more grieved than the letter he wrote her soon after, when his own sister died: "never has a blow struck so near my heart before." In May, just a month after Matilda's "dying struggles," Irving had apparently regained his composure (if indeed he had ever lost it): "I have in a manner worked myself into a very enviable state of serenity and self-possession, which is promoted by the tranquility of everything around me. . . . So time goes. If not in gaiety, at least in useful and agreeable occupation." And to his brother Peter, in that same summer, he joined a complaint about "feeble health" to a hope that a planned "jaunt" into Canada might "perfectly renovate me."

Surely a "jaunt" was not an adequate remedy for so deep a grief. Irving's letters and journals never suggested grief, never lost their studied and relaxed elegance, casualness, impishness, and sociability. It was many years until he first fully elaborated the account of his love for Matilda, and gave it the central place in his experience. At the time she died, in a little notebook he kept between 1808 and 1810, Irving jotted down a more believable summary of those years. And in it, he gave Matilda's "struggle" the status it probably deserved among the other comings and goings of the time:[25]

> Jan'y 1808—Went to Canada May
> ret'd June began Knick
> Winter in Canada
> 1809 ret'd Jan'y Peter gone
> Mat died in April

When Irving started "remembering" his love and grief, eight years later, what he probably was recalling was his own urgent need for some excuse to write. And it needed to be an excuse that would avoid the potential professional implication of the *History*'s success. In his "memory," Matilda served as the basis of one more evasion. Irving never wrote to overcome grief. But it is apparent that grief and writing were somehow tied together in his imagination. His error, and the error of a good deal of Irving iconography, was to reverse the causal relationship between grief and art.

[25] Irving to Mrs. Hoffman, May 19, June (?); to Peter Irving, August (?), *Letters,* 265, 272, 273. A notebook of Irving's (1810) in the Yale collection. *STW,* 1:119.

Grief did not cause Irving to write. Instead, he needed to grieve—or think he did—in order to be able to write. His "memory" of his own suffering, spelled out in a romantic convention, was a way of denying the extent of the professional commitment he actually was making in the years after about 1817. He could never be, nakedly, a writer by trade. He clothed his working identity, and mourning garb had the same purposes as the dress of a dandy or the black suiting of the scholar-relic. For Irving, writing was complicated by intimations of maturity and independence. In his fantastic retrospect of young love, these intimations could symbolically be invested in a possible marriage to Matilda. And when that possibility collapsed in grief, so did the need to write the *History* for practical reasons. Similarly, the myth went on, his second grief over the bankruptcy made it possible to write *The Sketch Book* "not so much for support."[26]

Up to the time Matilda Hoffman died, Irving's life did have a kind of coherence. His halting preparation for the law, his position in the Hoffman household, the Lads and their *Salmagundi* skits, his trip to

[26] A very instructive example of the kinds of critical distortions that can occur when a scholar takes a writer's autobiography too literally is Richard Ellmann's "Love in the Catskills," *New York Review of Books*, February 5, 1976, 27–9. Ellmann begins by accepting the simple truth of Irving's account of his love for Matilda, concluding that "This love story is one of the most affecting in a century distinguished for affecting love stories." He finds the lamentation scene Irving put in his 1817 notebook "moving." And Irving's grief, Ellmann thinks, accounts for some of the principal features of the story of Rip Van Winkle. "Following her death, Irving could look back on long years in which he moved like a somnambulist, alienated by grief in his native America, then by nationality when he became an American in postwar Britain, as Rip was a Briton in postwar America. . ·. . [The story] was a parable of his own monstrous dual vision, in which the history of New York took shape as farce, and the history of his own life took shape as tragedy, a vision followed by years of depression, and then by his reawakening, an artist once again, but a young man no longer."

The methodological project on which Ellmann was embarked is a fine one: to help reclaim works of art from the "purists" who think art has nothing to do with the experience out of which it comes. Indeed, he is quite fervent on this point, even fervent enough to tug William Butler Yeats into the matter: "As the work loses the auto-telic privacy which purist critics have sought to ascribe to it, it enters an interfusion of art and life. Or as Yeats said in a slightly different context, the stallion eternity mounts the mare of time."

What Ellmann does not see—and many contextualist critics seem to forget—is that the mare of time has ideas of her own. That is, we cannot suppose that the facts of the writer's life are a kind of notarized curriculum vitae, and that the problem is only to show how these facts of life find their way into works of art, being creatively transformed in the process, of course. Experience—quite apart from what we call "art"—is not matter-of-fact. It is creative, meditative, and reflexive. Experience is a wrought and rewrought affair. And art can be as much an instrument of experience as a mere outcome of it. As someone else once said, in a slightly different context, "The truth is no stranger to fiction."

Europe in 1804, beginning the *History* with one of his brothers, living at home and seeing all his brothers regularly—these elements hung together reasonably well. It was a simple enough matter to postpone any sort of reckoning with the problem of career, year after year.

After about 1810, though, Irving's life fell increasingly into disarray. He gave up even the pretense of the law. He passed many aimless months in Washington as an agent of his brothers. He spent a good deal of time arranging his life around what he called social "gaiety," but even the Lads fell into disuse. He did get up a minor revision of the *History,* and relished his $1,200 advance payment. And he did become the editor of a magazine in 1812 (*The Analectic,* he named it) at a substantial salary of $1,500. But even this venture he chose to treat as something slight, a mere pastime. "It is an amusing occupation," he wrote to Peter, "without any mental responsibility of consequence. I felt very much the want of some task in my idle hours; there is nothing so irksome as having nothing to do." However, the magazine itself soon became "irksome." Irving was happy, when war was declared with Britain, to accept a commission as an unlikely colonel in the New York militia. He was even happier when the governor took him along to Albany to help prepare for an anticipated British attack from Canada. He did still fuss a bit with *The Analectic,* but only a bit. The colonelcy was a harmless fraud. Nothing in his life seemed to make sense. Finally, in the winter of 1814–15, three things happened to set Irving altogether free from even his tenuous engagements: the governor abandoned the Albany "front"; the war ended; *The Analectic* foundered.[27]

Now completely at loose ends, Irving wandered back again to what he called "the gamesome city of the Manhattoes." And he *was* game, ready to snatch at the first random chance that fell his way, the first whimsical project that would fill his time. As luck had it, he was rooming with Brevoort in a house where Mrs. Stephen Decatur also happened to be staying. Her celebrated commodore husband, just paroled from British captivity, was offered command of a punitive expedition against the Algerine "pirates." Decatur asked Irving if he would like to go along as a curious kind of supercargo, and Irving excitedly had his trunks loaded aboard the *Guerrière.* Just as fortuitously, though, news arrived that Napoleon had escaped from Elba.

[27] Irving to Peter Irving, December 30, 1812, *Letters,* 350–1. Hedges, *Washington Irving,* takes *The Analectic* more seriously than one should, or at least more seriously than Irving did.

Decatur's mission was postponed, and Irving had to off-load his baggage. Then he decided not to waste the effort he had made to pack, and so took passage to Europe on his own.[28]

The odd chain of events, so full of contingencies that seemed to bounce a passive Irving first this way, then that, ended in a decision that was without any real purpose. Irving's planned trip to the Continent was nothing more than a "jaunt"; he only wanted to "see the armies." A few years later, in the draft letter to his prospective mother-in-law, he pictured the trip as a last fling. He would return home soon, he "remembered," to "settle myself down to a useful and honorable occupation." He would also "settle down quietly" beside his mother, "for the rest of her life." Here again, in this bit of reminiscence, Irving linked his inconstant actions to the latent issues of his life: career, and family. In truth, in 1815, he had not the slightest idea of what sort of "useful and honorable occupation" he might take up. Nor could he have expected to return to his mother, who was seventy-seven and already sick. (She died early in 1817.) Irving had simply reached the age of thirty-two with no clear sense of who he was or what he might do, and so was utterly vulnerable to the accidents of history—even to the whims of Napoleon or the Bey of Algiers.[29]

One more chance of history upset Irving's already fragile plan to "see the armies." When he reached Liverpool, the news of Waterloo had arrived; there were no more armies to see. Then still another chance intervened, this one medical. His brother Peter, onetime doctor and now manager of the European branch of the family firm, was ill with Saint Anthony's fire—an acute dermatitis. So Irving stayed in Liverpool to see to things. And as it happened, things were awful. Peter, like many merchants exporting to America, had bought on credit at the end of the war, anticipating a rush of American demand. But the demand did not come fast enough. As Irving began to sweat his way through the accounts—paying very novel attention to family business—it gradually dawned on him that the company could not meet its notes. There was no alternative but to declare the English branch bankrupt.

---

[28] Autobiographical Fragment; *PMI*, 1:308–10; *STW*, 1:144. For a different and unconvincing explanation of Irving's decision to go to Europe, see M. A. Weatherspoon, "1815–1819: Prelude to Irving's *Sketch Book*," *American Literature* 41 (January 1970): 566–71.
[29] Autobiographical Fragment.

For the first time since he had finished the *History,* Irving fell to
work with a sustained will. He scrambled for ways of extending the
firm's credit. He cared for his brother. He took almost no time out
to tour. And, as he worked, a disparity gradually developed between
the situation and his emotional responses to it. Every American
export firm in Britain was in trouble. Bankruptcy was already a
common practice, and Irving need hardly have felt disgraced by it.
His brothers certainly did not fall into despair, for the American end
of their enterprise was healthy. But Irving seemed almost to reach
out for pain and "humiliation." "I have never passed so anxious a
time in my life," he wrote Brevoort. "My rest has been broken, and
my health and spirits almost prostrated." Within a few months, by
the spring of 1816, he had completed the myth of his business grief—
the grief that would blend so neatly with his supposed grieving for
Matilda. "I find," he wrote to a New York friend, "every gay
thought or genteel fancy has left my unhappy brain, and nothing
remains but the dry rubbish of accounts. Woe is me! How different
a being I am from what I was last summer." A few months later, he
remembered how he had once been confident and free of care but
now was "weather-beaten." "It is not long since I felt myself quite
sure of fortune's smiles. . . . At present I feel so tempest-tossed that
I shall be content to be quits with fortune for a very moderate
portion."[30]

Gradually, too, he began to work out a vocabulary to describe his
state. And it was this vocabulary that would find its way, very
exactly, into the cathedral scene of lamentation in the 1817 notebook
and into his Dresden "Private Mems." When the bankruptcy hearing
opened, he wrote home a horrific description of his state: "humiliating . . . loathesome entanglement . . . murky cloud . . . withers
and blights me. For upwards of two years now I have been bowed
down in spirit, and harassed by the most sordid cares." All that
remained, really, was to introduce his lost Matilda into the picture,
and the portrait of the grief-stricken artist would be complete.[31]

The bankruptcy can hardly have wrought such drastic effects on
Irving. He had been an inactive partner. Peter's mistakes, not his,
had brought on the "humiliation." There must have been other
reasons why Irving took it so hard, and why he chose to say—and

[30] Irving to Brevoort, March 15, July 16, 1816, *ItoB,* 1:138–53, 163–74; Irving to Jane Ren-
wick, April 5, 1816, *Letters,* 440–1.
[31] Irving to Brevoort, July 11, 1817, in *ItoB,* 2:40–3.

perhaps even believe—his life had been so irrevocably changed. Irving seized on the bankruptcy, and used it for his own ends. He made it over into an occasion for his first furtive gestures toward personal and professional independence.

The circumstances were perfect. He was in England, away from most of his family. His mother had just died, and his father had been dead for several years. The only brother who was present was Peter, and he was ill (and had always been about as dependent as Washington on the older brothers anyway). The firm was also sick, and Irving found himself suddenly in the unaccustomed position of nurse to both business and brother. In the midst of all this death and infirmity, he could see himself as a source of strength and stability. He could even bring himself to worry about his brothers. To Ebenezer, the most sober, businesslike, and responsible, Irving could now write that "my heart is torn every way by anxiety for my relatives. My own individual interests are nothing. The merest pittance would content me if I could crawl out from among these troubles and see my connections safe around me." And to Brevoort, he sent the same pious message of concern and self-denial: "I feel very little solicitude about my own prospects . . . and am convinced, however scanty and precarious may be my lot, I can bring myself to be content. But I feel harassed in mind at times on behalf of my brothers."[32]

Irving began, now, to picture himself as a man who needed only a "pittance," who wanted only "bread and cheese." In part, this was a measured response to the bankruptcy proceedings. But there was another side to his reduced expectations. Bread and cheese he could earn himself, without anyone's patronage. He began to hint, in letters home, at a "plan," a scheme that could bring in a "scanty but sufficient means of support." He did not explain the scheme, but only wrote mysteriously that "a small matter will support a drowning man." It was with such dark sayings that Irving left Liverpool, and (as he later formulated it) "threw myself a stranger in London, shut myself up, and went to work."[33]

The "small matter" he had in mind was not *The Sketch Book* and a writing career. Not quite yet. Nor was it even his work on a third

---

[32] Irving to William Irving, December 23, 1817, *Letters,* 514–15; to Brevoort, January 28, 1818, *ItoB,* 2:61–4.
[33] Irving to William Irving, December 20, 1817, *Letters,* 514–15; Autobiographical Fragment.

and fancily illustrated edition of Knickerbocker's *History*—though that, too, was in the works. It was not even a scheme to "shut myself up." On the contrary, what Irving planned to do in London was to create a career for himself as an agent. He would work with the best British and American publishers, arranging for quick and honorable American editions of British books, and vice versa, protecting the rights of publishers and authors alike. The plan required, above all, inside knowledge of who was publishing what. And this meant that he not be shut up at all, but become instead something of a litterateur-about-town. This was perfectly consistent with the sauntering manner of a genteel bachelor. But it had a covert side, too. Into his notebook, Irving jotted an analysis of what amounted to the secret life of Geoffrey Crayon:[34]

> Periodical writers talk much of lounging about the town observing characters—& give the idea of an independent lounger as a happy being—life of a butterfly. It is because they do not know what it is. . . . These poor authors were generally on the keen hunt after a dinner.

Irving's own keen hunt for a dinner soon succeeded. Armed with his scheme (which never materialized), with letters of introduction, and with the reputation he had as Knickerbocker's creator, he managed to penetrate quickly to the inner circles of a very well organized and self-conscious literary and publishing cadre in London. It radiated out from the house of John Murray, master of perhaps the most distinguished and profitable publishing firm in Britain. Around Murray there clustered authors like Scott and Byron, as well as dozens of others who managed to earn very handsome incomes as authors. The tight elite centered on Murray's elegant drawing room, lined with portraits of his famous authors and friends. The establishment breathed sophistication, fame, and money. In New York, the profession of letters may have seemed a little makeshift and precarious. In London, it was a crystal-clear option, institutionalized, perfectly understood, and ably practiced.

For two generations or more, and especially after 1800, firms like Murray's and Constable's had capitalized on the rapid growth of literacy to transform printing and bookselling into something resem-

---

[34] *Notes While Preparing the Sketch Book*, 69.

bling modern publishing. Every year, John Murray played host at a fancy trade dinner, followed by an auction. His annual take from the book auction alone was on the order of £20,000. The publishers themselves had no figures, but guessed that the potential English market for books had shot up from about 20,000 to about 200,000 buying readers in little more than one generation. Actual sales had at least quadrupled in the quarter-century after 1780.[35]

The authors who provided the goods for publishers like Murray's or Longman's shared handsomely in the profits. Murray paid the poet George Crabbe £3,000 for rights to his complete poems in 1818. Byron got £600 each for the first two cantos of *Childe Harold,* and a grand £2,000 for the third. For the first two parts of *Don Juan* he was paid £1,575 outright. Scott was the champion. Campbell paid him £1,500 just to put together a compendium of Swift. At his peak, Scott probably earned something on the order of £30,000 a year (of which only about a third was from his novels, and the rest from other writing and editing chores).[36]

---

[35] McClary, *Washington Irving and the House of Murray,* xxxii ff.; A. S. Collins, *The Profession of Letters: A Study of the Relation of Author to Patron, Publisher and Public, 1780–1832* (London, 1928); Henry Lytton Bulwer, *The Monarchy of the Middle Classes,* 2 vols. (London, 1836), 1:54 ff.; T. Constable, *Archibald Constable and His Literary Correspondents,* 3 vols. (London, 1873); W. West, *Fifty Years' Recollections of an Old Bookseller* (London, 1850); Samuel Smiles, *A Publisher and His Friends,* 2 vols. (London, 1891). For similar developments in France, see Cesar Graña, *Modernity and Its Discontents: French Society and the French Man of Letters in the Nineteenth Century* (New York, 1964), chs. 1–4. It is impossible to date with any precision the actual beginnings of the literary "public" in England or in America. In any case, what counts for an understanding of writers like Irving is not the facts of literacy or even of book production and sales but the perceptions of authors and booksellers. Something drastic had happened to the conception of authorship between the time of Defoe's boast that "Writing . . . is become a very considerable Branch of the English Commerce. The Booksellers are the Master Manufacturers or Employers. The several Writers, Authors, Copyers, Sub-Writers and all other operators with Pen and Ink are the workmen employed by the said Master Manufacturers," and the time when Irving could think about his stories as a "capital." An extremely valuable essay on this point is "The Growth of the Reading Public," in Raymond Williams' fine *The Long Revolution* (American edition: Westport, Conn., 1975), 156–72. An intimate look at Samuel Johnson's earnings from his writing is J. D. Fleeman's "The Revenue of a Writer: Samuel Johnson's Literary Earnings," in *Studies in the Book Trade in Honour of Graham Pollard* (Oxford, 1975), 211–30. Johnson is sometimes called the first writer in English to depend truly on the literary marketplace, rather than on patronage or subscription. Fleeman's figures suggest, rather, that Johnson depended heavily on a royal pension that rewarded him for some political work—work sinister enough to place Johnson's name not on the civil list but on the crown's secret service list. (This last fact was pointed out to me by Johnson's biographer, Donald Greene.) Even in Johnson's time, the writer was rather more likely to be someone's "employee" than a free lance.

[36] These figures and similar ones are scattered through McClary, *Washington Irving and the House of Murray;* Collins, *The Profession of Letters;* J. G. Lockhart, *Life of Scott* (Edinburgh, 1902); and Williams, *The Long Revolution.*

Figures like these were not kept very secret. And no secret at all was the swift celebrity that success as an author could bring in London society. When Irving entered Murray's drawing room for the first time in August of 1817, with a letter from the poet Alexander Campbell, he looked at the portraits of Byron and Scott and Lady Caroline Lamb. He met George Canning. He returned that evening for dinner and listened to Murray boast about the number of guineas he had already paid Byron. He met Isaac D'Israeli. He savored what society called "Murray's famous port." In such a setting, the possibility of writing for a handsome income and an equally handsome reputation— not for a "pittance" or "bread and cheese"—was as plain as the possibility that one's portrait just might someday hang in Murray's drawing room. There was new point to Irving's determination to formulate some plan of life that "places me for the time above the horrors of destitution or the more galling mortifications of dependence."[37]

The galling mortifications of dependence would not go away so easily. Despite Irving's hints that he wanted to stay in Europe and support himself, his brothers continued to work away on their own solutions for his life. They could hardly realize that Washington was gathering himself for a belated thrust toward independence. So they continued to try to compose things for him back home. The eldest, William, was now a member of Congress and worked hard to get Irving an undemanding clerkship. He lobbied with Henry Clay and boasted that "my mind is full of the subject. I think on it night and day." On his side, Washington became increasingly explicit: He needed only a little, and hoped to get that "by my own exertions. . . . I feel that my future career must depend very much on myself." Still his brothers persisted. Just after the bankruptcy proceedings had finally ended, Irving had to warn Ebenezer that he was "able to rub along with my present means of support . . . so you need give yourself no solicitude on my account." Even this did not work. Ebenezer and William went relentlessly on—probably because Washington gave them no clear idea of what his "future career" was. Finally, they turned up a sinecure, a clerkship in the Navy Department with the impressive salary of $2,400.[38]

[37] Irving to Peter Irving, August 19, 1817, *Letters*, 488–9; to Brevoort, July 11, 1817, *ItoB*, 2:41–2; McClary, *Washington Irving and the House of Murray*, 3–9.
[38] William Irving to Ebenezer Irving, April 24, 1818, *Letters*, 522.

Ebenezer and William were working from a set of traditional notions about the man of letters as the object of patronage. And despite the changes being wrought by publishers like Murray's, even master professionals like Scott were still not reconciled to an entrepreneurial conception of authorship. Even when his income reached astronomical heights, Scott still clung to a sinecure in the Scottish court system. And Irving himself remembered hoping that the *History,* if it succeeded, might bring him some sort of patronage appointment. And so Ebenezer and William described the clerkship in what would once have been extremely attractive terms: "It is a berth highly respectable—very comfortable in its income, light in its duties, and will afford you ample leisure to pursue the bent of your literary inclinations. . . . You will be able to spend your days in the best of society and among the worthies of the land." They did not guess how impossible it would be to compete with John Murray's famous port.[39]

Irving refused the clerkship. He also assumed, wrongly, that his refusal would cause his brothers "chagrin." In fact, the distress was all on his side, not theirs, and was an accurate measure of the profoundness of the break he was making, a break not so much with his brothers, nor even with America, but with himself. He had several of his best sketches already written. He had a clear sight of things, and a new ambition. He had written some of his pieces in a real burst of energy, and he was beginning to speak of them as a professional "stock." When he did send the first number of *The Sketch Book* to America, it was to Ebenezer; and this gesture was practically pointless since he had asked Brevoort to take full charge of publication. But his decision to decline the clerkship needed justification, and Irving's covering letter to Ebenezer spoke directly to the point. Picking up his brothers' redundant phrase, Irving now asked definitely to be left alone, to follow the "bent of my own literary inclination. . . . If I ever get any solid credit with the public, it must be in the quiet operations of my own pen."[40]

"Solid credit with the public" was more than a metaphor; Irving had, after all, just seen a company through bankruptcy. In the same letter, he hoped that he might gradually "form a little stock of

---

[39] William Irving to Irving, October 24, 1818, quoted in *STW,* 1:170–1.
[40] Irving to Ebenezer Irving, March 3, 1819, *Letters,* 540–1.

literary property, that may be a little capital for me hereafter." He had made a momentous decision to earn his own bread by his own "exertions." And that decision had come in the midst of what he chose to define as a deepening crisis, and in economic terms. Now the new career was announced to his family in entrepreneurial language. At the same time, Irving's new vocational commitment obviously had other sorts of implications, familial and emotional. For one thing, Irving interpreted his career as one that required him to stay in Europe, instead of returning home to a "useful occupation." He also chose to read his decision as one that would liberate him from the "galling mortifications of dependence"; and a man who defined his decision in these terms might well expect that he would cause chagrin in those who had taken such generous care of him for so long. It was very important, then, that he present his decision, both to himself and to others, as one taken in desperation and grief, rather than aggressively and in hope. To be tolerable at all, his new sense of career had to be displayed as the outcome of sorrowful trial. And it helped, too, that his expectations could be put in spartan and self-denying terms. "I am living," he wrote, "in a retired and solitary way, partaking in little of the gaiety of life. . . . I only care to be kept in bread and cheese."[41]

The repetitious references to solitude, bread, and cheese in Irving's letter were a bit of a hoax. In London, he actually dined out often and well. His rooms were comfortable and even a little on the fashionable side. Peter was in town much of the time. He traveled to Scotland, where he spent several days with Scott. He had fallen in with as elevated a literary set as London had to offer. He had his Lads. But the hoax had a serious side. On some level, Irving probably was grieving and solitary. He did not grieve for Matilda. Nor was he solitary because of straitened circumstance. What had apparently died was a personality he had lived with for many years: the careless youth, the genteel amateur, the footloose bachelor. And what could be more solitary than deciding to place himself on one side of experience and an anonymous "public" on the other—with no family, no institutional buffers or nets, between; with no connection to that public, finally, but the lines on the printed page. His new career was precarious. Its independence was to be won only by what he thought of as "toil." And so it was suitable for Irving to grieve a little for the

---

[41] Irving to Ebenezer Irving, March 3, 1819, *Letters,* 541.

youthful amateur he had decided to leave behind, and to feel solitary in the bargain.[42]

Irving translated his time of crisis into very simple and straight-forward terms. In his view of things, he did undergo sorrow and abasement as a result of lost love and bankruptcy. Then, in a neatly ordered way, he wrote for escape and relief. On one hand was the problem, on the other the solution. But the real architecture of things was more intricate. Just as Irving had already begun the *History* when Matilda died, he was already at work on *The Sketch Book* when he learned about the impending bankruptcy of the Liverpool branch. *The Sketch Book* was not a cure for an already existing malaise. It was part of the malaise; in a sense, it *was* the malaise. Irving's personal stake in the book was enormous, and he hedged that stake with row upon row of defenses against psychic harm. Crayon was one such hedge—and a device Irving hit on only after he had begun the sketches. The London Lads was another, a sort of safety net in case his experiment in authorship should fail. The heart of the matter was what Irving now perceived as the "galling mortifications of dependence." And these became galling only once the possibility of a remedy came into sight. For Irving, the act of writing for the market had taken on an extraordinarily dense significance. It was a peculiarly aggressive thing for him to do, an odd assertion of the self against a past that had been so amiable and so dependent. And this assertiveness was not made out of grief, and not out of a fear of destitution, either. If anything, the reverse was true. Irving deployed grief and poverty—just as he deployed Crayon, dandyism, gentility, or romance—to protect himself. Writing for the market was extremely risky, not just economically but emotionally. And he found it easier to say that he had been driven to the market by sorrow or necessity than that he had chosen it. He had put his identity at issue. And this was the real meaning of the words "fate" and "fortune" in a letter he wrote his old mate Brevoort, as Irving waited anxiously for news of the reception of the first part of *The Sketch Book*:

> I am extremely anxious to hear from you what you think of the first number, and am looking anxiously for the arrival of the

---

[42] On *The Sketch Book* as "toil," see "Remarks of Col. Aspinwall," in William Cullen Bryant, *A Discourse on the Life, Character and Genius of Washington Irving, Delivered at the New-York Historical Society, at the Academy of Music in New York, on the 3d Day of April, 1860* (New York, 1860), 83–4.

next ship from New York. My fate hangs on it, for I am at the
end of my fortune.

When the news finally came four months later, and was good, he
cried.[43]

Experience does not intrude into art. It is worked into art. *The Sketch
Book* was whimsical, detached, and casual. Some of the sketches did
deal with sentimental and pathetic subjects like financial ruin or early
death. But Geoffrey Crayon's manner, even when dealing with pathetic subjects, was disinterested and unengaged. The effect Irving
strove for was one of easy and uninvolved grace. On its surface, at
least, his book showed few of the marks of the wrenching experience
out of which Irving wrote it. Even in the several sketches that bore
most directly on the writing for the market ("bookmaking," Irving
ironically called it), the manner was amused and superficial.[44]

But the two best and most enduring of Irving's stories were,
indirectly, about Irving's own traumatic attempt to gain personal
and vocational autonomy, and they were the stories that kept *The
Sketch Book* from being the "trifling" thing that Irving disingenu-
ously called it. The stories of Ichabod Crane and Rip Van Winkle
were the only two pieces in the first New York edition that dealt
with American subjects. They shared another peculiarity, too: They
were not told by Geoffrey Crayon. Ichabod Crane's story had been
"Found Among the Papers of the Late Diedrich Knickerbocker";
"Rip Van Winkle" was Knickerbocker's "posthumous writing." In
fact, both stories were sealed off from Geoffrey Crayon by layers of
putative authorship. The account of Ichabod's humiliation had been
told by "an old farmer" to another man, a "gentlemanly fellow,"
who had then recounted it at a meeting of "the Corporation" in New
York, where Knickerbocker had taken it down, to be left for Crayon
to discover and publish. The story of Rip Van Winkle was told by
Rip himself. Knickerbocker was only its recorder and Crayon its
editor. No fewer than four people stood between Irving and Icha-

---

[43] Irving to Brevoort, May 13, 1819, in *ItoB,* 2:95.
[44] All quotations and examples on the following pages are from the New York edition. I have
not troubled to cite page numbers, since the stories are so brief, and so many reprintings of the
sketches are available. There are some interesting observations on the Crayon figure in Thomas Cochran Buell, "The Professional Idler; Washington Irving's European Years" (Ph.D.
diss., University of Washington, 1965).

bod, and three between him and what had happened to Rip. No other pieces in *The Sketch Book* were so heavily framed. And no others were quite so informal and conversational.

Still, something more important than framing or tone linked the two stories. It was in them and not in Crayon's English sketches that Irving chose to try to come to grips with some of the implications of his own situation. He chose to invest himself most heavily in the two stories that were the most comic, the most removed from his life in England, and the most removed, too, from his own class and even ethnic culture. He was a sophisticated professional man, a man wholly defined by urban life; he had brought himself to the metropolitan center of British culture and had chosen the genteel Crayon as his main authorial voice. What could goings-on in rude Dutch villages, among ignorant farmers and hilariously ill-bred schoolmasters, have to do with him?

Ichabod Crane and Rip Van Winkle both pass through personal and vocational crises, and come out with profoundly altered lives. At the beginning of their tales, both heroes are enmeshed in lives that simply do not work, at odds with themselves and the world around them. Both have an experience that smacks of the supernatural and transcendent—though of course the reader is only asked to "half believe" it. The outcome in both stories is a resolution of the contradictions of the initial situation. Neither Ichabod nor Rip acts purposefully to bring this resolution to pass. Both are surprised and overtaken by powers outside their ken or control. They emerge, finally, not as self-made men but as men who have been remade by the intervention of something magical and spectral. (In much the same way, Irving liked to picture himself, at this point in his life, as having been made over by the caprices of death or the spectral market forces of transatlantic commerce.)

Most important of all, the problem around which both narratives were built is the difficult situation of the man of intellect and imagination, in a world that barely tolerates his presence. Ichabod and Rip, each in his own comic way, are idling men of letters. Their intellectual accomplishments, by London or New York standards, are quite negligible. But both, judged in their village contexts, are genuine sages, men of what Irving called "thought" or "learning." Both are dreamy storytellers. And it is on this most salient characteristic that their fates are balanced. Rip gains final peace, and harmony with his community *as* a storyteller—though at the cost of his farm and twenty years of adulthood. Ichabod makes good his escape *from* the scholarly life—though not as he plans, and at the cost of a terrific humiliation to his manhood and the concomitant loss of his job.[45]

Rip Van Winkle begins his remarkable career in a straitened situation, torn between his own inclinations and the nasty actualities of his life. He has one of those wives that inevitably get called "termagant," a sort of Xanthippe to his Socrates. His only "patrimony," his farm, has shrunk to an unkempt little plot that hardly will support him and his family. His son is a shiftless copy of himself, but totally attached to Dame Van Winkle, and so just another enemy. Rip has "an insuperable aversion to all kinds of profitable labor." Even in his sleepy village of subsistence farmers, he is in effect outside the economy, standing apart from the normal processes of production. In a world organized around patriarchy and property, he is a double failure. He is, in a radical sort of way, a marginal man whose only apparent solution to his own alienation is acquiescent good humor.

But Rip has a second and half-secret life, with three components that only emphasize and ratify his marginality. He loves to hunt squirrels in the Kaatskills, in the company of his dog, Wolf—who is just as henpecked and scruffy as Rip himself, but just as large-hearted, too. Rip also enjoys a kindly relationship with his neighbors, and especially with the women and children who seem to constitute his natural society. Finally, and most importantly, he loves to idle at the tavern. There, he and his colleagues have the unmistakable credentials Irving would have given any men of letters. They constitute a "kind of perpetual club of the sages, philosophers, and other idle personages of the village." They pass their time telling stories to each other, reading the occasional newspapers that chance to blow their way after a coach has passed through. They engage in

[45] In the 1812 edition of the *History*, Irving had prepared the way for his resolution to the careers of both Rip and Ichabod. The account of the later life of Diedrich Knickerbocker was expanded to cover the years since the first publication of the *History*. What Knickerbocker found, in this edition, was a pleasing reintegration into the life of his old village. He became a figure of affection, with the children of his neighbors and relatives constantly around him. He became, in a word, Rip. At the same time, Irving decided, it became clear that Knickerbocker could, if he had chosen it, have had precisely the kind of political career that eventually comes to Ichabod.

"profound discussions." They listen solemnly to the village school-master, "a dapper, learned little man." In such company, Rip is a recognizable version of one of Irving's own principal guises, the amateur dabbler, professional idler, and man of musings by inclination.

The problem, obviously, is in the very doubleness of Rip's life. His bent toward idleness and letters runs directly counter to the economic and social realities of his situation. In the simplest terms, in his world a man can either work or he can muse, talk, read, and write: a *man* of letters is a contradiction in terms. And so Rip is mastered by his situation, by his poverty, and by his wife, but also by his fatal propensity for what Irving had called in himself the "merely literary."

The solution to Rip's dilemma involves a mechanism that is a folktale in a number of different cultures. (In fact, Irving borrowed it from a German story in which Rip's part is taken by a man who actually is a poet by calling.) On one of his hunts, Rip falls in with the ghosts of Hendrick Hudson's crew, back in the Kaatskills on one of the "vigils" they are allowed to keep every twenty years. Rip drinks from their flagon—the same liquor that puts them back to sleep for two decades. When he awakes, all his problems have been dissolved.

Irving was asking his readers to be amused at something quite horrible, a kind of fractional murder of this amiable and harmless hero. Rip's initial reaction is fear. He wonders at once what his wife will say to his staying out all night. He calls pathetically for the faithful Wolf. He only gradually realizes, as he makes his way back to his village, what has happened—mostly because people stare at his odd clothes and white, long beard. Everything has changed. The sleepy village is now a bustling town, and it is full of Yankees where there had been only Dutch farmers. Before, a scrap of newspaper had been an important find; the town is now filled with printed matter—including a shower of election handbills. The tavern where he had whiled away afternoons with his fellow "sages" is now the Union Hotel, run by a man with the unmistakably Yankee name of Jonathan Doolittle. The sign over the door now bears the legend "GENERAL WASHINGTON" instead of "his majesty, George the Third." The face painted on the sign is the same "ruby" countenance, but the scepter has been changed to a sword, and George's red coat to Continental buff and blue. Rip's first encounters are confusing and frightening. People mock him, and point knowingly at their heads to signal that he is surely addled. An election crowd demands to know whether he is "Federal or Democrat," and when he can't understand, they cry him out for being a Tory.

The most miraculous thing about the story may not be Hendrick Hudson's crew but the ease and speed with which everything now falls into place. Within minutes, Rip's life takes on an admirable coherence. He discovers that his wife is dead. His daughter has married a cheerful and prosperous farmer with the studiedly non-Dutch name of Gardenier. The couple takes Rip in, and he soon becomes an established and fondly treated antique, a fixture of the town's life. He is a relic. But he has a function, a revered role that integrates him with the community. Idleness now becomes an acceptable career, and storytelling an appropriate vocation. And the bustling town offers what the old village had not: a continuously renewed audience for Rip's narrative. "Being arrived at that happy age when a man can be idle with impunity, he took his place once more on the bench at the inn door and was reverenced as one of the patriarchs of the village, and a chronicle of the old times. . . . He used to tell his story to every stranger that arrived at Mr. Doolittle's hotel."

This is the story of a transaction, a clever piece of double-entry vocational bookkeeping. What Rip gains in the bargain is a happy solution to his initial problem, and his story ends on that cheerful note. Indeed, generations of readers have grown up smiling with the story, not pausing to wonder whether the trade was worthwhile. But Rip pays dearly. Like a kind of village Faust, he has to swap something for the privilege of being a sage. And while his bargain is not quite as terrible as Faust's, it is bad enough. The physical topology of Rip's encounter with the ghostly Dutchmen may say something about the very large emotional stakes Irving was playing for.

Rip's encounter with the little men took Irving only two or three very condensed pages to tell. Into these few paragraphs, he was able to fit an astonishingly efficient parable on birth and rebirth. The setting he devised is almost a map of reproductive physiology. Rip, whose first and last names so nicely suggest death and sleep, stops hunting to rest. He lies down on a "grassy knoll," which turns out to be a kind of mons. He spies a curious little man toiling up a narrow gully, bearing that miraculous liquor. Rip joins him, and they climb the streambed to a narrow "cleft" in the rock. This cleft opens into a womblike "hollow, like a small amphitheater." And into this opening comes Rip (whom we should imagine to be about thirty-five, perhaps forty) with his "well-oiled fowling piece." When he awakens twenty years later, he has left his sleepy hollow, and is once more out on the grassy knoll. His gun has rusted away almost to nothing. In confusion, he tries to make his way back up the channel and into the amphitheater. But now the little stream is a torrent, and the cleft itself is hidden behind a waterfall of "feathery foam." These suggestions of parturition are confirmed by the most obvious kinds of temporal signals. Rip enters the cleft at the end of a day, and wakes at morning; his sleep begins in the autumn and ends in spring.

Rip's new birth is a birth of dependence and freedom at the same time. He becomes a sort of dependent child of his own daughter and her husband. He is aged, of course, but for the purposes of the transaction, age and childhood are interchangeable. For Irving and his contemporaries, the unmistakable conventional signs of adult independence for men were marriage and fatherhood, gainful work and property. By convention, the only respectable males who lacked such defining marks of status were those who were either too young or too old. But boys and old men were being joined in their prop-ertyless bachelorhood by men who pursued certain kinds of intel-lectual callings—preachers and schoolmasters, mostly, but also and increasingly by men who chose to be authors by profession. And so the problem Irving was addressing in Rip Van Winkle was complex and equally urgent—and not just for him but for other would-be writers, too. If men of letters were to become fully professional, writing openly and even aggressively for the market, always on a keen hunt after a dinner—if writing, that is, was to be their career—then what would be their social character? Would they live like other men, and have the same economic and sexual badges of masculinity? Or would they become a new, quasi-priestly caste, set off by expectations of bachelorhood and by at least a symbolic relinquishment of profits and property? And if they were women, how could they enter the market without surrendering all the sen-timental and pious attributes of well-bred females of the day?

The meaning of Rip's transaction is clear enough. What he cannot do—and what was so difficult for Irving—is to combine "manhood" and "letters." He does not choose between the two things in a deliberate way; Irving built the story in such a way that Rip cannot deliberate on anything, much less on so harsh a choice. But the choice is made. Rip pays out twenty years of adulthood to buy a life of superannuated storytelling, pays in what Emily Dickinson would later call "keen and quivering ratio."[46]

Irving addressed precisely the same set of questions in "The Legend of Sleepy Hollow." Even more plainly than Rip's, Ichabod Crane's story is a parable on the dilemmas generated by adulthood, masculinity, property, and marriage on one side and the career of letters on the other. Ichabod Crane is just as comic and inherently trivial a character as Rip. But he was Irving's vehicle for another meditation on the problems of authorship. Ichabod is, at the outset, what Rip becomes in the end: a man whose calling is to ideas, notions, and tales. He is a schoolmaster from Connecticut, which Irving dryly calls a source of "pioneers of the mind, as well as for the forest." He owns books, and has even read several from end to end. Like other village schoolmasters, Ichabod is regarded as "a kind of idle gentlemanlike personage, of vastly superior taste and accomplishments . . . and indeed, inferior only to the parson." He is a man of "superior elegance and address." Like Rip, he is a dreamy sort, who loves to idle in summer clover, reading and musing. In short, he is "our man of letters."

Ichabod's problem is ambition. In a farm village, his career is a thankless dead end. Like Rip, he is economically marginal, and dependent on the "patronage" of the farmers. He is a peculiarly oral character, an anaconda of appetites, longing to ingest everything around him and to "dilate" wonderfully to contain it. His career offers no means to satisfy his ambition. But Ichabod devises a scheme for escaping the mortifications of dependence. He will marry the buxom and bedimpled Katrina Van Tassel, daughter of a well-off farmer. Ichabod dreams of eating all of Baltus Van Tassel's great store of food, then selling the farm and setting off for Kentucky or

---

[46] The matter-of-fact differences between the details of Irving's own life and the life of a character like Rip have opened two possibilities to critics. The first, and most commonly chosen, is that the story has nothing to do with Irving's life at all—aside from such trivial connections as that Irving sometimes used a real-life printer named Van Winkle. The second is that the connection between the story and his life must be murky indeed. This has given a bit of a field day to some proponents of "Freudian" or "psycho-" critical methods. There are surely many "psychoanalytic" hypotheses that could find some justification in the text. One or more of them might even be correct, ultimately; but at the moment we have only the most limited kinds of means of guessing at which it might be. Psychoanalysis is no doubt a clinical art of considerable value. But such hypotheses probably ought to be confined to clinical practice, where they may sometimes do some good.

Tennessee to make his fortune. He dreams, in other words, of escaping the intellectual career altogether, and of joining the "great torrent of migration and improvement which is making such incessant changes in other parts of his restless country."

Like Rip, Ichabod is most comfortable when he is with women and children. He teaches singing to the ladies, and sits with them to tell the ghost stories he so loves. He does whip his pupils, but he gently spares the younger and weaker ones. And he joins the older boys in their sports. Among males his own age, Ichabod is only a hapless butt of jokes and pranks. He is especially victimized by Katrina's real suitor, the "formidable," hyper-masculine figure who carries the patriarchal first name Abraham, and the thrilling surname Van Brunt. His nickname is Brom, and his fellow "madcapping" bachelors call him "BROM BONES." Van Brunt is "Herculean," a "Tartar," the leader of a band of "Don Cossacks." He belongs integrally to the Dutch farming community, too, in a way that no ugly Yankee schoolteacher ever can. The reader and everyone else but Ichabod understands that Katrina Van Tassel and Abraham Van Brunt are meant for each other. The only surprise in the story, in fact, is the Headless Hessian trick with which Van Brunt finally humiliates Ichabod. And this surprise is rendered the more weighty by the fact that it is gratuitous. When he terrorizes Ichabod in the dark hollow, Van Brunt has already won everything; he is merely putting insult where before there was only injury to Ichabod's ambition. Ichabod has already failed; Van Brunt's assault just seals the failure with proof of an incompetence and disgrace so profound that Ichabod has to leave the village.

Ichabod Crane's ambition led at first away from books. Still, though he may have failed simply because he is ugly, he is humiliated by his own ardent faith in his "learning." He so avidly believes in mysteries, and in "old Mather's" scholarly disquisitions on witchcraft, that he falls quick prey to Van Brunt's impersonation of the Headless Hessian. Ichabod simply has too *much* head, and pays the price for it.

But he buys something with his defeat and disgrace. Irving tacked a second ending onto the tale. It is an awkward paragraph, and almost spoils the dramatic line of the piece. But it is indispensable to an understanding of the story's grave importance for Irving. Ichabod slinks away from Sleepy Hollow. Then he finds a new life, in which schoolmastering is only a first step toward resounding success. As it turns out, he had "changed his quarters for a distant part of the country, had kept school and studied law at the same time, turned politician, electioneered, written for the newspapers, and finally had been made a justice of the Ten Pound Court."

As a village schoolmaster, Ichabod had been outclassed by life, with no hope of marriage and the property it would bring. He is liberated only at the cost of humiliation. But—as with Rip—there is a balancing compensation. He moves into that "torrent of improvement" that had also transformed Rip's Tarrytown from dozing to bustle. And in this torrent Ichabod finds a type of success that had by far the most currency for Irving's generation, as it had had for Franklin's: the career of the lawyer-politician, public man, and scholar-turned-statesman—the career that anyone with Irving's experience would have recognized at once as a sure path to fame and fortune in the new Republic.

There is an important difference between the solutions to Ichabod's and Rip's problems. Rip gains his privileged position *as* a sort of village intellectual by sleeping away his adult life. Ichabod escapes *from* his own comic status as a man of letters to become a self-made man on his own terms and in a setting of his own choosing. But the difference only adds to the neat coherence of the two tales, and makes it all the more important to see them together as Irving's meditation on his vocational uncertainties. In both stories the pursuit of careers involving "mind" (on however comic a level) is plainly not compatible with success in "manly" things.

No matter what his conscious decisions on the subject may have been in 1818 or 1819, Irving's two-sided parable exposed a continuing suspicion in him that there was indeed something contradictory in the notion of the "man of letters." He was determined, at the time he wrote these stories, to make a living from his writing. There was even something a bit heroic in this determination, something remarkable in the effort and skill with which he went at it, and something gratifying about the large and quick success that came to him. But Irving still cherished and cultivated doubts. He still nourished the idea that there was some sort of inherent opposition between a life dominated by intellect and a life that was successful in worldly terms. His stories were built on an unstated principle that a life of "letters" was inevitably marginalizing, almost feminizing. Success in the world involved the sorts of manly power that belonged to men like Brom Bones or Baltus Van Tassel.

There was nothing new about this principle; it is at least as old as Jesus and Socrates. And such notions were not Irving's private ideas, either. Indeed, they were common to most of the poets, artists, philosophers, novelists, essayists—intellectuals of every description—in the first half of the nineteenth century. From Irving's day forward, a remarkable number of essays, poems, and books began with the same initial premise: The life of the man or woman of letters was, and even ought to be, defined in terms of an insoluble opposition; on one side was "art" or "learning"; on the other was "worldly" or "material" success. Across several decades, a curious idea blossomed into a cliché, at first among intellectuals and then more and more among their literate audiences: Spiritual elevation and existential failure were the proper twin conditions of experience for the writer, the artist, the radical reformer—for anyone whose purposes were intelligent expression and persuasion. What was new in Irving's lifetime was the paradoxical fact that a writer might do work within such an intellectual scheme of things, but then place that very work on the market, where it just might earn a small fortune.

Irving's own efforts made him, in modern equivalents, a millionaire. For a couple of years before he published *The Sketch Book,* and for a few years after, he was able to talk about this possibility in baldly economic terms, and to formulate it in his letters in precisely entrepreneurial language. For a brief time, he was an admitted capitalist of words, a striving captain of language. But it was not easy, and it did not last. Like many another entrepreneur, and like Benjamin Franklin before him, he began almost at once to yearn for a time when he would have enough money to retire into leisure, would be able to escape what he called the "necessity" of writing for money, would become once more the amateur dabbler. As years passed, and as success became a comfortable habit, he put on again the costume of Crayon. He also found that it was not at all difficult to accept the patronage of the Astor family, or to take a government sinecure like a diplomatic posting to Spain, cashing in on his solid credit with the public.

The letters of Irving's later years have little of the tension of the letters he wrote in England while he was at work on *The Sketch Book;* he never again wrote anything as full of anxiety (pinned on however false a myth of himself) as the Dresden "Private Mems." And it is no accident that he never again devised any stories as artful and compelling as the tales of Ichabod Crane and Rip Van Winkle. From the time he was forty, Washington Irving could hardly bear to think of himself, even in private, as a man who wrote for profit—though that is exactly what he was. Instead, he found his way back into the comfortable guise of the amiable and leisured gentleman.

There was a nice symmetry to Washington Irving's migration from the guises of youthful amateurism, through a moment when he confronted the imperatives of the market more or less directly, and then a lapse back into the comforting illusions of gentility, romance, or some other kind of mythic way of figuring himself. And the elements of this symmetry—the residual attractions of gentility and amateurism, the market with its risks and promises, and the illusory self-figurings—are found in the lives and work of many other writers during the half-century after *The Sketch Book*. Different men and women would of course arrange these elements into their own particular patterns, since all the manifold accidents of personal history would have their inevitable part to play. But the elements, and the contradictory relationships among them, would remain more or less constant, shaped by the persisting problems posed by the relationship of the writer and his or her work to the literary marketplace and its possibilities.

William Lloyd Garrison in 1824, an oil portrait by "Swain"

III

—

WILLIAM LLOYD GARRISON

Toward the end of 1825, William Lloyd Garrison commissioned a portrait of himself in oils. It was an extravagant thing for a young man in his position to do. He was only twenty, and just finishing an apprenticeship on the newspaper in his Massachusetts town, the *Newburyport Herald*. He was poor, and money to pay a painter was hard to come by. Indeed he was an orphan, a remnant of a broken family whose experience for many years had been mainly of failure, poverty, and humiliation. Also, he had grown up in two disciplines of frugality and self-denial: He was a devout Baptist, and an ardent student of Franklin's scheme of moral perfection. So he was more interested in "cultivating the seeds of improvement" than he was in the sorts of frivolous display he already thought were typical of "giddy youths."[1]

But he had ambitions. Three years before, he had worked his way to being shop foreman at the *Herald,* even though he was still just an apprentice. He was convinced he would have a gentlemanly career as an editor, and excited at the prospect. Still more, he had already

[1] Garrison's priggish remarks about "the seeds of improvement" and "giddy youths" were in a letter to his mother, May 26, 1823. Walter M. Merrill and Louis Ruchames, eds., *The Letters of William Lloyd Garrison,* 6 vols. (Cambridge, Mass., 1971–81), 1:10–13. These superbly careful volumes will be cited in this chapter as *Letters.*

published a dozen or so pieces in the newspaper—including some fiction and poetry—and had very definite ideas about becoming a celebrated writer. He had picked up a little Latin, and was able to toss off an occasional phrase in French. As the political accompaniment to these ambitions and pretensions, he had adopted the slogans and views of Newburyport's merchant elite, the Essex Junto. This made him part of the plaintive rear guard of a failed Federalist Party, but this political style was still fashionable in the town. All in all, he could think of himself as a young man poised for a triumphant vault into genteel respectability and even fame. He already cultivated the dress and manner he thought appropriate to his future. One of his associates described him as "an exceedingly genteel young man, always neatly, and perhaps I might say elegantly dressed."[2] Besides all this, he also believed he was turning twenty-one (since he mistakenly thought he had been born in 1804, not 1805). And that birthday, coinciding with the fact that he was completing his apprenticeship, seemed reason enough to have himself painted.

The portrait was the work of a local artist named Swain. He was probably only a workmanlike limner, but his picture accomplished William Lloyd Garrison's purposes perfectly. It showed a young man who might be a bit of a dandy, with his hair brushed forward in the Byronic manner. But this suggestion was carefully counterbalanced by the tightly wound neckpiece and the starched collar that braced the head and face, clear signals of a restrained gentility. There was more than either dandyism or gentility here, too. The eyes were earnest and looked with great frankness directly at the viewer. (Garrison already wore thick, metal-rimmed spectacles. But he would not have dreamed of wearing them for this portrait.) The mouth had something faintly somber about it, as though he had thoughts that were deep and memories that were burdensome. There was something apprehensive about the expression, as if the young man had taken on a task too heavy, or had an ambition that demanded too much of anyone with such limited resources.

William Lloyd Garrison was not content to mark this turning point in his life with a portrait. He also wrote a poem, a kind of

[2] This was the recollection of a fellow apprentice, Joseph B. Morss, colleague of Garrison's young years, as given in Wendell Phillips Garrison and Francis Jackson Garrison, *William Lloyd Garrison, 1805–1879: The Story of His Life, Told by His Children*, 4 vols. (New York, 1885–89), 1:55. This work is a monumental life and letters in the Victorian manner. But it is a mine of documentary material on Garrison and a model of editorial care and accuracy. It will be cited here simply as *Life*.

manifesto for the self, to publish in the *Herald*. It was a poor poem, hackneyed and declamatory—much more amateurish than the portrait. But it said a good deal about the consciousness of himself and his world that lay behind the expression in the picture. He called it—as he probably would have entitled the portrait—"The Spirit of Independence":[3]

> Spirit of Independence! *where art thou?*
>> *I see thy glorious form—and eagle eye,*
> *Beaming beneath thy mild and open brow—*
>> *Thy step of majesty, and proud look high:*
> *Thee I invoke!—O to this bosom fly;*
>> *Nor wealth shall awe my soul, nor might, nor power;*
> *And should thy whelps assail,—lank poverty!*
>> *Or threatening clouds of dark oppression lower,—*
> *Yet these combined—defied! shall never make thee cower!*

The first five lines of the poem merely call on the spirit of independence to enter his "bosom," to lodge behind his fashionable and carefully arranged clothes, lending them some of that "proud look high." But however trite the idea and the language may have been, this "invoking" was a call for help. And for good reason, for the next four lines place him on a fearsome gauntlet, more than threatening enough to justify a look of apprehension. On one side are all the things he has lacked: wealth, might, and power. On the other side are things he and his family have had plenty of: the lowering clouds of oppression and the whelps of lank poverty (a play on the popular imaging of poverty as the wolf at the door, but now attacking with her offspring, the "whelps"). All these threats must be "defied!" even if they come in awful combination. So the young man who would be independent is severely beset, always having to fend against danger, not so much to conquer as to resist being "awed." His single imperative is to make his passage through an ominous world, and never to "cower."

The portrait was a young man's attempt to make the important life he hoped for in the future seem concrete and manifest in the present. The poem was a kind of inventory of the sorts of perils he would have to endure in order to realize what the portrait promised. The

---

[3] The poem is reprinted in *Life*, 1:57.

ambition that lay behind the portrait, and the defiance proclaimed in the poem, were anticipatory and indefinite. All this young man of twenty knew with any certainty was that he was about to begin a career he hoped would bring him success and make him famous, and that along the way he must not cower. Exactly how the fame would come, and exactly what he would have to defy, were not yet clear.

During the next five years, he made a sequence of choices that finally gave definition to both ambition and defiance. The outcome was that he would seek his fame by writing and publishing a radical abolitionist journal. And in this journal, he would defy more or less every institution, custom, and law that constituted the society he found himself in. On the first day of 1831, he published the beginning number of his new paper, *The Liberator,* with a declaration addressed "To the Public." In it, he set down his most defiant sentences—the sentences that turned out be his most famous as well:[4]

> I *will be* harsh as truth, and as uncompromising as justice. . . . I am in earnest—I will not equivocate—I will not excuse—I will not retreat a single inch—AND I WILL BE HEARD.

He set the type for these sentences himself, and when he got to the phrase "I will be" he reached for the italic font. He went to his upper case for the type for "I WILL BE HEARD."

The ultimate subject of these remarkable sentences was, of course, slavery. And this might seem explanation enough for Garrison's passionate and drastically aggressive tone. But if the ultimate subject was slavery, the immediate subject was something else. The declaration "To the Public" that launched *The Liberator* gave much more attention to Garrison himself than to slavery. It had thirty-three sentences, and twenty-seven of them contained an "I," a "me," or a "my." The vows parse easily. The grammatical subject of each of them is "I," and the tense of the verbs is future. Garrison chose to begin his career as the writer and editor of this new journal by writing not about the institution of slavery at all, but about himself—and not about himself, exactly, but about a projective and abstract figuring of himself, an idealized writer who *will* never equivocate, compromise, or retreat; a writer who will, above all, BE HEARD.

---

[4] *The Liberator,* January 1, 1831.

And so the explanation for Garrison's rhetorical stance and manner, for the passion that became his authorial stock in trade, and the defiance that became his writer's signature, lies not just in slavery and its monstrous evils, but in his own life and career. The historian's problem is to explain how Garrison developed the intellectual habits and rhetorical manners that produced those sentences in the first issue of *The Liberator*—and hundreds of others like them. How did he develop the practice of placing his self (not *him*self but that figure of the self which was, in effect, his dramatic speaker) at the center of every question? What had fixed in him the habit of supposing that every moral judgment found its final warrant in the character of the singular first person who was publishing it? How did he come to insist so aggressively that the individual will—the will of *some* individuals, anyway—must endure whatever trials and not equivocate? And what was the source of that ill-tempered insistence that he must, above all, be heard?

Nor can the answers to such questions be found in intellectual "influences" that Garrison may have fallen under. To speak of him as a typical "transcendentalist" of the period is beside the point. Garrison probably never read any of Coleridge, and surely knew nothing of Kant. He began to publish *The Liberator* while Ralph Waldo Emerson was still a young and devoted Unitarian minister. David Henry Thoreau was a boy who had not yet decided he preferred Henry David Thoreau for a name, and his essay on civil disobedience was far in the future.[5] It is not very useful, either, to resort conceptually to some sort of vague intellectual current, climate, or movement, such as Romanticism; Garrison's youthful reading was centered much more on Franklin and Shakespeare than on Byron or Scott. And the moral philosophy being taught in American colleges has no particular relevance to Garrison; he quit school at eleven and read little or no formal moral philosophy. As for evangelical religion (which gets the credit and the blame for much more than it ought),

---

[5] Stanley Elkins linked Garrison with Emerson, and more particularly with Thoreau, in *Slavery: A Study in American Social and Institutional Life* (Chicago, 1959), ch. 4. He suggested, as many others had implied before, that there was something slightly unattractive about the way that "transcendentalists" repudiated any effort to find a practical, institutional solution to the problem of slavery, and did so in the safety of a New England world that protected their own persons and rights of speech completely. The problem, of course, is that these protections were not nearly so complete when Garrison began his work as they were when Thoreau took up the cause in the late 1840s. Also, it is quite imponderable whether any sort of "institutional" solution to the problem of slavery *could* have been found, or was in fact forestalled by antislavery radicals.

it did not by itself have the capacity to make men into radical abolitionist writers and speakers. If it had, there would have been hundreds of thousands, not just dozens, of figures like Garrison, North and South; and celebrated revivalists like Charles Grandison Finney would have spent their years writing and speaking against slavery instead of preaching mostly against tobacco and other such "evils." In fact, evangelical religion needs to be understood as one more upshot of the same kinds of social forces that produced abolitionism and other reforms, not as their source and origin. Men and women were not first undergoing religious conversion and then trying to reform society in order to satisfy the demands of a new piety; they were having the conversions and promoting the reforms for the same kinds of reasons. Nor can the influence of British antislavery writers and lecturers explain the way Garrison thought of his writing career. Their writings and speeches were available to every American who might take the trouble to read or listen, and in general they *were* prepared to equivocate, and to retreat any number of inches if they believed it would ultimately advance the cause.

Ideas like Garrison's conception of himself as a writer do not simply occur to people because of something they have read or heard, or out of the mere observation of a social fact like slavery. Such ideas are arrived at. And they are arrived at in the course of experience, on its terms and to serve its purposes. Even the simple idea expressed in the word "I" of Garrison's hammering negations— the "I" that "will not . . . will not . . . will not"—had no meaning apart from the complex of intentions, hopes, and fears with which it was freighted at the time he put the word into type. There can be no serious history of ideas that is not also the history of the social experience of the people who have them. Apart from that experience, where their meaning is grounded, ideas may have a chronology, but not a history.

The most important fact of William Lloyd Garrison's experience was that he came to his radicalism in the course of his attempt to establish a career as a writer, and not to writing through his dedication to antislavery or any other cause. He "turned author"—as he put it— before he turned reformer, and certainly before he turned abolitionist. The defiant writing stance he adopted for *The Liberator* was a stance he had articulated for himself during the preceding years, while he was working out his notion of a career as an author and journalist. The twenty-five-year-old abolitionist was the product of his efforts to realize the ambitions he had cultivated at twenty, when he had that oil portrait done and wrote his declamation on "The Spirit of Independence." So questions about the origin and meaning of his idea of the "I" that must be HEARD have to be translated into questions about why and how he decided to make a career as a writer.

It is possible, of course, that William Lloyd Garrison might eventually have decided that slavery was an evil thing, even if he had not first decided to center his life on writing and a hope for celebrity. There were many avenues through which men and women could find their way to one version or another of antislavery. But what is certain is that he would not have become the singular kind of abolitionist he was if he had not first become a particular kind of writer, with a very special notion of the way he ought to be heard by a certain sort of "Public." These career choices had given shape to his experience during the years when he was making the most important transition that a bourgeois society imposed on young men of the day—the passage out of family into work. That transition was the context for his decision to have his portrait done, and for his declaration that the world must above all be "defied!" Before he became convinced that slavery was the great social evil he must spend his life combating, he had already worked out a vocational formula for himself, a formula which required that as a writer he must combat *some* great evil, and never "cower" at the consequences.

Experience, in Garrison's time, place, and social class, began with family. And families had quite definite beginnings and endings. The parents-and-children family in which he grew up finally came to its end in the early morning hours of October 14, 1842, in the sitting room of Garrison's house in Cambridgeport, Massachusetts. The other members of his own, new, parents-and-children family were sleeping. He was resolutely awake, keeping a death watch over his last surviving sibling, James Holley Garrison. Their father was probably dead, though no one could be sure. Their mother was surely dead. And so were both of their two sisters. After this night, only William Lloyd Garrison would be left.[6]

---

[6] The death of James Holley Garrison is skillfully treated in the introduction to Walter M. Merrill, ed., *Behold Myself Once More* (Boston, 1954). This was the first publication of the text of a manuscript "autobiography" written by James Holley Garrison under his brother's influential supervision. Garrison's own account is in a letter of October 14, 1842, *Letters*, 3:106–7.

The fascination of a watch over the dying is to witness the precise moment of death, but Garrison somehow missed it. He quickly interpreted his lapse in a way that put it in a good light. He had been caught unaware, he decided, because James went so peacefully. From the signs, Garrison guessed that it had taken him at least half an hour to discover this "error."

He felt grief. But he also felt that rush of relief which softens grief. It seemed to him, as he spent the rest of the morning writing letters about James' death, that the "release from the flesh" had something about it that suggested consolation rather than sorrow. After all, James had been courting death for a long time. A few years back, he had even tried to kill himself. He had been—in Garrison's curiously Whitmanesque way of putting it—"habitancing" toward death for much of his forty-one-year life. Finally, in this dim room in Cambridgeport, the end had come. As Garrison chose to see it, James died bravely. In his last hours he had seemingly found something that had escaped him all his life: a measure of control over himself. Garrison did not give any specific examples of James' newfound self-control. He was merely exercising the exclusive right of a survivor to characterize others' deaths however he chooses. And Garrison decided to believe that his brother had looked death squarely in the face, "with all possible fortitude" (a trait he prized in his perception of his *own* character). James had never been able to master himself, and as a result life had utterly mastered him. But now his brother could see in James' death a novel triumph of the will. Finally, there was something in James to praise. "Death," Garrison wrote a few hours later, "had no power over his spirit."

The rhetorical gesture was typical: He could not write anything without saturating it with flourishes about things like "power" and "spirit." But it was more than a rhetorical flourish. The judgment was important precisely because death was the first thing anyone could have remembered that did *not* have power over James' spirit. He had been viewed for many years by everyone in the family as a hopeless disgrace. They called him "Crazy Jem." And he had accepted the role of family black sheep willingly. In fact, in the end, it was only this role that seemed to give him an identity: as an almost perfect foil for his brother's uncompromisingly upright character.

James Holley Garrison's life had been an astonishing succession of defeats and failures. He had been a sailor in the coasting trade, on a British man-of-war, and on American ships of the line. He had been a deserter and a thief. He had also been in prisons everywhere—in Cuba, in Portugal, in France—and in an uncounted number of American jails. Time and again, he had waked up with nothing but the clothes on his back. Sometimes not even with those, but naked and alone. Prostitutes up and down the seaboard had taken his money and watched him stagger away, drunk, sick, and broke. He had had women in some ports, men or boys in others. Finally, after all this, he had crept back to Massachusetts, too sick to serve in the Navy anymore. William Lloyd Garrison had taken charge, and sent James to dry out on a Connecticut farm owned by his wife's relatives. After an uncertain recuperation, James had come to live with his brother in Cambridgeport, and to write the autobiography that Garrison hoped would serve as a warning to other young men endangered by liquor and lust. Things did not work out, though. A final, fantastic binge along the Boston docks had brought James to his deathbed and William Lloyd to his deathwatch.[7]

As Garrison thought about the funeral that morning, his every instinct was to try to help James accomplish in death what he had not in life, to aid the cause of righteousness:

> I intend that the funeral arrangements and ceremonies shall be as plain, simple, and *free* as possible. Liberty of speech shall be given to all who may attend. I shall probably have a testimony to bear against the war system, the navy, intemperance, &c. in connection with James's history.

After the funeral, Garrison recalled that "My remarks were very pointed."[8]

William Lloyd and James Holley Garrison could hardly have been more different. William Lloyd had carefully managed his life, building his character, making himself into a model of piety and virtue. He had learned to control impulse, to resist temptation, and deny desire, to think of himself as his own master. James Holley, in pathetic contrast, had *been* mastered—by drink, by women and men, by poverty and illness, and by captains and lieutenants whose cruelty had left him scarred and frightened. Both the Garrison brothers had

---

[7] James Holley Garrison spelled all this out at delightful length in his manuscript autobiography, Merrill, ed., *Behold Myself Once More*.

[8] Garrison to George Benson, October 14, 1842; to Henry C. Wright, March 1, 1843, *Letters*, 3:106–7, 112.

been in jails. But William Lloyd always went there because of his heroic stands for righteous causes; James went for his sins and weaknesses. William Lloyd was a radical in the service of reforms: pacifism, temperance, women's rights, free speech, abolitionism—and an imposing list of others. James was a radical of vices: drunkenness, thievery, desertion, licentiousness, and promiscuity—and perhaps his own imposing list of others as well.

These contrasts between the two brothers were real, important, and obvious. But there were some veiled similarities between the two men, less obvious but no less real and important. Both lived lives that were mobile and uncertain. Each challenged powerful men and institutions. For their passions, both took great risks, placing their bodies and even their lives in jeopardy. Both brothers had their circle of intimates and friends. But each had chosen to confront society at large as a lone individual, and in angry and provocative ways. As a result, both James and William Lloyd Garrison had been branded as outlaws and outcasts.

These two lives of opposition had both involved an enormous preoccupation with the self. The Garrison brothers' self-consciousness knew almost no limits. Nor did their belief that the self was something the individual could make (or destroy) at will. And their individualism was not a merely intellectual choice, nor a philosophical judgment. For them, individualism was as much a habit as an idea, as much an emotion as a thought. It was a feature of social identity, of ideology in the richest and most complex sense, a product of the family experience they had shared, and of the sorts of practical economic and vocational possibilities that all the Garrisons, parents and children, had encountered during the twenty years before Garrison began to publish *The Liberator*.

The Garrison family that was dissolved with the death of James Holley Garrison had its origins in the middle part of the eighteenth century, in the Seven Years' War. That war was a struggle for empire between France and Britain, an event of truly world-historical proportions. But it had the most direct and concrete kinds of consequences for people, both men of wealth and prestige like Benjamin Franklin, and obscure men and women like the ancestors of William Lloyd Garrison. For Franklin, the war set in motion a chain of events that led him back to Europe, and eventually into the

Revolution. But the same war set off another chain of events that eventually led the Garrison brothers to their final rendezvous in Cambridgeport many decades later. The complete British domination of eastern North America that resulted from the peace settlement opened up Canadian land for emigrants from both Britain and America. In the Maritime Provinces, especially, this chance was seized by families from Massachusetts. A daughter of one of these families met and married a certain Joseph Garrison, who had emigrated alone, from England. The couple settled down to the arduous but ordinary task of rearing children, nine of whom survived infancy. And among these nine was Abijah Garrison, born in 1773.[9]

Abijah Garrison grew up to be a tall, strong, red-bearded, and prematurely balding man. He went to sea in the coasting trade, faring from Newfoundland to the Caribbean. He was almost surely a pilot and sailing master, though probably not the "Captain" that family tradition sometimes made of him. The only certain thing about him is that he was quite literate, given to an elevated prose style, and even to occasional poetry. His letters were elaborate and contrived, and full of the exaggerated, sentimental rhetoric of the Georgian period. He could write of "a Tempestuous Sky and Enraged Ocean." He was apparently a pious man, too, able to pray for "a Ray of Light from the Throne of God and Lamb."[10]

Abijah Garrison's sentimentality and piety found a new object to focus on when he reached his mid-twenties. She was Frances Maria Lloyd, a handsome young woman about as tall as he was. She was the daughter of another sailor, David Lloyd, an Anglo-Irishman who had come to Canada at about the same time as Abijah Garrison's parents. But Lloyd was no evangelical. He was a firm patriot and Church of England man. He watched apprehensively as revivalist preachers, most of them Baptists, wandered into the Maritimes from the newly independent American states, in search of converts. And one of the places they wandered into was his very own home, where they converted his daughter. He threw her out of his house, and she had to find a home with an aunt who was more sympathetic to her new faith, with its fervent preaching, its adult baptisms, and its relentless prayer meetings.

[9] The children of William Lloyd Garrison spent years, and even hired private detectives to help them, trying to reconstruct their father's family and his life. The result was their *Life*. The closest modern study of the origins of the Garrison family is Walter M. Merrill, *Against Wind and Tide* (Boston, 1964), especially in his "Notes," 335–6.

[10] April 22, 1804, *Life*, 1:16.

It was at one of those prayer meetings that Abijah Garrison and Frances Lloyd met. He followed her home, nicknamed her "Blue Jacket," and began courting her. He may have been looking for romance, but what he found was a young woman determined to live in the spirit no matter what the earthly costs. She had already allowed her new birth of faith to break the ties of her first birth of the flesh, and she would be ready to pay prices like that again if she had to.

Frances Lloyd and Abijah Garrison were married in 1798 or 1799, and began a series of moves around New Brunswick and Nova Scotia. In 1801, Frances Lloyd Garrison—"Fanny," as she was called—bore her first child, the son who would grow up to become "Crazy Jem." The little family found the going rough. They were the product of one war, and now they stumbled into the consequences of another. The Napoleonic Wars were good to the coasting trade, but Canadian vessels carrying the British flag were in considerable danger. And so, to escape what he called the "Ravages of War and the stagnation of business," Abijah Garrison decided to migrate to the United States.[11]

He chose Newburyport, Massachusetts, where he found plenty of work and cheap prices. Frances found Baptists in large numbers, and a couple of cheap rented rooms, large enough to contain her, Abijah, Jemmy, and a second child, two-year-old Caroline. She also found herself pregnant with the boy who would be born in December of 1805 and be named William Lloyd.[12]

Things were good for the Garrisons in Newburyport. Little Jemmy had a toy trumpet and a fife, and his father proudly wrote back to relatives in Canada that the boy could "Sing a Great many tunes." Wherever Abijah sailed, to Virginia or to Guadeloupe, he would write home to Fanny, ending his letters affectionately, with phrases like "May God bless you, preserve you in health, is the prayer of your affectionate Husband."[13] But history was waiting to happen to the family again. In 1807, the Jefferson administration

---

[11] Abijah Garrison wrote of these matters to his parents, April 4, 1805. A manuscript copy of the letter is in the collection of Garrison Papers in the Houghton Library at Harvard University.
[12] Frances Garrison chose to use "Lloyd" rather than "William" as the boy's calling name. This choice of names may have meant only that Frances hoped to patch things up a bit with her Anglican father. But her other children's names—James, Caroline, and Maria—managed to take in all the Catholic monarchs of England after Henry VIII. William was the name of the first king under the rule of the Protestant Succession.
[13] November 12, 1806, *Life,* 1:23.

placed its Embargo on all foreign trade. Newburyport, like the rest of New England, entered a sudden and deep depression. Abijah Garrison could not find voyages, and like the frustrated and unemployed men of many generations, he and his friends took to taverns and to drink. Sometimes, he even brought the friends and the drinking home. In the summer of 1808, five-year-old Caroline died. It was all too much for Fanny—who was pregnant again. One day, when Abijah and some of his mates were settling in for an afternoon of drink and talk, she shouted the men out of the house. Then, to add injury to insult, she broke their bottles. The birth of a second daughter in July was not enough to hold the family together—or may have been enough to break it apart. Abijah deserted. He left Frances; James, seven; Lloyd, three; and the infant Maria Elizabeth. He also left behind his sailor's hourglass, with his initials carved into its base. But that was all he left.

For three or four years after Abijah deserted her, Fanny Garrison managed to hold her family together by working as a casual nurse—still a menial occupation for the very poor. Then, at about the time the United States finally entered the European war, in 1812, she moved to Lynn, taking James. She left Lloyd and Maria Elizabeth to stay with two different Baptist families in Newburyport. (Abijah, meanwhile, returned to New Brunswick, where he became an anonymous casualty of the age. He did write to a cousin in 1814, referring mysteriously to "the Whirl I have taken in the World," and mentioning some poetry he was writing. But whatever his "whirl" and his poetry may have been all about, they did not include his family. He never saw Fanny or the children again.)[14]

In Lynn, James was bound out as an apprentice cordwainer, to work with the difficult kind of Spanish leather imported from Córdoba. In his master's shop, as in many other shoemaking establishments, it was the custom to pass around a heavy drink of rum and molasses. It would have shocked no one in the shop that a boy as young as James took his turn at the cup. But soon he began to establish an ominous pattern of "sinning," then repenting, begging his mother's forgiveness, and promising to sin no more:[15]

[14] A copy of this letter, in what looks like the hand of Wendell Phillips Garrison, is in the Houghton Library's Garrison Papers.
[15] Merrill, ed., *Behold Myself Once More*, 3–5.

I had never tasted liquor, but was persuaded by my fellow apprentices and likewise my master, to drink a little as it would not hurt me. I took a drink, and it was sweet, and from that fatal hour I became a drunkard. I soon got so I could take my glass as often as my master, and in a little while it required double that quantity to satisfy my appetite. I was now a confirmed drunkard. It soon reached my mother's ear, that her darling boy, one in whom she had placed strong hopes that he would be a comfort and support to her declining years, one who she had so often prayed to her heavenly father to guide and direct, had fallen before that monster *Rum*. I went, but with feelings I can not describe. She received me kindly, and pointed out in an affectionate and kind manner the path I was pursuing, what the consequences would be to my health, my reputation in this world, the many sufferings it would cause her, and the eternal damnation of my soul in the world to come. I promised to do better, and drink no more.

The promises failed, and soon James was spending time in a "house of ill fame" just outside Lynn, a "sink of infamy and vice . . . where many, many a poor young girl has lost her reputation."

Fanny Garrison had problems enough with James' "unsteadiness" and the lack of money. She was also constantly "tired with slavish work" as a nurse. Things did look up a bit in 1814 when she was able to bring eight-year-old Lloyd to live with her and be apprenticed to another shoemaker. Her youngest, Maria Elizabeth, soon joined them. The family was gathered again.[16]

But it was gathered for another mismatched encounter with history, an encounter the family would not survive. This time the challenge to the Garrisons was not war but the more relentless processes of capitalism and industrialization. Of course, people do not really experience grand abstractions like industrialization or capitalism. What people actually experience is much more concrete and particular. For the Garrisons, industrialization took the specific form of a proposal from a Lynn shoemaker who planned to go to Baltimore to open a shoe factory. Capitalism took the concrete form of

---

[16] The remark about "slavish work" is in a manuscript copy, also probably made by Wendell Phillips Garrison, of a letter of September 11, 1814, in the Houghton Library. Being a nurse meant little more than being a housemaid, and was likely to involve even more unpleasant duties.

low wages and failed enterprise. The entrepreneur invited Fanny Garrison to go along as a kind of nurse to the work force, and to bring the two boys along as workers. The Garrisons went, no doubt full of hope. The War of 1812 had just ended, and the boys might, after all, grow up in a world free of the "Ravages of War and the stagnation of business." But, like a lot of American enterprises that fell victim to the resumption of British imports, the shoe factory closed. By January of 1816, Fanny was complaining that "I walk the streets of Baltimore and feel myself alone." James was "a great trial," always carousing and fighting. Lloyd was "homesick" for Newburyport, for the house of the Baptist deacon who had taken him in when his father had disappeared. Finally, both boys deserted—Lloyd with his mother's blessing, and James without it. James followed his father's lead, and fled to the sea. Lloyd went "home" to Newburyport.[17]

Frances Garrison soon went into a dreadful and irreversible decline. At first, without the boys around, things went reasonably well. She was able to put Maria Elizabeth out to work as a servant girl, and to find work again for herself as a nurse in the new suburban houses of the rich. She was glad to be working for people she referred to as "the Quality." And she was proud that in their houses she was "treated like a lady." She also started a prayer group for Baptist women. But she was bound for grief. She was only in her forties, but she began to be more and more gloomy, sick, and tired. She started a diary and filled it with complaints about illness and fatigue, records of blood coughed up from the tuberculosis that flared in her from time to time. Most of all, she thought about death: her premonitions of it, her dreams of it, and, finally, her hopes for it. Even the institutional comforts of religion were denied her. In 1816, she became involved in some sort of controversy-by-mail with a member of her old congregation in Newburyport, where she still kept her membership. The dispute dragged on for two years; then, in 1818, the congregation voted to suspend her for at least four years.[18]

[17] Frances Garrison's comment about the streets of Baltimore is in a manuscript copy of a letter of January 7, 1816, Houghton Library.

[18] There is a handwritten copy of the Baltimore diary in Houghton Library. Entries for 1821 speak often of blood, disease, and the approach of death. The quarrel with the church is detailed in manuscript notes on the records of the Baptist church in Newburyport, Houghton Library. There is no indication what the complaint, brought against her by a man named Robert Robinson, actually was. The "Quality" remark is in a manuscript copy of a letter of September 7, 1817, Houghton Library. On this period of the family's trials, see *Life*, 1:32–3; Merrill, ed., *Behold Myself Once More*, 11–12; John Thomas, *The Liberator: William Lloyd Garrison* (Boston, 1963), 19–39.

Alone, sick, and tired, Fanny Garrison gradually worked out a systematic analysis of her life, a picture of her experience as one of progressive alienation and defeat. The analysis began with memories of early harmony and ease, described in a distinctly aristocratic tone and with a superbly genteel vocabulary:[19]

> At an early period of life, I was surrounded with every comfort that was necessary, nurtured with peculiar care and tenderness in the bosom of parental affection, blessed with the friendship of an extensive acquaintance, and beloved by all my relations. I had enough to attach me to this world. Gay and thoughtless, vain and wild, I looked forward to nothing but pleasure and happiness.

She became convinced that her conversion by the Baptists had led directly to her marriage, and this, in turn, had brought about her migration to Massachusetts, which had set the stage for Abijah's desertion. This causal chain, she thought, was all the more grievous in comparison with the giddy heights of her youth and expectations:

> But alas! have not my subsequent years taught me that all was visionary! How has the rude blast of misfortune burst over my head, and had it not been for an overruling Providence, I must have sunk under their pressure.

All this was conventional, though no doubt deeply felt. And so too was the next step in the analysis. If "this world" held only disappointment and pain, there was both justice and consolation in the experience:

> I was taught to see that all my dreams of happiness in this life were chimerical; the efforts we make here are all of them imbecility in themselves and illusive, but religion is perennial. It fortifies the mind to support trouble, elevates the affection of the heart, and its perpetuity has no end.

The language was clichéd—though impressive in a woman with her education—and the ideas were the stock notions of evangelical Protestantism. But conventions and stock notions sometimes work.

---

[19] The next three quotations are from a letter of May 24, 1820, from Frances Garrison to her daughter Maria Elizabeth, reproduced in *Life,* 1:39.

Hers fitted her case more neatly than they did the lives of many other people who tried to put them to use.

This analysis of the deep meanings of her own life clearly mattered a great deal to Fanny Garrison. And outside her diary, there was only one human object on which such notions could readily be fastened, one redeeming and redeemable human soul in all "this world," the small and distant son in Newburyport.

Whatever the eventual fate of his soul might be, it was very much this world and not the consolations of eternity that William Lloyd Garrison had set out to find at the age of ten, when he left his mother to go back to Newburyport. He went for a few months to school, but sat for his last lessons when he was eleven. Most of his training was religious. He sang in the Baptist choir, read sermons and tracts, and faithfully studied in Sunday school. Then he took up his second apprenticeship, this one in the gentler trade of cabinetmaking in the nearby town of Haverhill. There was a rebellious streak in him, though, a streak he shared not only with his father and brother but with countless other apprentices in those unsettled decades when traditional versions of apprenticeship were collapsing in many trades. Lloyd ran away, back to Newburyport. His master released him from his apprentice's bond, perhaps out of kindness, and perhaps out of a realistic recognition that the bond represented a social relationship that had become extremely difficult to enforce. Then, at thirteen, Lloyd began his third apprenticeship, this one at the *Newburyport Herald*.

Garrison always thought of it as "a Providence" that he won the apprenticeship at the *Herald*. Being a printer was the trade that was most likely to lead out of the ranks of artisans and into the life of a gentleman, perhaps even to a life of learning and reputation—as it had for Franklin and for dozens of other journalists, printer-publishers, and booksellers. Garrison was quite transformed by his apprenticeship, from a poor, practically orphaned waif into a young man who was certain that he stood on the threshold of something more than a livelihood—a career. He worked hard at it. He read constantly, avidly, and at random—Shakespeare, novels, political speeches, magazines, and newspapers. He picked up his fragmentary Latin from a fellow worker. He joined a local Franklin Club, a kind of Junto, where he and other ambitious youths would gather for "improving discussions."[20] While his mother endured the "rude blast of misfortune," Lloyd began to dress elegantly, and saved his apprentice's dollars to have the portrait painted.

All of this—the reading, the clothes, the Franklin Club, the portrait—was quite secular, and echoed his mother's language about the comfort, gaiety, and thoughtless expectations of her own youth. All the while, though, Lloyd did continue to serve his mother's piety—and his own. He attended church faithfully during his apprenticeship, trying to be what his mother hoped he would be, a "perfect Baptist." But there was something worldly straining in him, a vague but increasingly insistent determination that somehow he would earn "fame." This commitment to unbounded possibility was not some curious genetic trait he somehow shared with his father and brother. Breaking bounds—or at least seeming to break them—was a habit of mind that was plentifully revealed in the experience of many other young men and women in New England in the 1820s. He was, after all, a member of the Franklin Club, and he could take Franklin's autobiography as a plausible script for breaking with parental authority and prescription, for starting from scratch, choosing a career, and molding his own personality. It all made perfect sense in the most elementary existential way: He was, in simple fact, a young man on his own, apparently free and self-determining. It made sense, too, in vocational terms. At the end of the American Revolution, Massachusetts had only five newspapers, all of them in Boston. Now there were dozens, and scattered all over the state. The idea that he might become the owner and editor of one of them was perfectly plausible. And he did not need Franklin's example, either, to imagine that this career might make him into a celebrity.

William Lloyd Garrison and his mother were not just separated geographically. They were living within two different mental versions of what experience ought to be. He was aiming at a quite worldly success and fame. He could even reenact a specific scene from Franklin's autobiography—no doubt a scene that had been discussed at some meeting of the Franklin Club. When he was seventeen, Garrison submitted an anonymous contribution to the *Herald*. It was the crotchets of "An Old Bachelor," short pieces not very

---

[20] In 1878, Garrison gave a dinner speech to the Franklin Club of Boston, in which he described his first master as "a very Benjamin Franklin for good sense and axiomatic speech." The talk is reprinted in *Life*, 1:40–1.

different from Franklin's Silas Dogood essays, or Washington Irving's *Letters of Jonathan Oldstyle, Gent.* Garrison mailed them in, without a signature, just as Franklin said he had done at the *Courant,* and waited breathlessly the next day in the office as they were read. Like Franklin, he flushed with glory when his work pleased. This was, after all, the first step in a life that was headed upward, toward "comfort" and "extensive acquaintance," a life very unlike Fanny Garrison's sick and declining solitude in Baltimore.

Like the boy Franklin in Philadelphia, Garrison seemed to have broken free, to be poised on the edge of pure possibility. But not quite. His mother, unlike Franklin's father, always knew where he was. And, unlike Franklin, he was held by a truly sentimental piety about her. And so the two, mother and son, began to enact a verbal family melodrama. It was carried on in letters, and was an ideological tug-of-war in which the stakes were defined as nothing less than the fate of William Lloyd Garrison's soul.

Already, when Lloyd was still very young, there had been persistent and gloomy mothering cautions, with the figure of James hovering ominously, just off the pages of her letters. When he was only twelve, his mother had written:[21]

> Your good behavior will more than compensate for all my trouble; only let me hear that you are steady, and go not in the way of bad company, and my heart will be lifted up to God for you, that you may be kept from the snares and temptations of this evil world. Be a good boy and God will bless you, and you have a Mother, although distant from you, that loves you with tenderness.

As she became ill, Fanny introduced into her letters the theme of death's approach. Once, when she sent Lloyd a small trunk full of old clothes, she wrote that this might well be the last token of love she would live to give him. Whenever she wrote, she detailed her own symptoms and sufferings. When she could, she described the ravages of new epidemics of disease in Baltimore. And she would sign her letters, "Your Mother until Death," or, "Adieu, my dear, for I am tired."

[21] August 29, 1817, *Life,* 1:33.

When Lloyd told his mother about the "Old Bachelor" pieces (without sending her any of them), the ideological differences between the worlds of mother and son broke through the surface. She told him that she was "living on the charity of friends" and sometimes felt the "sensations of mortified pride because of that." Then she turned to his news. She expressed only guarded and conditional pleasure, and combined this with a warning and a "quizzing" joke:[22]

> You write me that you have written some pieces for the *Herald*. Anonymous writers generally draw the opinion of the publick on their writing, and frequently are lampoon'd by others. . . . I am pleased, myself, with the idea, providing nothing wrong should result from it. You must write me one of your pieces so that I can read on one side of your letter, and I will give you my opinion whether you are an old bachelor, or whether you are A.O.B., as A may stand for Ass, and O for Oaf, and B for Blockhead. Adieu my dear.

This was the letter she signed, "Your Mother until death." The joke could only have stung, because for the seventeen-year-old author these were not just "pieces" but the first steps in a career that he already hoped would bring him fame.

In March of 1823, the year following the Ass, Oaf, and Blockhead letter, Fanny Garrison wrote asking Lloyd to come soon for what would probably be a final visit. In her letter, she worried over the perils of adolescence, saying that he was "now at an age when you are forming character for life, a dangerous age. Shun every evil for the sake of your soul as well as the body."[23] He took two months to answer, and then said that he could not come at all unless she wrote

---

[22] July 1, 1822, *Life*, 1:44. When Fanny Garrison said she was "quizzing," she meant the word in the sense it still has, among some British users, of "mocking." The main literary convention of the pieces Garrison wrote as An Old Bachelor was the stock picture of women as "giddy" and frivolous creatures, always trying to lure men into marriage. But some of it may have been an indirect commentary on his own relationship with his mother: "The truth is, however, women in this country are too much idolized and flattered; therefore, they are puffed up and inflated with pride and self-conceit. They make the men to crouch, beseech, and supplicate. . . . Women generally feel their importance, and they use it without mercy. For my part, notwithstanding, I am determined to lead the *'single life'* and not trouble myself about the ladies." *Herald*, May 21, 1822, quoted in *Life*, 1:43. In the long run, of course, "the ladies" became a principal part of his constituency as an abolitionist, so much so that one of the public taunts with which he and other male abolitionists had to contend was that they were somehow effeminate.

[23] March 1823, *Life*, 1:48–9.

directly to the *Herald*'s owner asking his permission. But he also told her, no doubt with great pride, that he had continued to write. Even worse, he told her that his time had been "swallowed up in turning *author*." And worse yet, he was now writing "political pieces." In fact, during the two months between her pleading letter and this postponing reply, he had been publishing under a new pen name, "One of the People." The *Herald* carried one fiery essay after another, on subjects ranging from a gubernatorial election campaign to the Holy Alliance. And he was no longer anonymous, he told her, but on the road to fame: "But I am at last discovered to be the author, . . . and [it] has created no little sensation in the town." He defended himself, probably anticipating that she would be troubled by this news. He was only "cultivating the seeds of improvement in my breast," he said. And in any case the writing had kept him from wasting his time, "in the dull, senseless, insipid manner, which generally characterizes giddy youths."[24]

His defense failed. It was all too much for Fanny Garrison. She replied immediately, and this time there was no joking. She was simply appalled. She drew for Lloyd a clear line between piety and worldly ambition, and she fretted aggressively about what would become of him if he continued to stray across that line:[25]

Next, your turning author. You have no doubt read and heard the fate of such characters, that they generally starve to death in some garret or place that no one inhabits. Secondly, you think your time was wisely spent while you were writing political pieces. I cannot join with you there, for had you been searching the Scriptures for truth, and praying for direction of the holy spirit to lead your mind into the path of holiness, your time would have been more wisely spent, and your advance to the heavenly world more rapid. But instead, you have taken the Hydra by the head, and now beware of his mouth; but as it is done, I suppose you had better go on and seek the applause of mortals. But, my Dear L., lose not the favor of God; have an eye single to his glory, and you will not lose your reward.

The letter was remarkable, not only as a family document but for its canny grasp of the situation a young man on the threshold of a

[24] May 26, 1823, *Letters,* 1:10–13.
[25] June 3, 1823, *Life,* 1:31.

writing career faced. A generation earlier, or perhaps two, the problem might not have existed. Piety could find expression, in both life
and letters, in the ministry. It still could, of course. But Garrison
wanted more. He wanted fame, not the local reward that normally
belonged to the pulpit. He wanted to be certain that someday someone
would have the task of writing his biography. He knew, and his
mother tacitly allowed, that the ministry was not the solution. It
would not have been so difficult for him to become a preacher. Indeed,
it was much easier for a poor boy to enter the ministry in the 1820s than
it had been before.[26] But for someone with Garrison's burning ambition, the ministry no longer offered the most attractive way to turn
intellectual talents and a flair for words to account. In fact, one of the
reasons it had become easier to attend college and train for the ministry
was precisely that so many young men did *not* want the career. This,
in turn, was partly a result of the fact that being an "author by
profession"—if only as a journalist or magazine editor—had become
such a tempting alternative. Indeed, the only temptation more obvious
for a young man with a facility for language was probably law and
politics. And the kind of newspaper journalism Garrison was being
trained for was a writing career that was intimately involved with
political parties. Garrison's mother understood, implicitly, that once
such a choice was made, the Hydra really did have only a pair of heads.
"Turning author" could have only two practical outcomes, both of
them bad. It could lead to celebrity or to failure, to "the applause of
mortals" or a punishing isolation in some "place that no one inhabits."

It so happened that this would be Fanny Garrison's last letter to
Lloyd. And she drove her point home with great force, as though she
knew she was making what amounted to a deathbed plea:

> Now, my dear, I must draw to a close, and say that I love you as
> dear as ever, especially when you consider your dear mother and
> are trying by your good behavior to soothe her path to the grave.

She asked him, gently, if he came to Baltimore, to bring some of his
work for her to see. She signed herself, "Your affectionate Mother,
Frances M. Garrison." Two weeks later, Garrison did set out for a
visit, something he had often planned but just as often postponed.
He found his mother broken and emaciated and stayed for two or

[26] Cf. David Allmendinger, *Paupers and Scholars: The Transformation of Student Life in Nineteenth-Century New England* (New York, 1975).

three weeks. Then he left her, and in a few more weeks he heard that she had died.

Garrison himself wrote and set in type his mother's obituary in the *Herald.* "DIED. In Baltimore, after a long and distressing illness, which she bore with Christian fortitude and resignation, Mrs. Frances Maria Garrison, relict of the late Capt. Abijah G., formerly of this town."[27] For the next year, Garrison almost stopped writing. After the furious pace of the preceding years, he wrote practically no more "pieces" for several months, as though to assure his mother that he would not be worldly and "unsteady," after all. As for his father, Garrison raised his rank to "Capt." in the obituary, but then twice killed him, with the words "relict" (widow) and "late"—though in fact he had no idea whether his father was still alive. He did know that Maria Elizabeth had died the year before, that Caroline was long dead, and that James was somewhere, drowning in rum or salt water. In familial terms, at least, Garrison was alone, with his printer's trade, his skills as a writer and journalist, and the ambition those skills would have to serve.

But he had some important company. He had the emotional and ideological company of Fanny Garrison, and this presence was to be a very important one in his life from this point forward. Eleven years after his mother died, when Garrison was courting the woman he was going to marry, he wrote his fiancée a burning letter about his mother:[28]

> You speak of "a mother's love." An allusion like this dissolves my heart, and causes it to grow liquid as water. I had a mother once, who cared for me with such a passionate regard, who loved me so intensely. . . . How often did she watch over me—weep over me—and pray over me. "Oh, that my Mother were still living!" is often the exclamation of my heart. Alas! she cannot come to me.

He was inventing a childhood, of course. For most of the years since Abijah had deserted the family, when William Lloyd Garrison was three, he had not lived with his mother at all. Only in letters had she been able to care for him with "passionate regard."

[27] The obituary is reproduced in *Life,* 1:53.
[28] The letter, written in 1834, and the poem quoted next on "the masterpiece of womankind," are reproduced in *Life,* 1:34.

But this distortion of memory was not his only problem. He sent his fiancée a poem about his mother that revealed a more complicated kind of confusion:

> She was the masterpiece of womankind—
> In shape and height majestically fine;
> Her cheeks the lily and the rose combined;
> Her lips more opulently red than wine;
> Her raven locks hung tastefully entwined;
> Her aspect fair as Nature could design;
> And then her eyes! so eloquently bright;
> An eagle would recoil before their light.

The overt purpose of the poem was to provide a portrait of that gentle mother who had "cared." But the real effect—an effect Garrison can hardly have been fully in control of—was to present a picture of intimidating power. In the poem, Fanny Garrison appears as a woman of "majestic" height (Garrison himself was a few inches over five feet tall, considerably shorter than the average native-born American male of the day). She has an unusually vivid aspect, colored in lurid shades of lily white, wine red, and raven black. Her hair, while it is tastefully done, is "entwining." Her lips are not just red, nor even as red as wine, but "more opulently" red than wine. She has an eye that would frighten even an eagle.

The poem about his mother was thick with what seems to be a sexual excitement. Its language was an echo of the most charming and sensual thing William Lloyd Garrison ever wrote. Three years earlier, he had been editing a paper in Bennington, Vermont. He had confessed in its pages that he was "up to the eyes in love." Nothing came of it, except perhaps for one of the few letters that show the witty and humane William Lloyd Garrison that was usually hidden behind the relentless and unyielding public figure he created. A printer friend had written him, twitting him on the fact that his beloved was fond of cosmetics. Garrison responded by drafting a future scene in which he would paint her face. It is a seduction scene, quite comic and surprisingly smutty:[29]

---

[29] This paragraph is from a letter to Stephen Foster of March 30, 1829, *Letters*, 1:78–80. The "real" William Lloyd Garrison was a man with an inordinate fondness for puns, a doting father, a gentle and apparently affectionate husband, and had a good deal of the seductive irresponsibility of Dickens' Mr. Dick. The figure of the writer that he created for himself was

Hold your head steadily, dearest—so—very still—you shall look
in the glass presently—a little more vermillion, a denser flame of
health on this cheek—I like to see the *blood,* Mary, mounting up
to the very temple, commingling with that lily whiteness—your
eyebrows are hardly coal black—a little darker, in order to give
you a deeper brilliance to your starry eyes, or rather to their
light—shut your mouth, and draw back that little saucy tongue,
you pretty witch, for I'm going to put a ruby blush upon your
twin   (not   thin)   lips,   after   I've   kissed   them—there—
softly—softly—smack goes the brush. . . . *Cetera desunt.*

The scene is colored in the same aggressive shades of red, black, and
white that he later used in the poem about his mother. Either he had
a severely limited verbal palette, or there was some kind of connection between the two bits of writing. But in the lines about his
mother, the excitement is checked by the fearsome nature of its
object. Little wonder that when Garrison was well into middle age,
he could still say to his own children, "I still feel like a little boy
when I think of Mother."[30] Somehow he would have to find a way
to reconcile his ambitions with her awful warnings about the kind of
career he had in mind.

Garrison's relationship with his mother was certainly complex and
intense. It is one of those psychological knots that historians have only
indirect and imperfect means for untangling—and which might not
explain much, anyway, even if they *could* be untangled. But the
relationship occurred in a way that makes it unusually visible, in large
measure because the two were separated during Garrison's adolescence, and at least his mother's side of their dialogue was set down in
her letters and preserved. Whatever may have been the psychological
sources of her brooding and warnings (jealousy? guilt? some odd
confusion between her son and her own father? or the like), she found
a vocabulary for them that is perfectly accessible and comprehensible.
This was the vocabulary of her religion, amplified by her interpretive

---

of course none of these things. But it had its own reality, and often bled over into his "private"
life. In fact, for a man like Garrison (or any of the writers discussed in this book), the
membranes that separated the public and the private, persona and personality, were exceedingly permeable.

[30] This was the recollection of his children in *Life,* 1:34.

analysis of her own life. And when it is examined on this ideological plane, Garrison's relationship with his mother actually does explain a good deal about his life and career as a writer and speaker.

Garrison's mother defined for him a simple but severe ideological bind. She made painfully explicit a problem anyone would have had to face who yearned for both godliness, as it was preached in the evangelism of the day, and for success in the world. Many young men—and, increasingly, young women—of Garrison's generation had both these yearnings, and had to find some way of accommodating each to the other. But Garrison's version of the problem was particularly severe. His father's desertion and the family's poverty had made his earthly desires particularly acute. The career he had chosen—involving as it must the "applause of mortals"—was one in which material rewards alone could not satisfy, one that required fame as well. To make matters worse, the conflict between this kind of ambition and the spiritual demands of the religious life had probably been made considerably plainer by his mother than by the parents and advisers of other young people. She had put the issue into quite memorable and pointed prose. Her piety strained away from this world, toward the next. It pointed toward renunciation, not accumulation, toward self-denial, not aggrandizement, toward searching the Scriptures, not writing "political pieces." Ambition—in Garrison's case "turning *author*"—led in opposite directions. And, in addition to the threat to the soul posed by authorship, there was that other and more immediate danger: He might fail, and not only lose the way of God but "starve to death in some garret or place that no one inhabits."

For the next two years, he struggled with the problem, and worked his way to a partial solution. He would adopt the attitude of "defiance," and picture himself as the uncowering opponent of *both* the things his mother warned him about: the worldly temptations of wealth, might, and power on one side, and the oppressions of failure and poverty on the other. His mother had tried to teach him the consolations of the Christian life of suffering and defeat. He responded with a simple and brittle version of experience in which the task of the autonomous self was neither to prevail over the "rude blast of misfortune" nor to submit to it in the quiet hope of Christian consolations. The destiny of the man of "independence" was to publicly defy a world that beset him. To be real, the defiance had to be public, and its instrument was, purely and simply, language.

But for Garrison defiance was not its own end. Nor was it only a compensatory response to his original poverty or to the shame of his family's collapse after Abijah Garrison deserted them. "Defiance" looked forward, to the future. It was a strategy, a rhetorical device that might help bring a young writer and journalist the repute he yearned for. When he was just twenty-three, only three years out of his apprenticeship and already involved in a heated newspaper quarrel with another editor, Garrison thundered:[31]

If my life be spared, my name shall one day be known so extensively as to render private inquiry unnecessary; and known, too, in a praiseworthy manner. I speak in the spirit of prophesy, not of vainglory—with a strong pulse, a flashing eye, and a glow of the heart. *The task may be yours to write my biography*.

And so, when he completed his apprenticeship in December of 1825, Garrison's life was a complicated affair. He had his trade. But the printing trade was only a beginning. Now he had to transform a craft into a vocation, to become an editor, a man of influence and of affairs. The path that lay before him was clearly an entrepreneurial one. And since the journalism of the day was inextricably tied to politics, his calling would certainly lead him into party involvement—just as certainly as an Ichabod who "wrote for the newspapers" might end up going into politics and becoming justice of the Ten Pound Court. Garrison had chosen a career that would put him on the most intimate terms with "this world." And if he succeeded, he could expect to deal constantly with the dangerous Hydra of worldly realities: political parties and elections, questions of commerce and banking, and—most directly—with the daily economic realities of newspaper writing and publishing itself. But, always, there was the contrary tug of his mother's conception of the Christian life of sacrifice and consolation. The ideological issue was plain enough: Could the ambitions of a writer and a self-made man be somehow reconciled with the gloomy constraints of Fanny Garrison's kind of piety? But it was one thing to fix on mere "defiance" as a fighting stance. It was quite another to translate defiance into practice in a way that might actually bring him the rewards of fame without violating the requirements of faith.

[31] A letter published in the *Portland Yankee*, August 20, 1828, quoted in *Life*, 1:10.

His first practical step was in keeping with the Franklin model. He borrowed enough money from his former master to buy a recently founded—and already failing—Newburyport newspaper, which he renamed *The Free Press*. He spent about half of 1826 editing this paper, writing mostly party polemics in a failed cause. His motto was the motto of Massachusetts Federalism, "Our Country, Our Whole Country, and Nothing but Our Country."[32] And in the pages of *The Free Press* he adopted a rigorously conservative Federalist line. Already, as an apprentice, he had written a number of anti-Jackson pieces, condemning the general as nothing but a dueling, gambling, drinking, corrupted planter. But Garrison's politics went far beyond the conventional New England suspicion of Andrew Jackson. He resented all the political compromises of the 1820s, especially John Quincy Adams' acquiescence in the "loose" principles of the Jeffersonians. When Jefferson died, most New England editors were willing to forgive the old president in a quick flurry of bereaved patriotism, but Garrison would not relent. He still fussed over the fact that Jefferson was an "infidel." His unyielding editorials cost Garrison some subscribers, even in the Federalist town of Newburyport. After six months, his first venture had failed. But, in one important way, he had succeeded. He could say, in his final issue, that "This is a time-serving age; and he who attempts to walk uprightly or speak honestly, cannot rationally calculate upon speedy wealth or preferment. Men had rather be flattered than reproved."[33] He had defined politics in rigid moral and religious terms and had taken a reproving stand that had cost him a worldly penalty. He had courted the world's rejection. Now the question was, would he starve in some garret?

As for so many other young men of the time, the answer to that question lay in the city. For Garrison, this meant Boston, a place he had managed to avoid so far. He had been to Boston only twice—the first time on the way to his deathbed visit to his mother, when he had become hopelessly lost and confused; the second, a year or two later, when he had walked from Newburyport and arrived with bleeding feet, only to turn around the next day and take the stagecoach home. Now he came to Boston not as a man passing through, or just visiting, and this time he stuck it out. He went from one printing

---

[32] The motto Garrison devised for *The Liberator* was a turn on this Federalist slogan: "My country is the world. My countrymen are all mankind."

[33] Quoted in *Life*, 1:70.

house to another, looking for an opening, ready to hire himself out to any master to get a fresh start. It was several months before opportunity came his way. He took a position as editor of a struggling temperance newspaper, the *National Philanthropist.*

During his months on the *National Philanthropist,* Garrison began to change his political line in a way that implied a change in his idea of his mission as a writer. It was impossible to pretend, any longer, that the Federalist Party still existed. So, instead of using the old party as a point of reference for attacks on Jackson and his Democratic Republicans, Garrison turned to condemn party politics of every shade. He began to write about "the slothfulness and bane of party spirit." The important social questions—drunkenness, militarism, gambling, dueling, Sabbath-breaking, and a dozen other ubiquitous evils—were *beyond* party. Parties were saturated with the very sinfulness that reform journals like the *National Philanthropist* were trying to attack. Everywhere Garrison looked, but especially in politics and government, he now saw "depravity." Everywhere was a mighty host of evil, threatening "to subvert the purity of our institutions." And the means of national survival and salvation were not political parties, which were only one more subversive threat to "purity."[34]

This movement from last-ditch Federalism to a condemnation of all parties was consistent in an obvious way with the demands of piety. Parties are, after all, quite worldly instruments. But something else was at work, something a bit more strategic, and having more to do with career than with either religious faith or political loyalties. Editing a local newspaper like *The Free Press* established a close and

---

[34] The language about the "bane of party spirit" was taken from Washington's "Farewell Address" of 1796. A good deal of the significance of the emergence of the reform movements in the 1820s lies behind Garrison's use of such phrases. Washington's address had been a monumental expression of the kind of fear and contempt that the members of the revolutionary generation always had for political parties. Now, at the end of the 1820s, a new system of parties was taking shape. Its leaders were feeling their way toward new kinds of justifications for the permanent presence of political parties in a republic.

The most thoughtful account of the processes through which parties were legitimized by professional leaders like Martin Van Buren is Richard Hofstadter's *The Idea of a Party System* (Berkeley, Calif., 1969). But the traditional fear of parties did not so much disappear—as Hofstadter and others have suggested—as become channeled into a new course, the promotion of private, voluntary, and nonpolitical reform organizations whose ultimate purposes were the spiritual salvation of the whole nation. The typical reformer of the period worked in the hope that the successes of social reform would make government less and less important, and so make the parties harmless and irrelevant. In the 1850s, the practitioners of social reform and the professional party men would find each other, first in the American Party and then in the Republican Party. But for Garrison, and for people like him, reform was a remedy not only for social evils, but for the "bane of party spirit" as well.

demanding relationship between the writer and his audience, a relationship a bit like the one between a minister and a congregation. To succeed, an editor had to satisfy a constituency that was variegated and close at hand. But writing for a journal like the *National Philanthropist* was another matter. Here, the constituency was neither local nor varied, but a scattered audience tied together not by the chance bonds of locality but by the ideological bonding of Christian reform. The *National Philanthropist* had a small audience. But it was potentially grand. And anyone who wrote for it was emancipated from the task of satisfying diverse and erratic local opinions.

The shift from small-town editing to reform journalism redefined the relationship between the writer or editor and his audience. It was essentially the same as the shift Emerson would make a dozen years later by abandoning a pulpit in favor of the lecture circuit. It was the same vocational shift as the one involved in any preacher's decision not to have a local congregation but to become an itinerant, speaking to anonymous but large and enthusiastic revival audiences. The outcome of such career choices was the same: the substitution of a relatively homogeneous and potentially enormous audience of strangers for a small and intimate, but diverse and constraining, local audience. In fact, for anyone whose only stock in trade was words, the shift was in effect a move from an artisanal mode of production to a market economy of language. Local newspapers were still primarily organs of party, and party demanded local organization. But a reform journal like the *National Philanthropist* could break free of both party and locale by appealing to a limited but widespread market, an audience for which interchangeable parts of specialized fervor were better suited than editorial pieces carefully crafted for subscribers the author knew personally, and from whom he even had to collect money face to face, like a shoemaker dealing with customers. For a man like Garrison, this change in the relationship between the writer and his audience was especially appealing, since it promised to release him from the necessity of making accommodations to the requirements of his subscribers. Writing for a reformist journal held out the hope that "the applause of mortals" might be gained without making moral compromises.[35]

---

[35] Thomas L. Haskell, in "Capitalism and the Origins of the Humanitarian Sensibility," 2 parts, *American Historical Review* 90 (April 1985): 339–61; (June 1985): 547–66, has argued that "capitalism" promoted certain habits of mind, involving calculations of eventual consequences of action and a heightening awareness of human capacities to get things done, which made

This was precisely the possibility that Garrison tried to test during his brief stint at the *National Philanthropist*. His editorial view was that the evils that beset the nation were moral evils, not practical. They demanded solutions that were not political, but *prior* to politics. If men could be saved from drunkenness, kept from prostitutes, exposed to the saving influences of evangelical religion, then (and only then) might they be trusted to elect others to political office, to preserve the "purity of our institutions." The task of the reformer was nothing less than the salvation of the national soul. And it was, as Garrison defined it, a difficult and dangerous task, worldly perhaps, but worldly in a way that even his mother might approve. He and other reformers like him would have to risk everything. But he was willing to dare it. More than willing, in fact; he was delighted. For he could now view his career in sacrificial, though heroic, terms:

> While there remains a tyrant to sway the iron rod of power, or chains about the body or mind to be broken, I cannot surrender my arms. While drunkenness and intemperance abound, I will try to reclaim the dissolute, and to annihilate the progress of vice. I will reprove, admonish and condemn. My duty is plain.

The language and rhythms were little different from the language and rhythms of the 1831 *Liberator*. The implicit subject was not yet slavery, but drunkenness and vice. But the grammatical subject was very much "I." The voice he had found was already reproving, admonishing, and condemning, already armed and willing to dare power, no matter what the cost might be. And for Garrison's purpose, finding the right voice was much more urgent than finding the right subject. He was trying to make writing into a career. In the process, he was making written words into the credentials of social class.

---

abolitionism possible. "What, then," he asks, "did capitalism contribute to the freeing of the slaves? Only a *precondition,* albeit a vital one: a proliferation of recipe knowledge and consequent expansion of the conventional limits of causal perceptions and moral responsibility that compelled some exceptionally scrupulous individuals to attack slavery and prepared others to listen and comprehend."

Haskell's long essay is rhetorically brilliant. But his conclusion begs one question and risks muddling another. The begged question is, simply, what makes some individuals "exceptionally scrupulous" and others not? And why would only *some* scrupulous people attack slavery? What causes one person to turn the habits of mind induced by capitalism to abolitionism, another to become preoccupied with diet or dress, and another to turn those same habits of mind to advantage as a slave trader? Cf. David Brion Davis, "Reflections on Abolitionism and Ideological Hegemony," *American Historical Review* 92 (October 1987): 811. For the muddled question, see note 36.

Language was his medium, but it was more than that. It was the means through which he would identify the "dissolute," and reprove "vice." But vice and dissolution were characteristics that most often belonged to the social class from which he was trying to separate himself. And "reclaiming" the socially depraved was an activity associated with social privilege. On the other hand, the "iron rod of power" was something he always associated with decadent elites. And he was increasingly confident that defying power was the way he could become famous. What he was looking for—and eventually found— was a way of becoming celebrated—even infamous—by defying elite power but, in the process, gaining bourgeois respectability by claiming the social privilege of "reclaiming" the depraved classes or freeing those who were hopelessly oppressed. He almost never wrote or spoke explicitly about the question of social class. But the issue was always there, implicit in his figure of himself as the man whose "duty" is to "admonish" and to "condemn"—just as it had been implicitly present in that portrait he had commissioned at twenty, both in his decision to have it painted, and in the way he proposed himself to the artist.

Garrison sometimes talked and wrote as though there were only two parties to the reform struggle. On one side was the whole world of disorder, vice, and tyranny. On the other side was the lone individual, defiant and unafraid. It was as though a self-made, self-determined man had stepped full-grown into a world so alien to his own virtue that he could meet that world on no other terms than reproof and condemnation; as though, too, words themselves were the solution, the only necessary "arms" against the "iron rod of power."

In truth, as Garrison knew perfectly well, something did mediate between the individual and society, between the naked word on one side, and the rod and chains of the world on the other. Reform organizations were what gave extension and social meaning to the writing and speech of the individual reformer. Garrison did not have to invent reform to solve his ideological and vocational problems. He found it. When he went to Boston, benevolent organizations and "societies" were being formed in the city at a fantastic rate. The organizing mania dated back to the Revolution, but it was at a very high pitch when Garrison began his adult career. He lived in boardinghouses full of reformers and "city missionaries." It was in one of these boardinghouses that he first met the man who had founded the

National Philanthropist, and who invited him to be its new editor. The boarders invited a stream of reformers into the house, to give lectures and lead earnest discussions. But even this did not satisfy Garrison's appetite for the language of uplift and the condemnation of evil. He went from church to church, hearing sermons, listening to the Boston ministry's tireless plea for the necessity of reform—listening, too, no doubt, for the tricks of the rhetorical trade.

In such an ideological setting, reform was more than a list of separate evils, each being attacked by some separate organization. Reform was a schematic vision of reality and a systematic projection of the future, a version of life in which each particular evil—prostitution, say, or militarism—had its place, and each organization had its corresponding niche. Reform was an alternative to party, and becoming a reformer was, for Garrison, a way of identifying a constituency. Reform, no matter what its particular object, gave him membership in an organized community of like-minded people. He had already "turned author," but reform furnished him with a new kind of audience. And if he became radical enough—and wrote stridently enough—reform might win him fame, keeping him safe from his mother's dark vision of that "place no one inhabits," but still not losing him "the favor of God."

During the election of 1828, Garrison had one last fling at party politics and small-town newspaper writing. His dread of Jackson was so great that it could overcome, just once more, his other dread of the "slothfulness and bane" of party. He agreed to become the editor, for the election season, of the *Journal of the Times* in Bennington, Vermont, to write for John Quincy Adams—who, though he might be seriously flawed, was at least an acceptable alternative to the fearsome general. But even in this context, Garrison made the *Journal* a bit unusual among the local papers of the day by giving a great deal of space to the three reforms he now decided were most urgent: peace, temperance, and antislavery. His months in Bennington amounted to a kind of temporary relapse, a last flirtation with an orthodox set of journalistic practices he was about to abandon irrevocably.

Garrison was peculiarly vulnerable to the messages of other reformers—as though he were a kind of carrier of undifferentiated reform sentiment in search of specific articulations. While he was still in Newburyport, a leader of the peace movement had given a lecture in the town, and Garrison had become, overnight, a pacifist. Every new society in Boston for the suppression of one vice or another caught his fancy, and roused him to the most optimistic kinds of hopes—and the most intemperate kind of language. He was a man in search of movements, a moralist in search of outrages, and a publicist in search of causes.

So it was with slavery. Garrison had had almost no direct contact with slavery. He had never seen a plantation. He had seen very few slaves. When he had visited Baltimore at the time of his mother's last illness, he found her in the apparently voluntary and gentle care of an old black woman. But that woman was already free, and the racial implications of the situation did not make a very marked impression on Garrison. His hatred of Andrew Jackson had more to do with Jackson's drinking, gambling, and dueling than with the fact that the labor force at the Hermitage was made up almost entirely of slaves. But after 1829, slavery became Garrison's main concern. He never lost interest in other reforms, like women's rights or Sabbatarianism. When his brother James died in 1842, Garrison could still easily and comfortably make his pointed remarks about "the war system, the navy, intemperance, &c." But being an abolitionist writer and speaker soon became his vocation. Antislavery could do for him what no other reform movement could do so well: provide him with a cause over which there could be no compromise at all, propel him into fame (and infamy), threaten his life, and send him into jail cells in Baltimore and Boston.[36]

Garrison's conversion to serious antislavery work came in 1828, in the same quick way his conversion to other reforms had come. He was in Boston, still editing the *National Philanthropist*. Benjamin Lundy, a quiet young Quaker from Ohio—a saddlemaker by trade, and no taller than Garrison—came to town to lecture on slavery, and to

[36] A question that seems to be somewhat confused in Thomas Haskell's important essay, "Capitalism and the Origins of the Humanitarian Sensibility," is: If the mentality of the capitalist market is only a *"precondition"* for abolitionism, how can it "compel" anyone to do anything? A rudimentary distinction between necessary and sufficient conditions sometimes appears to have been lost in Haskell's statement of his case. In his "Convention and Hegemonic Interest in the Debate over Antislavery: A Reply to Davis and Ashworth," ibid., 850, Haskell suggests that when we say "*x* causes *y*" we imply this "violent fantasy": "in the absence of *x*, no *y*." He may have momentarily misunderstood something about the logic of implication. "If *x* then *y*" is (logically) true even if some *y* also happens to occur without the occurrence of *x*. Haskell's "violent fantasy" is actually implied by "if *y* then *x*," or by "*only* if *x* then *y*." This is not a trivial or merely technical error. In fact, it is the source of a good deal of the murkiness of the current debate among historians over the relationship between capitalism and abolitionism. Cf. note 35.

promote his journal, *The Genius of Universal Emancipation*. Before his public lecture, Lundy spoke to a smaller, earnest group at Garrison's boardinghouse. Garrison was urgently moved. He began to make slavery one of the principal topics in the *National Philanthropist*, first, and then in the *Journal of the Times*. After Jackson's victory in the fall of 1828, Garrison was out of work (for many small-town editors, newspaper writing was almost seasonal work; the seasons were elections and the potential harvest was victory and local spoils). Luckily, Lundy invited him down to Baltimore, to become a co-editor of *The Genius of Universal Emancipation*. Garrison jumped at the chance.

When Garrison went to Baltimore, he was in his mid-twenties. He had been a marvelously "steady" boy, and an assiduously workmanlike adolescent. He plainly expected to become a successful man. But he had failed in his first publishing venture. He had had to borrow money. He had moved quickly and unprofitably through two editorial positions, on the *National Philanthropist* and the *Journal of the Times*. In economic terms, at least, he brought only a record of failure to *The Genius of Universal Emancipation*. But he also brought something else. He had developed a definite and powerful writing style, an equally definite idea of the proper writer-to-audience nexus, and a propensity to adopt unpopular—and unprofitable—causes. Even before he reached Baltimore, he decided that Lundy's antislavery strategies were too cautious. Gradual emancipation or colonization were not the answers. What was demanded was an immediate, unconditional end to slavery, with no compensation for slaveholders, and no concern for solutions to the problem of what should be done with ex-slaves. In effect, he decided that *slaves* were not the issue; *slavery* was. Slavery was a sin, and he would not accept any slow and incomplete solution. He had already reached similar conclusions about temperance and pacifism: He had demanded nothing less than the total prohibition of drinking and war. Now he applied the same logic to slavery. And within a few months he was in jail.

In Garrison's experience, Baltimore and Newburyport had been the poles of a moral axis. Newburyport was the place of his youthful and ambitious embrace of this world. Baltimore was the place of his mother's lonely vigil for the next world. Now, again, in Baltimore, Garrison set about to tempt "the rude blast of misfortune." And he chose, uncannily, a Newburyport trader as his means. In the fall of 1829, Garrison printed in *The Genius* a pair of brief items accusing the merchant (who like Abijah Garrison followed the coasting trade) of transporting eighty or so slaves from Baltimore to New Orleans for sale. The transaction itself was utterly commonplace and perfectly legal. But Garrison singled the man out for an angry and somewhat inaccurate attack. The result was a suit for libel. He was found guilty and fined. He refused to pay, of course, and was sentenced to a six-month jail term.[37]

He was happy. The jail was large, old-fashioned, and relaxed. Garrison took his meals with the warden and his family, and had time to read and write. He got up a pamphlet giving *A Brief Sketch of the Trial of William Lloyd Garrison*. But his relaxation, his sense of harmony—almost of ease—did not come only from the comforts of jail life, or just from the pleasure of writing about his own victimization. Garrison was delighted on a level deeper than physical comfort or verbal narcissism. All the elements of a new picture of himself, components of a self-image that he had been devising gradually for years, now fell neatly into place. It was almost as though his life had, for a few weeks at least, an unambiguous and dramatic moral script.

The central theme of the drama was not really slavery, nor even reform in general. It was Garrison's final realization of his own "freedom." As he put it in a half-joking letter that he proudly dated "Baltimore Jail/May 12, 1830": "I pay no rent—am bound to make no repairs—and enjoy the luxury of independence divested of its cares." Thoreau could have written the lines, but only much later, for Thoreau was only thirteen. Emerson would eventually have some sentiments of the same sort, but not yet. Garrison was working from a kind of informal transcendentalism that was older than the formal schemes which would one day be worked out in Concord. His vocabulary of "independence," "luxury," and "cares" echoed the autobiography of Benjamin Franklin as much as it anticipated Emerson. He had, in hard fact, "divested" himself of much. He had cast off, one by one, the garments of social identity that men and women ordinarily use to buffer and organize experience. He had no family, no job, no property, no protection of law or sanction of custom, no control, even, over his own body. He had actually transcended every tie of kinship, membership, or institution. He had become, so it seemed in his quiet room in the jail, the complete

---

[37] Thomas, *The Liberator*, 108–13, has a good account of the jail episode.

master of his own fate and soul. Like many other prisoners of his
age, real and fictional, Garrison scratched a poem onto a wall of the
jail. It was a sonnet, a reworking of Richard Lovelace's popular
"Stone walls do not a prison make, /Nor iron bars a cage":

> *High walls and huge the* BODY *may confine,*
> *And iron gates obstruct the prisoner's gaze,*
> *And massive bolts may baffle his design,*
> *And vigilant keepers watch his devious ways.*
> *Yet scorns th'immortal* MIND *this base control!*
> *No chains can bind it, and no cell enclose:*
> *Swifter than light it flies from pole to pole.*[38]

In a curious way, this kind of "freedom" had been the unacknowl-
edged quest of the whole Garrison family for years. Abijah's desertion was one way of claiming liberation from "cares." James'
drinking and defections were another way of asserting "independence." Fanny Garrison's yearnings for the "release" of death and
the consolations of heaven were her version of the quest for individual immunity from the world. But William Lloyd Garrison had
found what his parents and his brother never did, a way of giving
"freedom" an organized focus, and in this world. He had found a
way of defying social institutions, and even breaking laws. But his
criminality was pious, not drunken and fleshly. He could surrender
to power, as he did in jail, confident that he could surrender the body
and keep the "immortal MIND" free as light. And he had worked this
magic, which was both philosophical and existential, within a career,
as a writer. He had seized the only calling he could follow in jail as
well as out. In a primitive sort of way, at least, he not only owned
the means of production for his career, but they were eminently
portable and could be operated as well inside a cell as out. And he had
made his own self his real writing subject, a subject he had immediate access to, wherever he was. Armed with this seemingly coherent sense of his own absolute freedom, Garrison could comfortably
accept the offer of the wealthy New York merchant Arthur Tappan
to pay his fine after forty-nine days in jail. He could leave his cell,
and begin to make preparations for the first issue of *The Liberator*,
ready to set the italic type for those metallic words, I *will be . . .*

---

[38] The poem is reproduced, along with much other material on the jail episode, in *Life*,
2:179 ff.

*   *   *

The type Garrison used for setting his declaration "To the Public" in that first issue of *The Liberator* was borrowed, from a friend at another Boston journal. This was fitting, because he was living, in effect, on borrowed time. He had left his jail cell on the patronage of Tappan. That kind of patronage would come to him again, and with increasing frequency, not only from the Tappan brothers but from a number of other wealthy merchant-philanthropists as well. And patronage would also come in other forms, too—even as sad little gifts from the free blacks who for many years were the largest group of subscribers to *The Liberator*. Garrison's career did gradually bring him the celebrity he had always wanted—especially after he was the victim of a spectacular mobbing in Boston in 1835. It brought him travel to Europe and the welcome attention of the British antislavery movement—which included many peers and even a royal duke. With the passage of time, it brought him audiences for his lectures and speeches, audiences that at first numbered in the dozens, but then in the hundreds. But for most of his years it did not bring him an income he could count on. What he did live on was various forms of patronage—loans everyone knew would not be repaid, gifts to abolitionist societies that were directly intended to make up his salary, and even campaigns to collect money for a fund to help support him and his family.

By a circuitous route, the young man who was so obsessed with "independence" had become almost completely dependent on patrons and benefactors. But there was a logic to it. Out of the way he had defined the writing career for himself had come a figure so resolute and unyielding, so determined to pursue perfect moral justice, that it was made safe for patronage. That figure was as impervious to temptations to trim and compromise as it was invulnerable to prisons. If only his "body" could be jailed, then only his body was dependent on the gifts he accepted. He could accept the support of benefactors—black as well as white, poor as well as rich—because he had defined the writing career itself as a kind of public benefaction. He had made himself into an institutionalized civic conscience, reproving and admonishing, not for his own purposes but for God's.

So the solution to the moral dilemma his mother had confronted him with became as well a solution to the problem of how he was to live. The literary marketplace, with its promises of fame and success, had called him to the writing career in the first place. But his resolution of the conflict with moral piety that those promises posed had taken him away from the writer's market altogether. In his completed identity as an abolitionist writer and speaker, the contradictions between ambition and piety were quieted. And so were the kinds of excitements that had been generated by the authorial career that the young man in the oil painting had planned for himself. He had relinquished any hope of reaching vast and sympathetic audiences—what his mother had called "the applause of mortals." He had committed himself to a cause that had little chance of success in the present, or in any short-term future he could plausibly have foreseen in the 1830s. He had made *his* audience into a constituency in a holy cause. But this meant that he could lean on that audience for support in a way that short-circuited the market relations between other writers and their audiences. He could accept direct patronage from people like his wealthy colleague Wendell Phillips precisely because it was not himself but the cause the patronage was supporting.

But Garrison's moral equations had to be reaffirmed from time to time. As the antislavery movement grew, as he became more and more famous, he had to keep moving to new and increasingly radical positions, in spasms of righteousness that split organizations and alienated a remarkably long list of friends and allies. This was no mere quirk of personality. If anything, it was a quirk of persona. The figure of the writer that he had created to make his extraordinary career possible was a fragile thing. It required that he be always in danger, always at the margins, on the verge of suffering and privation. If anything that smacked of practical success—let alone real power—came near him, he had to move quickly away, and affirm once more his unshakable "independence."

In the end, though, Garrison was able to find a permanent and comfortable resolution to the requirement that his relationship with his society at large be one of perpetual defiance. When the Civil War came, he faced some difficult choices. For years he had scandalized audiences by reviling the Constitution as a "covenant with death." He had even burned it in public. He had called for the secession of the free states. And his initial response to Southern secession had been to argue that the Union should be dissolved peacefully. He had also been an ardent pacifist and a proponent of nonviolence. So when Lincoln issued his first call for volunteers, and made it clear that he intended to use every means to maintain the Union, Garrison had to decide whether to continue his long career of uncompromising opposition to power.

But his choices were not mere moral choices between abstract principles. They also gave him a chance to work a fundamental change in his way of conceiving his own career. The sequence of events beginning with Lincoln's election and ending with the Emancipation Proclamation worked a rapid inflation of Garrison's public reputation. The crowds that gathered to hear him became dramatically larger and more enthusiastic, numbering now not in the hundreds but in the thousands. He found himself becoming something of a public hero. And, step by step, as Northern audiences began to lionize him, he began to lionize them, their Union, and, in the end, their president. During the first two years of the war, while Lincoln wavered on the question of emancipation, Garrison searched for a middle ground between the administration and its aggressive abolitionist critics, who included his old friend Wendell Phillips. And when Lincoln did at last issue the Emancipation Proclamation, Garrison's rewards came quick and fast. An official copy of the Proclamation reached Boston on New Year's Day, during a Jubilee celebration in the Music Hall. The orchestra was hard at Beethoven's Fifth Symphony when it arrived, and the symphony was interrupted as the audience broke into twelve hurrahs, nine for Lincoln and three for Garrison, who was seated in a place of honor in the gallery. That evening he went out to Medford in a company with Emerson and other dignitaries to see a new statue of John Brown. Many abolitionists were still finding fault with Lincoln for not doing something sooner, or something more drastic, about slavery. But Garrison had been completely won over to the president. The next day's *Liberator* called the Proclamation "a great and historical event, sublime in its magnitude, momentous and beneficent in its far-reaching consequences, and eminently just and right." The following year, Garrison was invited to Washington, where he met twice with Lincoln and passed whole days with cabinet ministers and senators.[39]

The peace Garrison was making was not just with Lincoln and the Republican Party. It was a peace with society. And it was his separate

[39] For the Music Hall scene, see *Life*, 4:69–70. The assessment of the Emancipation Proclamation is in *The Liberator*, January 2, 1863.

peace. Other abolitionists, following Phillips' lead, continued throughout to criticize Lincoln. Indeed, when it came time, after Lee's surrender, for Garrison to take the final institutional step and propose that his American Anti-Slavery Society be disbanded, the resolution was defeated by a large majority, with 118 delegates voting against him, and only 48 in favor of his proposal to "abolish the now happily obsolete antislavery society." But for him, the temptation to make his peace was overwhelming. He was determined now to think of the Americans—those who rallied to the Union, at least—as "a people, united in sentiment." For the first time in his long career, he could say "Let us mingle with the mass, then, and endeavor to work with the mass, and not affect isolation or singularity, nor assume to say, 'Stand by, we are holier than you,' when we are no better." For the first time, the "applause of mortals" did not seem threatening.[40]

Garrison picked up the popular expression "Jubilee" to describe the progress of events—the unification of the Northern public in "sentiment," the Proclamation, the Union victories, Lee's surrender, and finally the Thirteenth Amendment. But Jubilee not only gave him the chance to relax his defiance and become a public hero; it also brought a permanent solution to the nagging material problems that had been implicit in his way of defining his career. In the spring of 1865, he decided to discontinue *The Liberator*—though he announced this nine months in advance and raised the subscription price substantially for the remainder of the year. That fall, he set out on an extended lecture tour that earned the sizable sum of $1,400 in a little over four weeks. Then he came home in time to set the type himself for the last issue. In it, he said "Farewell, tried and faithful patrons! Farewell, generous benefactors! . . . Hail, ye ransomed millions! Hail, year of Jubilee." During those last months of *The Liberators'* publication, those benefactors and patrons were busy indeed, organizing a fund to "put him at ease."[41] Within a year and a half, they had raised over $35,000, enough to make him truly "independent" for the rest of his life. He would continue for more than another decade to write and speak, and for substantial fees. But he did not

[40] Garrison's own account of his last meeting with the American Anti-Slavery Society is in *The Liberator*, May 19, 1865. When he published this, Garrison had already announced, the preceding March, that he would discontinue *The Liberator* at the end of the year. An admirably succinct summary of the meeting is in Merrill, *Against Wind and Tide*, 299–300.

[41] *The Liberator*, December 29, 1865. "Put him at ease" is from a letter of October 16, 1865, quoted in Merrill, *Against Wind and Tide*, 309.

have to do it. His long labor of defiance had finally brought him both fame and financial security.

Garrison's new version of the public as a "mass" to which he might finally surrender his "singularity" was not a straightforward result of the impact of events on his consciousness. He was putting the war to his own uses, investing it with his own meanings. Nothing in the progress of events forced him to decide that the Northern public had suddenly had a miraculous accession of holiness, or that it was now his proper "duty" not to challenge the "iron rod of power," but to hover near senators and cabinet members and presidents as a collaborator in the glorious cause of a redeemed Union. Most of his fellow abolitionists did not make these decisions with anything like Garrison's haste or enthusiasm, though they read the same war news he did. But most of them would have had difficulty grasping the extent to which Garrison was finally liberating himself from a self-definition that—while it had worked well—had been precarious and extremely demanding. When the time came for what he called "Jubilee," his jubilation was not only for the Union, and not only for the freed slaves, but perhaps most of all for himself.

Ralph Waldo Emerson, Sarah Goodridge's 1829 miniature

IV

RALPH WALDO EMERSON

In 1829, Ralph Waldo Emerson posed for a miniature. It was an appropriate thing for a man in his position to do, for he had come to two important junctures in his life, one of them romantic and the other vocational. He was going to marry Ellen Louisa Tucker, and he was about to be ordained to preach at the Unitarian Second Church in Boston. So it was fitting that R. Waldo Emerson—as he had chosen to call himself—and Ellen Tucker have themselves painted, if only in miniature.

The two events Emerson was marking were obviously important. He had already passed some institutionalized waypoints in the life of a man of his social class and background in New England. He had graduated from Harvard eight years earlier, when he was still only seventeen. Four years later, as he was about to turn twenty-one, he had been very conscious that he was about to become *"legally* a man."* A month before his birthday, he had made a commitment in his journal: "I deliberately dedicate my time, my talents, and my hopes to the Church."[1] Then, in 1826, he had been approbated,

---

[1] Entry for April 18, 1824, in William H. Gilman et al., eds., *The Journals and Miscellaneous Notebooks of Ralph Waldo Emerson,* 16 vols. (Cambridge, Mass.: 1960–82), 2:237. These invaluable volumes will be cited here as *Journals and Notebooks;* dates for entries will be given only if the exact timing of an entry is material to the point under discussion.

licensed to give sermons occasionally, but not yet to hold a pulpit in any Unitarian church. But all this—finishing college, dedicating himself at twenty-one to a ministerial career, and even being permitted to preside over church services from time to time—had been only so much preparation. Now he was about to take two extremely serious steps, the two steps that he understood would mark a definite passage from youth into "manhood." He dramatized the moment in his journal in a way that linked his coming marriage and the anticipated beginning of his professional career, and then prayerfully draped over both events a mantling of divine will:[2]

> My history has had its important days within a brief period. I enjoy the luxury of an unmeasured affection for an object so deserving of it all & who requites it all. I am called by an ancient & respectable church to become its pastor. I recognize in these events . . . the hand of my heavenly father . . . I feel my total dependance [sic]. O God direct and guard and bless me.

This rounded and harmonious version of his life was one that Emerson had devised quite deliberately and self-consciously. As he described himself in his journals and letters during the year before his marriage, the elements of his life appeared to fall neatly into place. His "unmeasured affection" for Ellen Tucker was in harmony with his call to the respectable Second Church, and both these things had been wrought by the same heavenly hand. It would be important to try to convey this sense of harmony and rightness not just to his journal, but to the miniaturist.

For his sitting, he chose some rather conventional ways of trying to signal that he was a man in whom the mysteries of love and the burdens of professional office were met and fused, without tension or discord. As marks of maturity and respectability, he wore a formal coat, and a high, heavily starched collar that cradled his face in the best class fashion of the day. But he balanced these badges of station with a faint smile, suggesting not amusement but a certain intimate knowledge of affairs of the heart. His hair was brushed forward a little, in a way that hinted at a capacity for passion but still kept well within the bounds of good grooming. His eyes, at least as the artist caught them, conveyed some of the same suggestions of

---

[2] January 17, 1829, *Journals and Notebooks*, 3:149–50.

benign romantic readiness. They were not the eyes of a mature professional man of divinity only, but of a young man not entirely unacquainted with matters of "affection."

The artist, Sarah Goodridge, was a woman of considerable talent, who had studied with Gilbert Stuart. She produced a quite striking portrait of Ellen Tucker. But the miniature of Emerson was not a successful piece of art. Worse yet, it failed to convey Emerson's characterological message. The Waldo Emerson it showed looked rather more stuffy than seriously responsible. And whatever marks of sentiment and affection Emerson and the artist may have tried to put into the picture collapsed into a vacuous, almost simpering, complacency. Part of the problem was no doubt that the task itself was difficult, for both subject and artist: the clichés of sentimental romance and the stiff-necked conventions of middle-class respectability were not easy to harmonize. But Emerson had a particular problem of his own, a problem he was very much aware of. He believed that some people could control their expressions completely with what he called "great power of face." But, he wrote in his journal some months before he posed for the miniature, "I have none. I laugh; I blush; I look ill tempered; against my will."[3] He had difficulty looking the parts he had laid out for himself in his journal. And the result was that he really appeared in the miniature not as a serious cleric in love, but as something else, something he very much feared he might actually be: only a self-satisfied and decorous young man of no particular merit, but with a faultless pedigree, a man about to claim what mere ancestry and breeding entitled him to—the pulpit of a fine Boston church and, to go with it, the pretty and extremely bright daughter of a wealthy family.

Waldo Emerson was quite willing to admit that his pulpit and his marriage were not the earned rewards of his own efforts. The "dependance" he chose to acknowledge in his journal was only on his "heavenly father." In truth, the snobbish-looking man in the miniature was dependent in many other ways on more earthly kinds of unearned benefits. From his birth on, he had enjoyed a

[3] July 1828, *Journals and Notebooks,* 3:13. Moncure Conway said that Emerson once said to him that "My portraits generally oscillate between the donkey and the Lothario." Quoted in John McAleer, *Ralph Waldo Emerson: Days of Encounter* (Boston, 1984), 423. This rambling and chatty book is a feast for anyone fond of Emerson anecdotes.

rather imposing set of familial and institutional advantages. He had been a creature of privilege, entitled to what he referred to as "great expectation." He had, in truth, every New England expectation but one—money—that any young man of his social class could imagine.

Ralph Waldo Emerson was the son, grandson, and great-grandson of ministers. (He was even the step-grandson of another, since the eminent Reverend Ezra Ripley of Concord had married the widow of his predecessor, the woman who was Emerson's paternal grandmother.) Grandfather Emerson had held the pulpit of the church at Concord. Emerson's father was minister of Boston's grandly prestigious First Church. Step-grandfather Ezra Ripley still ministered to the Concord church while Emerson was growing up. These men, living and dead, presided over the beginnings of Emerson's own ministerial career. The first sermon he ever preached was given from his Uncle Samuel Ripley's pulpit in Waltham. He preached his second sermon in his father's old church, the First. It was also in the First Church that he gave his first sustained series of replacement sermons during the years between his approbation and his ordination. And when it was time to be formally ordained at the Second Church in March of 1829, the ceremony was a tableau of ancestral and institutional continuity. The first ritual step, the "charge" to the new minister, was administered by Grandfather Ripley—who had also charged Emerson's father thirty-seven years earlier. The ordination sermon was delivered by Uncle Samuel Ripley. The "right hand of fellowship" welcoming the new minister to his congregation was offered by the man who had replaced Emerson's father at the First Church, Nathaniel Frothingham.[4]

This intricate and dense network of family and professional relationships was the defining context of Waldo Emerson's youth. It limited the choices he could consider, perhaps; but it sanctioned the choices he did make. It took him through Harvard College. It guided him gently toward the Divinity School and the ministry. It made his selection of a bride plausible—not only to him, but also to Ellen Tucker and both their families. It made his ordination much more than the formal ratification of a contract between him and the Second Church—made it into a public ritual of acknowledgment of the claims and privileges of family and history. By and large, then, the

[4] *Journals and Notebooks*, 2:98n; Ralph L. Rusk, *The Life of Ralph Waldo Emerson* (New York, 1949), 119; Gay Wilson Allen, *Waldo Emerson: A Biography* (New York, 1981), 93–4.

expression of self-congratulation that found its way into the 1829 miniature was more than justified.

But there had been one persistent problem that had darkened the inherited entitlements which defined young Waldo Emerson. There had been no money. Very little of the merchant wealth that belonged to his mother's side of the family found its way to her. So when his father had died in 1811, he had left a forty-three-year-old widow with six children, ranging in age from eleven to three. And from that point on, Emerson's life had been shaped by charity.

The charity had been a form of patronage, channeled through the same familial and professional systems that eventually led Emerson to his marriage and his position at the Second Church. When his father died, the First Church had provided the Widow Emerson with a seven-year annuity of $500. (When the Emersons needed more money, as they often did, members of the congregation stepped in with private donations.) Waldo had been only eight when his father died, but the seven-year annuity lasted until he was ready to enter Harvard. Then the church, whose minister, Frothingham, would later give the hand of fellowship at Emerson's ordination, voted money to help pay for his education. (It was the income on a bequest, and it was this same legacy that had already been used to help Emerson's older brother through Harvard.) The man who had been Emerson's headmaster at the Boston Public Latin School was able to get him appointed "the President's Freshman"—a sort of messenger and orderly—which paid his tuition and room for the first year. And Emerson's Uncle Samuel Ripley completed the arrangements. He was running a school, and said that Waldo could teach there during the winter vacations to earn money.[5]

When he graduated from Harvard, Emerson tried to get a position teaching at the Latin School. This choice was as predictable as the decision to go to Harvard in the first place; boys who intended to become ministers, but who were too young when they finished college, customarily taught school for a few years. But Emerson's record at Harvard had been so poor (he ranked below the middle of his class) that he was turned down. So he had to fall back again on family connections, and teach for several years in a school for girls that his older brother William had started in Boston. And when he became convinced that he had tuberculosis—though no doctor

[5] James Elliot Cabot, *A Memoir of Ralph Waldo Emerson*, 2 vols. (Boston, 1895), 1:27; Allen, *Waldo Emerson*, 38; Rusk, *The Life of Ralph Waldo Emerson*, 62.

would make a definite diagnosis—he resorted once more to family patronage. In 1826, during the winter after his approbation, he traveled to South Carolina and Florida, with the financial help of his Uncle Samuel Ripley.[6]

This tight web of inherited "expectation" and practical "dependance" occasionally chafed. Emerson grumbled from time to time over his family's preoccupation with "pedigree." He could even declare that ancestry was irrelevant, and that "my business is with the living." But such moments of impatience were exceptional (and confined to the journal). When he was ready for what he thought of as "manhood"—career and marriage—his deepest sense of himself was as a man who would finally be able to earn a good living doing what generations of Emersons had done. From the time he was an undergraduate, he had dreamed of "fame." And he pinned his hopes for it on his capacity for "eloquence." Occasionally, during his apprenticeship as a minister, he joked that he might leave the profession and "commence author," if only the "muse" were not "unwilling." But such speculations were few and not at all serious. For his ambitions, the Unitarian establishment seemed an ample stage. Indeed, for him it seemed the only stage, the only plausible institutional setting for a satisfactory career. And this career was what made it possible for him to have the "luxury" of being able to fasten unmeasured affection on a girl like Ellen Tucker.[7]

And so, as he set out on his marriage and career, Emerson thought of his life as one that was defined by continuities of time and place. "History," he stuffily said, "is premiere in the cabinet." And he could write to a friend, before he had even met his future wife: "I am in the pleasant land of my fathers, and of my sons and sons' sons peradventure." He could travel to Charleston and Saint Augustine—and be quite amazed by their bizarre foreignness—but the idea of a life at any distance from the land of his fathers was unthinkable. A year after he

---

[6] Allen, *Waldo Emerson*, 60–80; Ralph L. Rusk, ed., *The Letters of Ralph Waldo Emerson*, 6 vols. (New York, 1939), 1:80. These volumes will be cited here as *Letters*.

[7] Emerson's most famous complaint against the idea of "pedigree" was in a journal entry of January 1825, which ended: "But the dead sleep in their moonless night; my business is with the living." *Journals and Notebooks*, 2:316. Two years later he labeled the front cover of a notebook "Genealogy," and set down about fifteen pages of notes on his ancestry. *Journals and Notebooks*, 3:349-53. The notion that he might "commence author" was put in a very lighthearted letter to his brother William in 1827, *Letters*, 1:201.

was licensed to preach, the possibility developed of a call to a congregation in New York. He recoiled, saying that he would rather "be a doorkeeper at home than bishop to aliens."[8]

This satisfied sense of history and place was part and parcel of Emerson's basic idea of what it meant to be a minister. In an early sermon, he began by asking the congregation, "When we came up this morning to the house of God, did we come up in savage solitude, each from his lonely house, a congregation of hermits to whom society is unwelcome?" His answer, emphatically, was no. The assembled congregation was a close community, knit together by bonds of family and friendship:[9]

> We have taken sweet counsel together. We do not live for ourselves; we do not rejoice, we do not weep alone. Our lives are bound up in others. Our blood beats in our breasts pulse for pulse with a true accord at the honor and shame of a hundred other hearts to which God has united us in family or friendship.

To be a minister, for him, was to take up what he called a "priestly" vocation, to become the moral voice of such a community. It was a career that led emphatically away from nature toward institutions, away from solitude toward community. The ideal congregation was not an audience but a constituency. The ideal priest spoke not to strangers but to families he knew intimately. And this relationship was manifested concretely in the legal contract that bound the minister to his congregation, with a definite income, in principle for life. The duties were clear and fixed by powerful traditions. He could count his visits to the sick and the grieving; he could keep track of the numbers of people he married or baptized. There were sermons to prepare, and he could carefully number these, too. There might be times when the prospect of having to write one every week seemed "terrifick." But being a preacher meant having definite, limited tasks, performed for an almost changeless audience, done at close range, and for a measured reward.[10]

[8] Emerson to John Boynton Hill, June 19, 1823; to William Emerson, January 6 and October 31, 1827, *Letters*, 1:132, 185, 218.

[9] This sermon was written in June of 1827, during Emerson's approbation. It is in *Journals and Notebooks*, 3:90–1.

[10] Emerson's inaugural sermon at the Second Church was on "The Christian Ministry." It is printed, along with a number of other early, fugitive pieces, in A. C. McGiffert, ed., *Young*

Emerson's understanding of his profession was almost perfectly opposed to any possibility that he might "commence author." In the career of a writer, the tasks were undefined; the work was produced for a marketplace full of strangers, and it carried no certainty whatever of profit. Little wonder that the idea of becoming a writer surfaced in his mind only from time to time and as a joke. Little wonder, as well, that whenever his older brother hinted that he might abandon his own budding career as a lawyer in New York to take up lecturing or newspaper editing, Emerson was alarmed. He urged William to stick to the "comfort and respectability" of his learned profession.[11]

In less than three years after Emerson had his miniature painted and set out on his own career of comfort and respectability, everything fell apart. Ellen Tucker Emerson died early in 1831. A year and a half later, in September of 1832, he went into the pulpit of the Second Church to resign.

His disagreement with the Proprietors of the Second Church was one that he provoked. He refused to continue to administer the Lord's Supper. He was ready enough to defend his decision, even to use a kind of close scriptural reasoning that was very atypical of his sermons. But he had understood the problem of this sacrament from the beginning, and could quite easily have continued the practice as a "symbolic" gesture. He had a great deal of support in the congregation, and it is obvious that he could have worked out a compromise if he had wanted. But instead he chose to challenge the Second Church, and then to insist on his position in a way that forced an end to his contract. After he resigned, it did not take Emerson long—not more than five years—to became a professional man of letters. In fact, he eventually became one of the most famous and financially

Emerson Speaks: Unpublished Discourses on Many Subjects (Boston, 1938). The remark about the "terrifick"obligation to write four sermons a month was in a letter to his step-grandfather, Ezra Ripley, March 22, 1829, *Letters,* 1:26.
[11] The cautions to William about lecturing and newspapers were in letters of April 3, 1828, and June 29, 1831, *Letters,* 1:230, 326–7. Michael T. Gilmore, *American Romanticism and the Marketplace* (Chicago, 1986), ch. 1, has some interesting observations on Emerson's attitudes toward the market economy at large, though he does not connect these very closely with Emerson's own professional practices and anxieties. Gilmore's best chapters are those on Hawthorne, which follow rather closely some brilliant leadings of Stephen Nissenbaum, set out in "The Firing of Nathaniel Hawthorne," *Essex Institute Historical Collections* 114 (1978): 57–86, and in his introduction to the Modern Library edition of *The Scarlet Letter* (New York, 1983).

successful American writers and orators of his age. It is tempting to see his resignation from the Second Church as the liberation of a talented writer who had decided to free himself from the constraints of a clergyman's life, and to take his chances in the literary market-place. Over the years, Emerson did much to promote such a picture of himself as a man who had been ready to renounce tradition, "dependance," and "pedigree," seeking always after "self reliance." But in truth he left the ministry with no very clear idea what he might do, and no firm plan to "commence author." He defined his vocational crisis precisely, but only on one side: he was clear, pub-licly and privately, about what he would *not* do. But he pictured himself as a man who had set himself adrift. His decision had been prompted in some measure by his very real grief for his dead wife. And he may have been lured on by the expectation that when her will was probated he would inherit enough money to equal twenty years of his starting salary at the Second Church. But if he had plans, he only hinted at them, even to his brothers and his own journal.[12]

On the other hand, he understood quite well that there was a literary career to be made. He knew he could try editing a journal, and he even joked a little with his brothers about founding one. He also knew he could try public lecturing, which had already become a cultural institution in New England, and paid well. But he was unwilling or unable simply to launch himself on the new career without some further step of preparation. In discussions with his family about his situation, he adopted a mixture of irony and sheep-ishness: "Projects sprout and bloom in my head," he wrote to William a few weeks after the resignation, "of action, literature, philosophy." Though he was at a critical vocational juncture, he had real difficulty confronting it directly. He was precisely where Irving had been in 1815, and at almost exactly the same age. And, like

---

[12] His brother Charles understood that the moment was immensely critical, but could only speculate on the outcome: "Now things seem to be flying to pieces, and I don't know when they will again be put together and he [be] harnessed in . . . the labors of a daily calling. . . . I do not doubt he may write and be a fine thinker, all alone by himself; but I think he needs to be dragged closer to people by some practical vocation, however it may irk his tastes." Quoted in Cabot, 1:174. Emerson's own journals and letters for this period hardly ever use language like "daily calling" or "practical vocation," except in a gallows-humor way. The sermon Emerson preached on the occasion of his resignation is in Edward Waldo Emerson, ed., *The Complete Works of Ralph Waldo Emerson*, 12 vols.(Boston, 1903–04), 11:8–25. It contains much more scriptural citation and close theological argument than he customarily used in the pulpit. The episode can be followed in *Journals and Notebooks*, 4:27, 29, 30, 32, and in *Letters*, 1:352–3. Emerson's financial expectations during the months preceding his resig-nation can be tracked in ibid., 1:323, 327, 349.

Irving, he seemed vulnerable to chance and impulse. He planned another trip to the South in December, for his "health." But when a vessel offered itself for Italy, he jumped at the chance with little or no explanation to anyone—not even to his own journal.

But—as with Irving—what appeared to be accident and whim had a logic. Like Irving, he was interested in literary, not physical, landscapes, monuments, and ruins. He did visit cathedrals and catacombs, but impatiently. It gradually became clear that the real purpose of his trip was to see men who had made triumphantly successful careers as writers. He visited Coleridge and Wordsworth, and acted as though his only real purpose were to confirm that they were indeed ruins, quite ordinary men and not inimitable masters with qualities of genius that he might lack. And when he met Carlyle, he was willing to regard him as a true monument precisely to the degree that Carlyle was willing to see *him* as a potential one. What he was looking for in England was the same thing Irving had looked for there: a sense of assurance, a conviction that he might indeed "commence author," and might do so without being either sheepish or ironic about it. [13]

By the time he was ready to take ship for home, in September of 1833, Emerson was able to tell himself without confusion or embarrassment that his experiences with Wordsworth, Coleridge, and Carlyle had comforted and confirmed him in his vocational "convictions." And a few days later, aboard ship, he made it clear what these convictions involved. "I like my book about nature," he said in his journal. Then he added, in the same sentence, with only an ampersand to join the thoughts, "& I wish I knew where and how I ought to live." He seemed to be certain about one thing—that he would write a book—and uncertain about the other—how he would live. But the two fell together easily in one sentence exactly because his "conviction" was clear that the first was part of the answer to the second. The very first thing he did when he arrived in the United States was to make arrangements to give a public lecture. He had given some lectures during his time at the Second Church, but they

[13] Warner Berthoff's introduction to *"Nature" . . . A Facsimile of the First Edition* (New York, 1968), vii–lxxxi, has some very intelligent observations about the relationship among Emerson's resignation, his trip to Europe, and the writing of *Nature*. Some similar arguments are well put in B. L. Packer, *Emerson's Fall: A Reinterpretation of the Major Essays* (New York, 1982), 236,n.26. See also Merton M. Sealts, "The Composition of *Nature,*" in Merton M. Sealts and Alfred Ferguson, eds., *Emerson's "Nature": Origin, Growth, Meaning* (Carbondale, Ill., 1979), 175–93.

had been avocational gestures. Now, the first public lecture after his trip to Europe was like a second ordination, the announcement of a new career. And from this point onward, Emerson's experience would be organized almost entirely around the fact that he was a writer by calling. And this was made easier—perhaps made possible at all—by Ellen Tucker Emerson's will. Her estate was settled in his favor, and the resulting capital of over $11,000 would yield a steady income. It was not enough to live on comfortably. He would have to continue for years to serve as a substituting minister in a number of Unitarian pulpits. But from September of 1833 on, his central purpose was to make his living as a writer. Over the years, he would produce a great many books, essays, lectures, and poems, and all of them in the hope that they would bring him a return.[14]

To be sure, Emerson's writing was always full of "ideas," ideas that even passed in his own day and since as a kind of philosophy. And he also had some quite definite esthetic commitments, which manifested themselves in a distinctive style and address. But his ideas and his esthetic practices cannot be reduced to the level of mere intellectual belief, with no connection to the requirements and imperatives of the fleshly and the material. He himself could not only admit this, but joke about it with a charming lack of embarrassment. After the probation of his wife's will, he wrote a quite witty letter to his brother William, making an analogy between having money and living a life of Reason, as against being broke and subject to the demands of the Understanding, "that wrinkled calculator, the steward of our house, to whom is committed the support of our animal life":[15]

> Reason is the highest faculty of the soul—what we mean often by the soul itself; it never *reasons,* never proves, it simply perceives; it is vision. The Understanding toils all the time, compares, contrives, adds, argues, near sighted but strong-sighted, dwelling in the present, the expedient, the customary. . . . The Tucker estate is so far settled that I am made sure of an income of about $1200. wherewith the Reason of Mother and you and I might defy the Understanding upon his own ground, for the rest of the few years in which we shall be subject to his insults.

[14] September 6, 1833, *Journals and Notebooks,* 4:237. A levelheaded and even courageous discussion of the significance of the inheritance is in Joel Porte, *Representative Man: Ralph Waldo Emerson in His Age* (New York, 1979), 55–63.

[15] May 31, 1834, *Letters,* 412-13.

"I need not say," he pointedly added, "that when I speak in play I speak in earnest."

Emerson was on the way to becoming a consummately professional man of letters, who understood that such ideas as Reason and Understanding were not ideas only, but also instruments, the materials and tools of a trade that he prosecuted with extraordinary vigor and efficiency. If he declared himself on an almost limitless range of broad questions—God, nature, immortality, truth, beauty, goodness, and the like—it was partly because he was presenting himself as a "thinker," a man whose legitimate calling was to traffic in such heady abstractions. And if he worked hard and self-consciously at developing a style and voice that were peculiarly his, it was not for esthetic purposes, merely, but also to mark his prose as "original."

As a minister, he had had a more or less conventional body of doctrine, and an equally conventional prose form, the sermon, as the instruments of his practice. There was a settled understanding between him and his congregation about the particular *capacity* in which he spoke. Now, as a writer and lecturer on the open market, he had to face both the freedom and the necessity of adjusting doctrine and form to satisfy expectations that were not at all settled. And, most urgently of all, he was free to propose a new notion of the capacity in which he would speak and write. His primary task was to develop a conception of the career of the writer, a figure of himself as an artist. And it was extremely important to him—and to his audiences too—that this figure be one who was moved by purposes much more elevated than profit. The plain fact, as he knew, was that people would not pay to hear or read anyone who was explicit about wanting to be paid. There could be little doubt, then, what Emerson's first subject would be. His "book about nature" would not be a book about nature at all, but a book about the figure of a man *in* nature: a man whose characteristic mode of experience was insight, whose medium was language, and whose purposes quite transcended any considerations of the marketplace—a man, indeed, for whom the "material" world existed only as "symbol." This was to be his first book, entitled simply *Nature,* published in 1836, three years after his return from Europe.

★   ★   ★

Emerson began *Nature* in a way that was meant to draw his readers into a shared disquiet, as though they were part of a vast congregation, and in spiritual crisis:[16]

> Our age is retrospective. It builds the sepulchres of the fathers. It writes biographies, histories, and criticism. The foregoing generations beheld God and nature face to face; we, through their eyes. . . . Why should we grope among the dry bones of the past, or put the living generations into masquerade out of its faded wardrobe?

Emerson was using this cultural diagnosis to set the stage for a compressed and half-disguised narrative he was going to spell out in the next section of his book, the section he called simply "Chapter I." The narrative would be the story of a conversion experience, in which "a man" found an exalting salvation from this secondhand deadness of the age. It was, in other words, to be the story of a spiritual pilgrimage. But the "man" was to be no ordinary pilgrim, like Bunyan's. He was the figure Emerson called "the Poet"—the same figure he sometimes called the "scholar" or the artist. He was a fairly obvious figuring of Emerson himself; the poet's quest was a dramatized version of Emerson's own progress out of the ministry into his new career.

In his account of the poet's experience, Emerson was careful not to address vocational questions directly (though he did drop plenty of clues for readers who were in the know). Instead, he elaborately laid out three alternative contexts as frames for his narrative, none of them having anything directly to do with vocation or career. The first was familial, melodramatic, and in a very loose sense, sexual; the second was Christological; the third was philosophical. He put all three in place to prepare for the same narrative outcome, the poet's face-to-face, ecstatic reunion with "NATURE."

Emerson couched his introductory cultural diagnosis in language and metaphors that would have been appropriate to family melodrama. He cast the tyranny of the past as patriarchal. The age "builds the sepulchres of the fathers." It "gropes" among their "dry bones." It "masquerades" in their "faded wardrobe." And against this motif of patriarchal darkness, desiccation, and deprivation, he set a char-

---

[16] *Nature* (Boston, 1836), 5. Except where noted, all quotations on the next several pages are from *Nature*, 5–14.

acterization of Nature that was fulgent, liquid, and nourishing—in a word, maternal: "We are," he said, "embosomed for a season in nature, whose floods of life stream around and through us. . . . The sun shines to-day also."

(It might be tempting to see all this talk about fathers' graves and embosom-ment in nature as evidence that Emerson was giving voice to some kind of desire to slay a father and possess a mother. This would drive him, plausibly, to want to sanitize the story by having the poet become as a child—to avoid the obvious pitfalls. And this in turn would promote a paranoid fantasy that he might actually devour the mother in order to attain complete possession of and union with her. And something of this sort does happen in the essay. The poet becomes more and more aware of himself as a child. Finally, he becomes perfectly helpless and harmless: "I am nothing," he will say. But this very helplessness entitles him to possess Nature, at least with his voracious eye: "I see all," he will exclaim in triumph, and "currents of Universal Being circulate through me." But there was nothing necessarily "psychological" about any of this. Emerson's own infantile fantasies about fathers and mothers—whatever they may have been—were not breaking out in prose. He was deploying very conventional language designed to evoke the paternal and the maternal. If he associated the fathers with death, dryness, and falsity, if he introduced nature with metaphors that were mammary, if he made poets into babes, such associations were not "free" but controlled, purposive, and artful. There was no mere intrusion of unconscious matter onto his pages; on the contrary, he was lending emotional force to his own potentially vacant abstractions of Nature and "the past.")

Emerson's opening was meant to set the stage for the narrative of the poet's escape from the faded masquerade of the dead. And it was important for him to frame his narrative in such psychologically freighted terms because his plot was going to be quiet and well-mannered, as quiet and well-mannered as his own resignation from the Second Church had been. Indeed, the familial terminology he was using was taken directly from his private definition of his crisis of career. During the month after he provoked his decorous quarrel with the church, he had written into his journal:[17]

---

[17] *Journals and Notebooks*, 4:27. He made an equally direct connection between his own ministerial tasks and the claims of "foregoing generations" during the dark months after Ellen Emerson's death. He had to write a sermon for a fast day, and he had no stomach for it. But he lashed himself to his duty with this formula: "I will respect this Fast as a connecting link by

I have sometimes thought that in order to be a good minister it was necessary to leave the ministry. The profession is antiquated. In an altered age, we worship in the dead forms of our forefathers.

But the latent connection between the story he was setting out to tell and his own restrained life generated a serious writing problem. It was somewhat like the problem Franklin had faced in his autobiography. Franklin's difficulty had been to find ways of making the potentially tedious account of a tradesman's effort to become "good" into a story with some dramatic intensity. Emerson's task was to find ways of making a potentially placid story of spiritual self-discovery seem bold and arduous. In the narrative Emerson was setting the stage for, the poet was going to vault confines that were no higher than his own books, the walls of his room, and his quite ordinary relations with friends and family. But for Emerson, the story was very urgent indeed, both intellectually and personally. So he insinuated sexual struggle and familial strife into its setting, as one way of making the poet's pilgrimage into nature seem valiant and full of portent. When the poet went into nature, he would be doing nothing less than breaking free of a father's dry bones and faded wardrobe, to nourish himself on the floods of life at nature's bosom.

Emerson also wanted to convince his readers that the poet's spiritual adventure had great religious significance—the same kind of significance, in fact, as the birth, death, and resurrection of Christ. So he laid a trail of none-too-subtle markers to establish this second contextual framing for the poet's quest. He spoke of "sepulchres," knowing full well that the most obvious reference was to Christ's entombment. He talked about knowing nature face to face, confident that his readers would recognize the obvious allusion to Paul's letter to the Corinthians. Perhaps fewer readers would see that "dry bones" was an allusion to a verse in Ezekiel that was conventionally interpreted as a promise of Christ's resurrection. And even fewer might pause over a curiously worded exhortation, "Let us interrogate the

---

which the posterity are bound to the fathers; as a trump through which the voice of the fathers speak." *Journals and Notebooks*, 3:246. A good deal of the meaning of his emancipation from the ministry lay in the fact that he was absolved from such dutiful performances. It would take him some time to learn to submit to the other set of conventions that constrained the professional lecturer and writer.

great apparition, that shines so peacefully around us." The phrasing was odd, and only a religiously sophisticated reader could have picked up the connection Emerson was trying to establish between his poet's experience and the life of Christ. "Apparition," he knew, was from the Greek word that also gave "epiphany"—the feast celebrating the twelfth day in the life of Christ, when his divinity was made manifest to all the world, as represented by the Wise Men.[18] Anyone who was alert to this might also have seen that "interrogate" suggested the solemn days of rogation—asking or supplication—preceding the day of Christ's ascension. With his somewhat awkward sentence, Emerson was suggesting a connection between what was going to happen to the poet and Christ's infancy, death and resurrection, and reunion with God in the ascension.

The third context for the tale of the poet was philosophical. Emerson defined Nature—famously—as "all that is separate from us, all which Philosophy distinguishes as the NOT ME." And he made it very clear that what he meant by this was *everything,* including the body, that is outside consciousness. This not only defined Nature in the most inclusive possible terms, it also defined the mind or "Soul" by exclusion, as *nothing*—as a kind of vacancy or potentiality. Emerson was pressing the limits of his own philosophical competence here. But it did not matter, for his purposes were dramatic, not technical. He was laying out a radical position not because he wanted to make a radical point, but because he wanted to give the poet a radical mission. So he placed consciousness, without dimension, on one side of an epistemological line. On the other side was everything else, "both nature and art, all other men and my own body." So the philosophical errand of the poet was as bold as his familial and his religious tasks: He was going to find a way to gain dimension for consciousness, dimension as infinite as Nature's, so that the poet's soul could contain the whole boundless world of the "NOT ME."

After setting the stage so intricately, Emerson began his account of the poet's experience very innocently:

To go into solitude, a man needs to retire as much from his chamber as from society. I am not solitary whilst I read and

---

[18] Later in *Nature,* Emerson used the term "apparition" to mean precisely the manifestation or revelation of divinity: "The noblest ministry of Nature is to stand as the apparition of God."

write, though nobody is with me. But if a man would be alone, let him look at the stars.

But there was an argument implicit in this gentle beginning. The "man" is not just any man, but a man of letters. He is not leaving just any room, either, but a "chamber," a room given over to reading and writing—a minister's study, perhaps. Even the "whilst" that Emerson chose over the more common "while" reinforced the signal that the man is a person of breeding as well as learning, who could manage a period of leisured retirement not only from society but from his scholarly undertakings.

Out of his study, away from his books and papers, Emerson took this "man" through a sequence of three solitary encounters with the NOT ME, preparing for a fourth in which he and Nature become at last one. Each of the three preparatory encounters is given a specific time of day. The first comes during a night, the second on a morning, the third during a twilight. (He may even have meant these separate experiences to suggest the three Rogation Days before the feast of the Ascension.) In each of the three preparatory encounters with Nature, the man—soon identified as "the Poet"—engages the world in all of the three contexts Emerson had laid out in his introduction, until they are gradually merged, each into the others. He becomes as a child, getting clear of the sepulchres of the fathers. He has his moment of epiphany when it becomes manifest to him that the whole world is divine, and he with it. And he wins freedom from his epistemological nonentity when the initial division of the world, into the soul on one side and everything else on the other, is denied; the poet finally realizes (experientially, not argumentatively) the complete identity of his soul with all the world of the NOT ME. Then, with all this preparation, the poet is ready for his fourth and final encounter with Nature, in which he utterly possesses it and is possessed by it.

The poet's first sight of Nature, once he has gained the necessary solitude, is the stars: "Seen in the streets of cities, how great they are!" Neatly, and in the briefest possible compass, Emerson proceeded to invoke each of the three contexts he had established in his introduction. The stars have a religious meaning: They are a "remembrance of the city of God," they are the "preachers of beauty," and they "awaken a certain reverence." Epistemologically, they hint to the poet that the NOT ME, though still "inaccessible," is somehow "kindred." And this incipient kinship triggers the poet's awareness that "all the wisdom of his best hour" is somehow linked to the way the things of Nature had "delighted the simplicity of his childhood."

From the stars seen in the streets of cities, Emerson took his poet to a hillside, from which he could look out over the neat New England countryside on a clear morning:

> The charming landscape which I saw this morning, is indubitably made up of some twenty or thirty farms. Miller owns this field, Locke that, and Manning the woodland beyond.

But the "indubitably" turns out to be ironic. For the poet has come here precisely to cast doubt on the titles of Miller, Locke, and Manning. He has come, it turns out, to expropriate their farms, to transform their land into landscape.

> But none of them owns the landscape. There is a property in the horizon that no man has but he whose eye can integrate all the parts, that is the poet. This is the best part of these men's farms, yet to this their land-deeds give them no title.

The poet is gradually repudiating the kinds of relationships that bind men and women in "society." He has left his own "chamber," where he pursues his learned profession. Now he rejects—spiritually, at least—the economic fact that Emerson knew was the very basis of polity in his social and legal world, the institution of private property. In real life, and in law, the land-deeds of Miller, Locke, and Manning were protected by what the Supreme Court of the United States called the "sanctity" of contract. But the poet has found another kind of holiness in the horizon, a sanctity that has nothing to do with "real" estate. And he has laid an exclusive claim to this "property." But the wording is careful. The poet does not "own" this property; he "has" it. Emerson knew the philosophical principle of identity, that whatever *has* the properties of a thing, is that thing. So the poet is gaining an identity with what he sees. And he is able to do this because in his solitude he can see in a way other men cannot, he can "integrate" the landscape with his eye. As a result of this epistemological sleight-of-eye, the poet also makes more progress in the other two contexts of the narrative, progress both toward his spiritual epiphany and toward his properly childlike capacity to take Nature as his food and drink:

> To speak truly, few adult persons can see nature. . . . The sun illuminates only the eye of the man, but shines into the eye and the heart of the child. The lover of nature is he . . . who has retained the spirit of infancy even into the era of manhood. His intercourse with heaven and earth, becomes part of his daily food. . . . In good health, the air is a cordial of incredible virtue.

The poet is ready for his third preparatory interrogation of Nature. Emerson was now able to fuse all three dimensions of the experience into one encompassing "exhilaration," one that does not require any "thought" or any inventory of the various sorts of "good fortune" involved. There is only a perfect gladness—so perfect, in fact, that the poet is brought to the verge of fear:[19]

> Crossing a bare common, in snow puddles, at twilight, under a clouded sky, without having in my thoughts any occurrence of special good fortune, I have enjoyed a perfect exhilaration. Almost I fear to think how glad I am.

The surprising word order—"Almost I fear" instead of "I almost fear"—might have been intended as a verbal signal of the exhilaration itself. But the introduction of the element of fear into the story pointed immediately toward a new kind of place, a fourth place where the poet's experience would be consummated. The place was "the woods," away from city streets, cultivated landscapes, and village commons. It was a place of dangers—snakes, perhaps—where timid and well-bred men more used to chambers than to wilderness

---

[19] Emerson had worked this passage, like many others, through his journals. In 1834 he wrote—with an astonishing lack of control of emotional tone—that "I do not cross the common without a wild poetic delight notwithstanding the prose of my demeanor." But this must not be taken to mean that he actually had one or more such experiences of wild delight. The journals, like the essays and lectures he took from them, are at least as much about experiences as they *might* be as about what actually happened to him. The journals are, obviously, a writer's journals. And the passages that record the experiences that went deepest—like the one recording Ellen's death, or the entry where he reported that he had opened her coffin months after she was entombed—are usually quite brief, and without flourish. See *Journals and Notebooks,* 4:355. The laconic entry about opening Ellen Tucker Emerson's coffin is at 4:7.

might fear to go. But the poet, encouraged now by three rewarding interrogations of Nature, is ready. In this Edenic setting, he himself will become like a snake, but an innocent one, sloughing his skin the way he has cast off the wardrobe of the sepulchres. He will discover then that the woods are farms of a sort. To him, they will be a place of decorum, a place where he can be a welcome "guest." In the woods, he can recover childhood, God, and epistemological union with the world. And he can soar out of time, out of the confines of "the age" and into the perpetual, the perennial, and the millennial. In the process, he will even discover a solution to the ancient theological problem of the relationship between reason and faith:

> In the woods, too a man casts off his years, as the snake his slough, and at what period soever of life, is always a child. In the woods, is perpetual youth. Within these plantations of God, a decorum and sanctity reign, a perennial festival is dressed, and the guest sees not how he should tire of them in a thousand years. In the woods, we return to reason and faith. There I feel that nothing can befal me in life,—no disgrace, no calamity, (leaving me my eyes,) which nature cannot repair.

In these woods, the poet completes his bold and arduous project. He becomes as completely at one with Nature as Emerson's most careful use of the language could make him. He vanishes into the world, but simultaneously takes the whole world into himself. There is a transaction, in which he loses his private identity and becomes nothing in order to see all. But in the transaction, he gains spiritual liquidity. His head is "bathed." "Currents" flow through him:[20]

> Standing on the bare ground,—my head bathed by the blithe air, and uplifted into infinite space,—all mean egotism vanishes.

[20] Emerson had also anticipated this passage in his journal. In 1835 he wrote, "Standing on the bare ground with my head bathed by the blithe air, and uplifted into the infinite space, I become happy in my universal relations." *Journals and Notebooks,* 5:18. But, again, this does not necessarily mean that he was reporting an actual experience. In fact, this entry's rhetorical awkwardness (with rich words like "bathed," "blithe," and "infinite" trailing off into the meager phrase "happy in my universal relations") is very like the journal entry in which "wild poetic delight" decays into "notwithstanding the prose of my demeanor." (See note 19.) It is always a mistake to reason from the seeming urgency of prose to the urgency of any experience that might have given rise to it. But it may make some sense to think that if an expert writer uses stilted and ill-managed prose, it ought to cast some slight suspicion on any claim that it is a report on an intensely felt personal experience.

I become a transparent eyeball. I am nothing. I see all. The currents of Universal Being circulate through me; I am part and particle of God.

As a result of this, the poet is finally able to cut the last remaining ties that bind him to the world of ordinary men. He has already abandoned whatever learned profession kept him in his chamber, reading and writing. He has relinquished property, and even the idea of property. Now he surrenders what remains of his social identity. Family and friends, acquaintances and servants—all the relationships of town and village life—are quite lost to consciousness.[21]

> The name of the nearest friend sounds then foreign and accidental. To be brothers, to be acquaintances,—master or servant,—is then a trifle and a disturbance. I am the lover of uncontained and immortal beauty. In the wilderness, I find something more dear and connate than in streets or villages.

The figure of the poet that emerged from Emerson's narrative was a radical one. In fact, the three contexts for his radicalism—sexual, religious, and philosophical—set the stage for an assault on the three essential institutions of middle-class culture as Emerson knew it: family, church, and property. The poet in the narrative breaks free of every conventional obligation of family—and with it, other forms of "acquaintance." He subverts churches and ministries by becoming himself part and particle of God. And he sabotages property relations by trivializing ordinary men's contractual claims to their portions of Nature.

This kind of talk might have shocked some of Emerson's readers, but it can hardly have frightened them much. There is a profound

---

[21] What the poet is experiencing here is a kind of dying, the obliteration of ego. And Emerson might well have said that the poet is almost afraid to think how glad it makes him, for in the midst of the personal and vocational rendings that followed Ellen Emerson's death, he had pointedly made his own equation between death and the possibility of infinite vision. He was meditating on suicide—though probably only in verse—and wondered whether it might bring an immeasurable reward:

> *And o perhaps the welcome stroke*
> *That severs forever this fleshly yoke*
> *Shall restore the vision to the soul*
> *In the great Vision of the Whole*

Journals and Notebooks, 3:230–1. Something like this "welcome stroke" comes to *Nature*'s poet, making him dead to the world in order to baptize him in Universal Being.

difference, Emerson said, between the "timber of the woodcutter" and "the tree of the poet." He meant to celebrate the poet's tree, of course. But what he left unsaid was that while the woodcutter might take the poet's tree to market, the poet could not lay hands on the woodcutter's timber—or on any other relation of contract, commodity, or obligation that bound men and women who were *not* poets. Emerson always insisted on a strict "correspondence" between the two orders of reality, material and ideal. But in his account of the poet's experience, the world of "Spirit" and the world of ordinary people are skewed, and the poet's radical insights have no civic implications. Miller, Locke, and Manning can still go about their business, secure on their freeholds; preachers can preach and the faithful can pray in their churches; parents can put their children to bed without dread for the coming day. Emerson had simply doubled the world—not "integrated" it—claiming one order of experience for the poet and leaving the other, "lower" order to ordinary men with their ordinary ways of understanding. Explicitly, his argument was always for unity and wholeness. Implicitly, the poet's errand demanded a complete separation from the world of "other men" and their ways.[22]

In one of the many journal passages he decided to appropriate for *Nature,* Emerson observed that one of the evidences of "discord" between man and Nature was that it is impossible to "admire a prospect" and at the same time "sympathize" with two Concord farmers, "Wyman and Tuttle who are digging in the field." In the book, he used this idea to end his chapter on Spirit, and also to establish a punning meaning for the next chapter's title, "Prospects." The passage became: ". . . for you cannot admire a noble landscape, if laborers are digging in the field hard by. The poet finds something ridiculous in his delight, until he is out of the sight of men." In the process of rewriting the journal passage, Emerson made exactly the kinds of changes that were required by the way he had defined the poet's experience. He decided not to give the diggers names—

[22] Emerson's readers have pondered the question of his "radicalism" for a long time and from a variety of political and philosophical angles. Much of the discussion in the twentieth century has been shaped by the desire of anti-communist liberals to define the "American experience" as potentially radical in itself, as though realizing the sort of "American vision" of a writer like Emerson were an ultimate political project. Certain popular front advocates in the 1930s took a similar view, and argued that the truest "Americanism" and the truest "Communism" were the same thing. They even quoted Emerson, from time to time. The difference may be that the anti-communist liberals have not believed they were making propaganda, while the popular front leaders probably understood that they were doing exactly that.

even fictitious names—or to number them, but made them anonymous figures in a group that could have been of any size. He demoted them to the rank of "laborers," something any sturdy Wyman or Tuttle would have feared and resented. He did not give the poet a choice between two worthy purposes—admiring the prospect or sympathizing with his neighbors. Instead, he made the other men a mere obstacle to the poet's single purpose. He also insisted that the poet's landscape was "noble," making the distinction between the poet and the "laborers" much more telling than Emerson's own differences from Wyman and Tuttle. Finally, he made it plain that the poet's cosmic voyeurism is an activity that has to go on in secret. He cannot have his delight in the presence of other men, cannot really *see* if he is seen. The laborers are a problem precisely because they are digging "hard by" (not because their digging is hard, like Wyman's and Tuttle's, inviting sympathy). From an appropriate distance, they could have been part of a "charming landscape." But if they watch, instead of just being watched, they make the poet's delight seem "ridiculous." Earlier, just after the poet's ecstatic moment of being uplifted into infinite space, Emerson had said that the greatest delight of the woods and fields was "the suggestion of an occult relation between man and vegetable." Now, near the end of his book, he was playing a complicated game on this idea. The root meaning of "occult" is "covered over." But the diggers are uncovering the land, cultivating it—a word with no real connection to "occult," but still homonymic. The diggers' relationship to vegetables is patent and instrumental, and very much at odds with the poet's delight.[23]

There was an interesting undertone of shame and fear in the way Emerson handled the poet's spiritual transformation. In the woods, those "plantations of God," he likened the poet to a snake. This was a metaphorical way of denying the reality of evil, an important part of Emerson's philosophical program. But it also suggested that the poet's enterprise might not be impeccable. The poet came to Nature like a bridegroom. He has put off his faded wardrobe. He is "bathed." He is the "lover of uncontained and immortal beauty." He

---

[23] John Barrell, *The Dark Side of the Landscape: The Rural Poor in English Painting, 1730–1848* (New York, 1980), is brilliant on the sorts of painterly conventions that Emerson may have had in mind as he worked over this passage.

"beholds somewhat as beautiful as his own nature." Similarly, the poet's momentary interruption of his delight, by saying "Almost I fear to think how glad I am," hints at something dark. And Emerson ended his chapter-long narrative by shifting, without any preparation or transition, from joy to grief. Nature, he said,

> always wears the colors of the spirit. To a man laboring under calamity, the heat of his own fire hath sadness in it. Then, there is a kind of contempt of the landscape felt by him who has just lost by death a dear friend. The sky is less grand as it shuts down over less worth in the population.

This mournful conclusion of the poet's pilgrimage was sandwiched between the description of the poet's triumphant discovery that the wilderness was "dear" and the coming chapters—all very cheerful—in which Emerson would methodically count the ways that Nature served man. In these chapters there would be nothing that counted as loss, nothing for which to mourn. Nature, he would argue, serves man incessantly and prodigally. Even the "private poor man" lives in luxury, for he enjoys the fruits of social and economic development—which are all part of Nature. The poor man[24]

> hath cities, ships, canals, bridges, built for him. He goes to the post-office, and the human race run on his errands; to the bookshop, and the human race read and write of all that happens, for him; to the court-house, and nations repair his wrongs. He sets his house upon the road, and the human race go forth every morning, and shovel out the snow, and cut a path for him.

This poor man seems to have money to buy stamps and books, and the leisure to read them. He can pay lawyers. He has a house, and apparently pays the property taxes necessary to support snow removal. But in the synoptic vision of the poet, even the poorest of widows and orphans (and their close relatives, men of genius) benefit from the instructive and disciplining effects of the economic side of the "NOT ME." This kind of moral instruction is the "good office" that[25]

---

[24] *Nature*, 17.
[25] *Nature*, 47–8.

is performed by Property and its filial systems of debt and credit. Debt, grinding debt, whose iron face the widow, the orphan and the sons of genius fear and hate;—debt, which consumes so much time, which so cripples and disheartens a great spirit with cares that seem so base, is a preceptor whose lessons cannot be forgone, and is needed most by those who suffer from it most.

Over the years, Emerson has taken a good deal of criticism for such Panglossian transports, as though he were merely smiling on the ways Property invents to grind the faces of the poor.[26] In fact, he did treat poverty and debt as unhappy and hateful things in themselves. They become beneficial only within the poet's integrating vision of a world that is ruled everywhere and always by a "final cause." Emerson may have been naive, but he was not cruel. And his naiveté was philosophical and rhetorical, not personal or social. The naiveté belonged to the figure of the poet, not to Emerson's own life and practice, where debt had often had a very iron face. In *Nature,* there was a single-minded purpose: to lay out a conception of the poet's career that would be heroic. His poet must be bent on something much grander than a "practical vocation," or a "daily calling." Emerson had chosen to ground his notion of what it meant to "commence author" on the idea that there was a kind of vision that was peculiar to the poet—infinite and whole. And if the poet was to see Nature aright, Nature had to *be* aright, even in those details that caused suffering.

There was nothing very original about this, or very puzzling, taken as mere philosophy. The idea that the whole world must have some final cause and the idea that God's creation must be good in all its parts both were old and worn teleological conceptions. What is interesting is the way Emerson stretched the seams of the poet's cheering assessment to let hints of shame, fear, and grief show through. In the passage that ended the story of the poet's ecstasy in the woods, Emerson suddenly reached into his own experience for the memory of his loss of "a dear friend." But his own private grief

---

[26] Dennis Donoghue, in *Reading America: Essays on American Literature* (New York, 1987), 31, calls the passage on debt an "extreme scandal." Emerson was not being hard-hearted, Donoghue concedes, but only "pedantic." But in his pedantry, he was "offering the poorest people an educational program when what they need at once is bread and money." Kenneth Burke once noted that *Nature's* enemies rated it a "Happiness Pill." "Eye, I, Aye—Emerson's Early Essay 'Nature': Thoughts on the Machinery of Transcendence," in Sealts and Ferguson, eds., *Emerson's "Nature,"* 150.

had been linked very directly to the choice he had made, to "write and be a fine thinker, all by himself." He had experienced in real life what Irving had experienced only in fantasy. He had been moved by grief to make a vocational decision that had led to his becoming a writer. But, like Irving, he had been led along by ambition and calculation, too. It was important to him that this not be obvious. And the best way to accomplish this was to have the figure of the poet seem to be perfectly innocent of any worldly ambition, and even incapable of any worldly action. But the poet's quick lapse into grief came exactly at the point of transition between his private ecstasy and his militantly naive inventory of the way the world "ministers" to every human want. Immediately after the lamentation about "less worth in the population" came a fresh page, headed with the title of the next chapter, "COMMODITY." The joinery between the closing phrase, "less worth in the population," and the subject of commodity was carefully done. His own "loss" had helped make him a writer, and he was now producing his little book for sale.[27]

Nature was not just a meditation, or only a manifesto about artists. Of course it was not *just* a commodity, either. But it was an attempt to legitimate a particular kind of vocational enterprise, the production of such commodities by men whose subject matter was defined much more by terms like his other chapter titles, "Beauty," "Language," and "Spirit," than by considerations of marketability. But this meant, in turn, that the figure of the poet might be suspected of having pecuniary purposes that needed to be kept covert, or translated into carefully controlled hintings at shame or grief. Emerson made a number of strategic choices in *Nature,* choices that were designed to shield the poet from any visible sign of ambition for fame, success, or profit. He took the poet into the woods, far from his house and from "other men." He gave him "currents of Universal Being" for food and drink, as though a poet needed no other. But still he hinted that the poet might be doing something slightly illicit, something he could do

[27] James M. Cox, "R. W. Emerson: The Circles of the Eye," in David Levin, ed., *Emerson: Prophecy, Metamorphosis, and Influence* (New York, 1975), 71–5, suggests that Emerson fed off death, particularly the deaths of Ellen Tucker Emerson and of his brother, Charles, during the time he was finishing *Nature.* Whatever truth there is to this (or meaning, for that matter) may be much more practical and less psychological or spiritual than Cox supposes. For an interesting discussion of Emerson's response to his brother Charles' death, see Packer, *Emerson's Fall,* 48–57. Packer treats the poet's ecstatic "transparent eyeball" experience as Emerson's way of dealing with his grief for his brother by "mastering anxiety through denial and reversal in fantasy." Packer's study of Emerson is often brilliantly insightful. But she does surrender—and at critical junctures—to the temptation to confuse Emerson's construct of the poet with Emerson himself.

only in private, something that made him unexpectedly and unaccountably sad, or something that might make him feel ridiculous in the sight of other men. The poet was simultaneously a figure of boundless ambition and a man of no consequence whatever. On his own terms he was a perfect success, but by common standards, a failure. In the language of the epitaph Franklin wrote for his parents' grave, the poet was without estate, and without gainful employment. He might well be embarrassed, afraid, or sad, unwilling to have other people see him at it, or know what he was thinking.

In his own life, the "practical vocation" Emerson was working very hard at required precisely that many other people see him and know what he was thinking. He did not expect to make much money from *Nature,* although he was pleasantly surprised to find that the first printing of five hundred copies sold out as fast as it did. But he did need the book to help establish a reputation, so that the enterprise he *did* hope would be profitable could gain momentum. He still had to do a lot of preaching to help make up the difference between the income on his inheritance and what he needed. (There were other mouths to feed, too. He had recently remarried, and Lidia Emerson was seven months pregnant when *Nature* was published.) But he was also giving lectures, as many and as often as he could manage. During the winter season following the publication of *Nature,* he gave a series of twelve talks, on "the philosophy of history." He read them in Boston, at the Masonic Temple. But he repeated many of them in surrounding towns like Plymouth and Salem. He wrote his own advertising, hired the hall, paid to have the tickets printed, and arranged to have them sold by a friendly bookseller—all with an eye to maximizing his net profit.[28]

This kind of activity was as public as the poet's ecstasies were secret, and as aggressively entrepreneurial as the poet's career was

---

[28] His average audience in Boston that winter was about 350. They paid two dollars for a ticket to the entire series, and his net profit after all his expenses was $350. This was only about one-fifth as much as the interest he earned on Ellen Emerson's bequest, but it equalled about 10 percent of the price of the house he had bought for himself and his new wife in Concord the year before. It would be two more years until he could afford to give up preaching altogether, and earn enough from writing and speaking to make life comfortable. There is a good discussion of this lecture series in Allen, *Waldo Emerson,* 287–92. On the cost of Emerson's house, see *Letters,* 1:447. For an admirably careful history of the publishing life of *Nature,* see Robert Spiller, Alfred Ferguson, et al., eds., *The Collected Works of Ralph Waldo Emerson,* vols. 1– (Cambridge, Mass., 1971–), 1:6. These superbly edited volumes will be cited here as *Collected Works.*

retiring and unpaid. What Emerson needed to do, in intellectual terms at least, was to devise a way of bringing his figure of the poet back from those woods, across that bare common, through the streets of cities, and into his chamber, so that he could function in public in front of audiences. The poet in *Nature* was a figure of fantasy. But Emerson now got his chance to discipline that fantasy, to speak about his conception of the artistic career in the most formal and demanding setting he could have chosen. In 1837, he was invited by the Phi Beta Kappa Society to give the oration it sponsored every year at Harvard. The customary topic that the speakers labored over was the scholar in America. The occasion framed the questions for him very neatly: Could he give the Harvard audience a revised picture of the life of a man of intellect that would somehow rescue the figure of the poet from the danger of inconsequence, triviality, or ridicule? Could he speak of things the scholar might usefully *do,* giving a version of the scholar's employment that, while it might not be explicitly gainful, would at least be in demand? And could he do all this in a way that preserved the passion and the radicalism of the figure of the poet in *Nature*? But behind such abstract questions lay another that was full of concrete risks. Could he explain his idea of the calling of "the scholar" in a way that made sense out of his own notorious decision to forsake his pulpit for the literary marketplace?[29]

The occasion was of as much moment as the questions. It was the end of August, the season of commencement. There would be a grand, gowned academic procession from University Hall to the First Church. Many older members of the Society would be there, as living evidence that scholarship had a continuous and comfortable

---

[29] On Emerson as a lecturer, see the very valuable work of William Charvat, *Emerson's American Lecture Engagements: A Chronological List* (New York, 1961); C. E. Schorer, "Emerson and the Wisconsin Lyceum,"*American Literature* 24 (1953): 467; and Eleanor M. Tilton, "Emerson's Lecture Schedule—1837–38—Revised," *Harvard Library Bulletin* 21 (October 1973): *passim.* The standard work on the Lyceum is still Carl Bode's *American Lyceum: Town Meeting of the Mind* (Carbondale, Ill., 1968). An extremely useful discussion of the relationship between lecturing and publishing is Donald M. Scott, "Print and the Public Lecture System, 1840–1860," in William Joyce et al., eds., *Print and Society in Early America* (Worcester, Mass., 1983), 278–99. Even more important are the same author's essays, "The Popular Lecture and the Creation of a Public in Mid-Nineteenth Century America," *Journal of American History* 66 (March 1980): 791–809, and "The Profession that Vanished," in Daniel Calhoun, ed., *Professions and Professional Ideologies in America* (Chapel Hill, N.C., 1983). An interesting contemporary comment, by a friend of Emily Dickinson's, is J. G. Holland, "The Popular Lecture," *The Atlantic Monthly* 15 (March 1865): 187. Another friend of Dickinson's—her most important literary friend—described the lecturer as "moving to and fro, a living shuttle, to weave together this new web of national civilization." Thomas Wentworth Higginson, "The American Lecture-System," *Macmillan's Magazine* 18 (May 1868): 49.

institutional home in Cambridge. Most of the faculty would be present. Indeed the two hundred or so gowned students would be joined by men of all ages. The aisles would be filled, and there would even be people standing outside, listening at the windows. And there would be invisible presences, too, as the audience recalled the distinguished speakers who had given the address in other years: the president of Brown University in 1836; the Chief Justice of the Massachusetts Supreme Court the year before that; and behind them an imposing file of men of letters, stretching back for decades. The rhetorical situation invited—even demanded—gravity and decorum.

But everyone in the church—everyone, at least, who was at all versed in the current intellectual atmosphere—knew that something different might happen this year. A new style of speaking and writing was abroad, a style that one impatient member of the audience described as the "misty, dreamy, unintelligible style of Swedenborg, Coleridge, and Carlyle."[30] Most of the audience probably knew that the speaker cultivated that very style. He also was a man whose local fame derived mainly from his repudiation of his own ministerial career—a repudiation, as it happened, of the very career that was still the most likely choice of any member of the class of 1837 who had been inducted into Phi Beta Kappa. There were rumors that the speaker had been complaining to his friends that "genius" in America was much too "tame." Surely he would have something indecorous to say; surely he would disturb the gravity of the day.

Emerson understood perfectly well that the dramatic components of the occasion were contradictory. He would be expected to be exquisitely well-mannered, but also expected to shock with touches of verbal anarchy like "A thought too bold—a dream too wild." He could be as decorous and ceremonial as the moment demanded, and still play the subversive. He could be all gentility and restraint, and at the same time be something of a ranter, with a plea for "savage nature." In this setting of solemn formality, he could say that "out of terrible Druids and Berserkirs, come at least Alfred and Shakspear." In fact, he could deploy an ominous vocabulary—"bold," "wild," "savage," "terrible," and the like—to good effect precisely because

---

[30] This was the language of John Pierce, a minister who was in the audience, impatiently timing Emerson's talk. Pierce said he understood nothing of what Emerson said, and could not tell how many others in the audience shared his "predicament." But he and everyone else had no trouble recognizing the general drift of the speech. Bliss Perry's detailed account of the occasion, in *The Praise of Folly, and Other Papers* (Cambridge, Mass., 1923), 93–4, is still useful, if somewhat sentimental. See also *Collected Works*, 1:49–51.

the occasion was so formal, so ceremonial, so nicely bounded. In a building that strained toward tradition—standing on the same plot of ground where John Winthrop had interrogated Ann Hutchinson two hundred years before—he could speak of a "giant" come to "destroy the old." At a moment whose purpose was to exalt education, he could deplore "systems of education" that have "exhausted their culture." He could do this because he and his audience alike knew that the occasion *was* rhetorical, and that later the speaker and other members of the Society could attend a dinner, where he would listen with care to a formal toast offered in his honor: "Mr. President, I suppose all know where the orator comes from; and I suppose all know what he has said. I give you, *The Spirit of Concord. It makes us all of One Mind.*"[31]

No one was better than Emerson at exploiting just this rhetorical boundary between the decorous and the "savage." In his pulpit, at the lectern, and in his essays, he knew how to measure out heteropathic doses of provocation and reassurance. He knew how to invite audiences and readers to contemplate thoughts too bold and dreams too wild. But he knew equally well how to draw back from such moral verges, to lard his lectures and essays with comforting references to the old, the tired, the familiar. He knew how to deploy an unsettling new figure, like Emanuel Swedenborg, with his "theory of insanity, of beasts, of unclean and fearful things."[32] But he knew, too, how to

[31] Emerson himself recorded this toast, *Journals and Notebooks,* 5:376. The man who gave it was Charles Warren, of Plymouth. Emerson chose to see no irony in Warren's formula, though several possibilities were there. Warren could have meant something like "He makes out that we are all of one mind, when everyone knows perfectly well we are not," or "He pretends to bring concord, when everyone knows that his sort are sowing discord among the churches." Most likely, though, Emerson was right, and Warren was just yielding to the temptation to play a game with the name of Emerson's adopted town.

[32] All quotations in this discussion of the Phi Beta Kappa address are taken from the version printed in *Collected Works,* 1:52–70. One study that is keenly aware that Emerson was a consummate rhetorical strategist is Jonathan Bishop, *Emerson on the Soul* (Cambridge, Mass., 1964). Another, which is also nicely conscious of the historical contexts of those strategies, is Porte's *Representative Man.* An ambitious and impressive effort to place the question of style at the center of Emerson's work is David Porter, *Emerson and Literary Change* (Cambridge, Mass., 1978). Porter argues that what drove Emerson's writing career was a long search for a new "mode," one that was "adventurous" and even "revolutionary." In fact, Porter suggests, Emerson was as self-consciously revolutionary as the Cubist painters were to be in art. As Porter sees it, Emerson was trying to work a fundamental alteration in the way language itself was employed: "He reattached language to process rather than to conclusion." What is not clear is how much of this "reattachment" can be found in Emerson's actual practice as a writer (either of poetry or prose), and how much belongs merely to Emerson's speculations about what a new "form" or "mode" might be like if one could be devised. It is one thing to really do something "revolutionary" as an artist. It is quite another to make a career out of saying that something revolutionary ought to be done.

hedge such gestures about with assurances that the highest culture was still to be sought after in the comforting old names—Chaucer, Shakespeare, Plato, and the rest. Emerson cannily exploited the possibilities latent in the dramatic contradiction offered by the moment. What he managed, in fact, was a performance whose intellectual content was very nearly submerged by its theatrical maneuverings between the decorous and the unsettling.

He began in perfect docility, identifying himself with the occasion, the audience, and its usages. "Mr. President and Gentlemen," he said, "I greet you on the re-commencement of our literary year." But, in the space of less than a minute, he was talking about casting usage to the winds, promising that the American scholar's day of "apprenticeship" and "dependence" was coming to an end. He was even suggesting, a little loosely, an astronomical metaphor for the great change he had come to announce—pointing out that a star in the "constellation Harp" was going to become a new polestar, as though the heavens themselves would declare the newness of the day.[33] But, just as swiftly, he dropped back into a reassuring conformity with tradition and its prescriptions: He tranquilly agreed to "accept the topic which not only usage, but the nature of our association, seem to prescribe to this day."

Throughout the lecture, Emerson repeated this kind of maneuver, moving deftly from safe and predictable ground to language that was meant to jolt and even threaten, but then coming to rest again on the familiar and congenial. For example, when he came to his discussion of the relationship between the scholar and nature—about ten minutes into the lecture—he put himself on a kind of verbal trapeze, swinging between sentences meant to unsettle and sentences meant to calm. He introduced nature in lines that might shock (including a quite daring turn on what it means for men and women to look upon one another). He could even have set them as lines of poetry:

> *Every day, the sun; and after sunset, night and her stars.*
> *Ever the winds blow; ever the grass grows.*
> *Every day, men and women, conversing, beholding and beholden.*

---

[33] As the editors of the superb modern edition of Emerson's works astutely point out, Emerson was mistaken about the next polestar. *Collected Works,* 1:254n. Emerson did not intend it, of course, but his error lends irony to the difficulty he had in defining with any exactness the kinds of activities his scholar ought to engage in to help bring about the new age.

But no sooner did he provoke his audience with this gesture toward the "unintelligible" than he introduced the figure of the scholar, not caught up in the holding and beholding at all, but musing over it, assessing it, and from a very safe distance. "The scholar must needs stand wistful and admiring before this great spectacle. He must settle its value in his own mind." Then, a minute later, Emerson was churning the audience again, offering them a picture of a feminized Nature infinitely turbulent:

Far, too, as her splendors shine, system on system, shooting like rays, upward, downward, without centre, without circumference,—in the mass and in the particle nature hastens . . .

But what Nature was hastening *to* quickly turned out to be quite safe—much safer than the corresponding moment in *Nature*. Instead of a transparent eyeball, Nature now finds only a "mind," cool and assessing. The sentence ended, lamely, " . . . hastens to render account of herself to the mind." If there were no center and no circumference, at least there was bookkeeping. "Classification begins," he went on. And it turned out that what the scholar was to do with Nature—by classifying—was to discover law, not random "shooting . . . upward, downward." So, Emerson made clear, what he had in mind was really only astronomy, chemistry, and the other familiar subjects of the curriculum. But then, as soon as he had given this innocent cast to the relationship between the scholar and Nature, he swung again toward the misty and dreamlike. All science finally leads to the same conclusion, he said: Nature and mind have the same "root." So the true scholar sees that what he shares with Nature is a common fundament, which is nothing less than the "soul of his soul." And—just in case anyone did not see that this was a radical idea—he characterized it himself: "A thought too bold," he insisted, "a dream too wild." To complete the rhetorical circuit, he gently lowered himself and his audience from this carefully framed verbal climax back onto stable ground. Was not their ancient precept "Know thyself"? And was not the current conventional wisdom "Study nature"? Well then, his doctrine of the unity of mind and Nature was nothing more than a recognition that these two unexceptionable precepts were in fact "one maxim." Solid comfort indeed for an audience that lived off precept and maxim, and for whom a

Nature in which men and women beheld and were beholden, or a Nature that shot rays without center or circumference, might seem an uninvited and unwelcome guest at an academic ceremony.

Emerson followed this same strategy throughout the lecture—as he would do throughout his career. Again and again, he shifted into phrases that anyone in the audience might suspect *ought* to be shocking, then shifted back out again, into formulas that were amply sanctioned by tradition and usage. By the time he had come to his conclusion, the audience must have known what to expect. As he had done at the outset, he started with decorum. As though conscious that his hearers might be tiring after more than an hour, he alerted them that the end was near: "Mr. President and Gentlemen," he said—repeating his opening words. But this feint toward "usage" set up a thundering condemnation of American culture. The "spirit" of Americans was "already suspected to be timid, imitative, tame." The very air was made "thick and fat" by greed, both in public and private life. "The mind of this country, taught to aim at low objects, eats upon itself." The scholars were no better than the rest of the people; they were "decent, indolent, complaisant." And for young men of talent and promise, for the "thousands" of potential artists, poets, and scholars who were "crowding to the barriers for the career," the result was "tragic." "There is no work for any but the decorous and the complaisant." So young men of promise can only be "hindered from action by the disgust which the principles on which business is managed inspire, and turn drudges, or die of disgust,—some of them suicides."

The point could hardly have been more emphatic. He hammered away, even repeating "complaisant" and "disgust" within seconds, as though he were at a loss for words. He had gone to a rhetorical limit with this indictment of the business society of his day, of its "avarice" and its disgusting "principles." He had spoken wildly, like a prophet who had been "inflated by the mountain winds, shined upon by all the stars of God." But there was no possibility that he might leave the matter here. He was clearly determined to honor not just his own opinions but the opinions and habits of discourse of his audience as well. So he was bound to end more gently, and in safety, bound to offer a mild cure for the "tragic" social and cultural disease he had just diagnosed. He had no choice but to ask, as he now did, "What is the remedy?" In his answer, he could return his audience to terrain more cultivated than the lexical fens of "avarice," "disgust," and "suicide." And so he did. As a "remedy," he counseled softly, "Patience—, patience." He encouraged the scholar to take comfort in the fact that he was not alone, for he had the company of "the shades of all the good and great"—presumably the ghosts of Plato, Chaucer, Shakespeare, Goethe, and the rest. He also offered "solace" in terms vague enough to calm any fear that he might recommend a real change in the way scholars actually behaved in the world: He told them to be consoled by "the perspective of your own infinite life." The "work" he offered his audience was as vague as the solace. But to this concourse of ministers, would-be ministers, and might-have-been ministers, it was a most familiar idea of work. Their task, Emerson said, was "the study and the communication of principles." And if this labor could make "good instincts prevalent," they might bring about the "conversion of the world."

Now Emerson had only one brief turn left, one more swing from a hint of anarchy to a resolution in tried formulas. He told his audience they were all "units"—that is, discrete individuals—who could not be lumped together and "reckoned" as a class, a party, or a section. No, they were all separate, private men, each of whom could walk on his own feet, work with his own hands, speak his own mind. But, lest this suggest that he was promoting eccentricity and idiosyncrasy, he invoked two formulas that made it perfectly clear that he was not encouraging private excesses: First, he addressed them familiarly as "brothers and friends"; then he said they would go into the world as independent individuals, "please God." With this benediction securely in place, he finished with a vision of the future admirably designed to leave no doubt as to his own suitability, not only for this lecture and for the coming dinner and its toast to concord, but also for a career lecturing to audiences composed overwhelmingly of morally earnest and earnestly moral middle-class men and women. "A nation of men," he said, "will for the first time exist, because each believes himself inspired by the Divine Soul which also inspires all men."

The lecture (and the essay that was published soon after) was a brilliant achievement in rhetorical engineering. Its thrusts toward radicalism of style and manner were carefully hinged to balancing gestures toward the familiar and safe. This strategy seemed to promise that whatever there was about him that was "misty, dreamy, unintelligible," whatever was bold, wild, and savage, whatever it was that had prompted him to quit his pulpit, had already been tamed. On the other hand, this strategy gave a certain energy and tension to his obviously ministerial manners, manners that would, by themselves, have been mere gentility and decorum. In effect, Emerson offered his hearers and readers a choice—either quite satisfactory to him: They could see him as a product of their own world, who had taken on some peculiar but harmless habits of what people were calling "the newness"; or they could see him as a determined apostle of the newness, but one who was able to translate it into terms they could feel at ease with.

The Phi Beta Kappa lecture was one of the most important moments in Emerson's career. It was his most significant public appearance since his resignation. It was his chance to declare that he still had a foot in the Harvard College–Unitarian Church establishment. The impression he meant to leave was of a man who could be critical perhaps, but not really destructive; difficult to follow at times, but not dangerous. But there was a second, related question implicit in the occasion, a question that needed to be addressed not through rhetorical manipulation but through exposition and argument. This was the question of what he called "the career." In just what capacity did he speak? If "young men of the fairest promise" were not to preach, what were they to do? If they were to leave politics and government to clerks, and if they could only be disgusted by business, then what was "the career"? Emerson knew that his resignation, and his recent debut as a writer, posed the question sharply. He was still giving sermons—and would have to continue to do so for two years more. But he had made it clear that he was going to abandon the ministry, to be a "unit," to "speak his own mind." Still, the notion of being an intellectual without any institutional connections or credentials was new to his audience, and it had a number of puzzling implications. He was not like the university presidents, the judges, the professors, and the ministers who had given the Phi Beta Kappa lecture in other years. He was no more and no less than the writer of his essays and the speaker of what he sometimes called his "harangues." But if he was only a figure of speech and writing, what kind of "office," what sorts of "duties," did he claim for himself? And, perhaps most important of all, what sorts of real social and institutional *means* were there through which these duties and offices could be performed? Or did the career of the scholar exist in some sort of social and institutional vacuum?

In the lecture, Emerson approached such questions very gingerly.

He even offered up a decoy subject, opening and closing on a "topic" that he resolutely ignored in the body of his talk. He opened with five minutes about the peculiar position of the scholar in America, and ended with five minutes on the same nominal subject. But between his opening and his closing stretched a full hour without one remark that bore specifically on the American situation. He was self-conscious about it. Three-quarters of the way through, he even apologized for having dwelt too long, "perhaps tediously," on an "abstraction of the scholar," and said he would now return to "the time, and this country." But so saying, he went on to discuss not "this country" at all, but "the time," and meditated some more on Shakespeare; on Goldsmith, Burns, and Cowper; on Goethe, Wordsworth, and Carlyle, and on "the melancholy Pestalozzi." Emerson's point—his decoy point, at least—in his first and last pages was the same: the time of the *American* scholar has at last come. Americans, he said in his opening, "cannot always be fed on the sere remains of foreign harvests"—one of the most frequently quoted passages in the address. At the end—in the other sentence that has probably been most often repeated—he said that American scholars "have listened too long to the courtly muses of Europe." But between these remarks, he said nothing at all about the situation of poets, artists, writers, and other American scholars.[34]

Emerson was not just a man trapped in a subject sanctioned by usage, who really wanted to talk about something else. The idea of the scholar in the abstract, the intellectual for whom time and place were not binding or confining, was crucial to the conception of the writer's career he was trying to formulate. He wanted to present the scholar as a figure of limitless possibility, poised between traditional careers he must now abandon and a future that he could envision only as an "abstraction." Like Emerson himself, this figure of the scholar would be free of background, education, and scholarly profession—free of everything that might define him as a product of "the time, and this country."

Emerson introduced his argument—and it was an argument, with a very definite progression—by dredging up an ancient fable, that

---

[34] O. W. Firkins, nearly three-quarters of a century ago, pointed out that "The American Scholar" had little or nothing to do with scholars in America. *Ralph Waldo Emerson* (Boston, 1915), 160. It is easy to understand Emerson's ruse: He was practically required at least to appear to speak on the American situation. It is probably just as easy to grasp why so many scholars—particularly those who have been institutionally identified with the academic project of "American Studies"—have been so hypnotized by Emerson's obligatory feint.

the gods had made society by dividing up a unitary Man into so many men, as the hand is divided into fingers, to increase productivity and efficiency. But the division of labor had alienated men from themselves. Every man tended to become defined by his tasks, a reified embodiment of his own tools:

> Man is thus metamorphosed into many things. The planter, who is Man sent out into the field to gather food . . . sees his bushel and his cart, and nothing beyond, and sinks into the farmer, instead of Man on the farm. The tradesman scarcely ever gives an ideal worth to his work, but is ridden by the routine of his craft, and the soul is subject to dollars. The priest becomes a form; the attorney a statute-book; the mechanic, a machine; the sailor, a rope of a ship.

The scholar, it followed, is in his "right state" the "delegated intellect. . . . *Man Thinking*." But the scholar was subject to the same kind of alienation and reification that the division of labor inflicted on other men: "In the degenerate state, when the victim of society, he tends to become a mere thinker, or, still worse, the parrot of other men's thinking."

The general idea behind this assessment of the crippling effects of the division of labor was one that would have been familiar to most of Emerson's audience. He was announcing that he was going to take up the epistemological dilemma that had surfaced so emphatically in English writing a half-century earlier—the same dilemma that Franklin had addressed with such skill in his autobiography. The idea that the scholar, no less than any tradesman, was a specialist whose mind was distorted by his profession was an old one. It had been put succinctly by Samuel Johnson in his description of the learned mind as "crippled and contracted by perpetual application to the same set of ideas." Adam Ferguson had neatly ridiculed the man of letters, living "at a distance from the objects of useful knowledge, untouched by the motives that animate an active and vigorous mind," able to "produce only the jargon of a technical language." Emerson was going to work his way toward an idea of the scholar's "right state" as one that enabled the scholar—and no one else, no planter, no tradesman, no priest, no attorney, no mechanic, not even a sailor—to lay an immediate and direct claim to the truth. His scholar would be whole and healthy. He would think and live originally, in intimacy with Nature, truth, and action.[35]

But if the audience was familiar with the epistemological problem Emerson was going to attack, and could even anticipate the general directions he might move in, they must have been curious to know how the matter related concretely to *him,* and to his own recent decisions to quit his pulpit and take up writing and lecturing. Was he going to argue that recovering the "right state" of intellect required every scholar to quit posts, forsake ranks and titles, put off gowns and institutional paraphernalia? And, if he was going to claim that he had somehow healed himself of the crippling effects of the learned professions, what exactly was *he* going to do as *Man Thinking*?

Of course, no one would have expected Emerson to lapse into detailed or explicit autobiography. But he made a point of saying several times in the lecture that true artists speak from experience, and that the best orator always delivers his own "frank confessions." And what he delivered was another implicit figuring of himself, a meditation on his own career choices, and a reckoning of the sorts of things he feared and hoped such choices might lead to.

He began his argument with an obscure promise and an odd warning. The obscure promise was that "the true scholar" is "the only true master." The warning, delivered immediately, was taken from an ancient saying—in Epictetus—that "All things have two handles. Beware of the wrong one." Neither the promise nor the warning made much sense, immediately: The rest of the lecture would be his explanation. All that was clear for the moment was that he was presenting himself, in effect, as his own dramatic speaker, ready to claim some kind of mastery, but still wary of wrong handles.

Next, Emerson made an inventory of the "influences" that create the scholar. He presented it as a list. But it was really a dialectical progression, a sequence. The influences were three: Nature, books, and action. Nature he described in terms altogether good. Nature ministered always to what is best in the scholar, teaching him, leading him toward the exhilarating discovery of his oneness with a world that is not fact but spirit, whose laws are the laws of mind, and so the laws of the scholar's own intellect.

[35] For a discussion of Johnson, Ferguson, and other eighteenth-century writers' fretting over the epistemological problems posed by the increasingly specialized divison of labor and social function, see pages 57–62, and note 37, page 58. I have found John Barrell's conversation and lectures on this matter to be as enlightening as his fine book.

But this time Emerson chose to reverse the narrative progression of *Nature*. There, he had taken the poet from books to Nature. Now he began with the scholar in Nature, then brought him to the second "influence," "the mind of the Past." It is inscribed in art and in institutions, but it influences the scholar most directly through books. In theory, books are "noble." In books, the innocent, ancient "scholar of the first age" had wrought life into truth, action into thought, business into poetry, and "dead fact" into "quick thought." But books—said this bookish speaker to his bookish hearers—can become "noxious," both for ordinary people and for scholars. "The sluggish and perverted mind of the multitude" takes its stand on some book. Men of intellect do worse even. They found colleges, build libraries, form churches, and ordain ministers. He passed his judgment on this tendency in what was probably the most flat-footed sentence he ever spoke: "This is bad; this is worse than it seems."

Emerson had posed his problem. He had done it abstractly, to be sure. Still, he was implicitly proposing himself—his figure of himself, at least—as a man who had known Nature and the infinite mastery it promised. But he had also been beset by books, had even been what he called "the bookworm." The task, for him and for any man who would become *Man Thinking,* was one of synthesis, of finding a way to fasten the innocent wisdom gotten from Nature to the sophisticated learning gotten from books. The synthesis, the final step in the progression from the enspiriting influences of Nature, through books and the afflicting institutions they gave rise to, lay in "Action." This was the "right handle" the scholar must grasp if he were to become a "true master."

Instead of launching immediately into his discussion of action, though, Emerson paused for a transitional moment to make a rude gesture toward ministers, as though to make it clear that they were the most pathetic victims of books and creeds, colleges and libraries. He set the stage for this by saying that it was common wisdom that men of letters were as unfit for real work "as a penknife for an ax." A penknife was still, of course, a knife used to prepare quills for writing, so the image was apt. But the simile also had potentially sexual implications, and Emerson quickly worked them out. He said (as though he were just innocently repeating an ugly but common rumor) that he had "heard" an unpleasant thing about ministers. The rumor was that the clergy are "addressed as women," fit to hear only "mincing and diluted speech." Indeed, he noted, "there are advocates for their celibacy."[36] An alert listener might have remembered that some minutes before, Emerson had characterized the scholar in nature as a "boy." Now he was about to make it clear that the vague notion of *Man Thinking*—whatever else it meant—did imply *manliness,* and a related nest of notions like "ripening," "heroic," "vanquishing," "dominion," and "power." Books, and the kinds of institutions and careers men made on them, were potentially feminizing. Action was the cure:

> Action is with the scholar subordinate, but it is essential. Without it he is not yet man. Without it, thought can never ripen into truth. . . . Inaction is cowardice, but there can be no scholar without the heroic mind. . . . The true scholar grudges every opportunity of action past by, as a loss of power.

Some of the boys and men in the church must have strained forward a little, now, alert to the possibilities for action the speaker would offer. And he went on in a way that seemed to suggest that he had much to say along these lines. The world, he said, lies "wide around," waiting for the ripened and courageous man. The scholar need not stand safely away from it, as the boy from nature, wistful and assessing:

> I run eagerly into this resounding tumult. I grasp the hands of those next me, and take my place in the ring to suffer and to work. . . . I pierce its order; I dissipate its fear. . . . So much only of life as I know by experience, so much of the wilderness have I vanquished and planted, only so far have I extended my being, my dominion.

Here was the solution to the antithesis of books and Nature. Action would enable the scholar to realize the mastery of the world promised by Nature, and not only to read books in safety but also to write them without merely adding to their "mischief." If the man of letters took his place in the ring, grasped the hands of the others there, and

---

[36] Here, as he had done in *Nature,* Emerson was reaching into his own professional past for both notions and language. Just after he had initiated the polite controversy that led to his resignation, he wrote in his journal that the ministerial career was bound up in "an effete superannuated Christianity." *Journals and Notebooks,* 4:27.

heroically conducted life and business, he might become like those scholars of the first age who had been able to transform life into truth, business into poetry.

What Emerson was asking for, clearly, was a suspension of the effects of the "old fable" of the division of labor. He was proposing that scholars might somehow—and *as* scholars—take up the tasks of the "planter" and the "tradesman" he had introduced at the beginning of the lecture: "Years are well spent in country labors; in town—in the insight into trades and manufactures. . . . Colleges and books only copy the language which the field and the work-yard made."

He had come to a critical moment. It was time to say what *kinds* of actions he had in mind. If scholars were to embrace the world, just how were they to do it? For himself, the private and practical answer was that he would exercise his talents not in any traditional learned calling, but in the literary marketplace. His own "action" would be to produce and sell essays and books and lectures, hoping for celebrity and profit. But of course he could not openly propose that as the kind of action appropriate to the scholar. What then? Business or politics? It was true enough, he said, that men "such as they are" seek after money or power. But money and power are not for the scholar, who should leave them to "clerks and desks." Nor did he even so much as hint that the proper field of action for a man of talent and learning might be the active promotion of any of the reform causes that swirled around him, even in his own family. The audience could only wonder what kind of action was left to them.[37]

At this important juncture, Emerson was resolutely evasive. He had proposed action as the solution to the problem faced by the man of letters. But he had no agenda. He had offered a diagnosis of the

---

[37] It says much about Emerson's ideas of "action" that just a few months before this lecture, when his friend Bronson Alcott was forced to close his experimental school because of a public scandal over his unusual methods, Emerson counseled him to forget about actually *having* a school, and instead to try to change the system of education by *writing* about it. *Letters*, 2:75. Harriet Martineau left an apt characterization of Emerson's attitude toward abolitionism in her recollection of a visit to his house during the year before his Phi Beta Kappa lecture: "He did not see that there was any particular thing for him to do in it then: but when, in coaches or steamboats or any where else, he saw people of color ill-used, or heard bad doctrines or sentiment propounded, he did what he could and said what he thought." Martineau, *Autobiography* (London, 1877), 1:375, as quoted to good effect in Allen, *Waldo Emerson*, 253. Emerson had recently quarreled with his famous Aunt Mary Moody Emerson, who was an avid abolitionist and did not understand his passivity on the slavery question. Allen also has a very nice account of their dinner-table fight—a shouting match that led her to swear never to enter his house again. A little while later, she wrote him that she had lost him "in the chaos of modern speculation—I knew not on what ground you did anything—nor where to find your principles—they were an enigma." Ibid., 254.

scholar's problem, telling many of the members of the audience that they had grasped the wrong handle in their professional lives. He had pointed in the general direction of a remedy—that they manfully lay hold of the right handle of action. But he had no particular categories of action to suggest to them, nothing beyond vague references to "country labors" and the "insight of trades." He talked under the heading of action for almost fifteen minutes. But most of what he said was really about observation. The manly and heroic scholar he set running eagerly into the world turned out to be a man who loved to watch, a man bent less on having experience than on learning from it: "Drudgery, calamity, exasperation, want, are instructers in eloquence and wisdom." In the end, Emerson's discussion of action went nowhere in particular. For his audience, he had only the bucolic admonition: "There is virtue yet in the hoe and the spade, for learned as well as for unlearned hands."

This refusal to say anything concrete about the kinds of actions the scholar ought to engage in put Emerson precisely where he wanted to be. He might have to come to the lecture with a set of specific proposals—that scholars try to reform political parties, for example, or write and speak against slavery, or lobby for the rights of the Cherokee, or try to do something about poor men and women's "drudgery, calamity, exasperation, want." But whatever he may have thought about such possibilities in private, he knew that having practical goals would set practical limits to both failure and success. And the conclusion he was driving toward was that for the man of letters who rejects "the mind of the Past," there are no practical limits. When he steps outside the kinds of careers sanctioned by the institutions of culture, the scholar has unlimited possibilities for both defeat and victory.[38]

So Emerson moved toward his conclusion with a ten-minute fan-

---

[38] Frank Lentricchia, in his fine *Ariel and the Police: Michel Foucault, William James, Wallace Stevens* (Madison, Wis., 1988), 116, observes that it is simply not possible to derive a political practice from Emerson, that, in fact, "there can be no Emersonian practice." This may be true, but it runs the risk of overlooking the fact that most of what Emerson has to say about such things as freedom, rights, and property are not really about the civic freedoms, rights, and properties of citizens, but about the spiritual freedoms, rights, and properties of *poets*. Taking the word "practice" to mean political activity, Lentricchia's judgment ought to read: "For the scholar or the poet, as Emerson conceived him, there can be no practice." Cf. the uncharacteristically stressful denunciation of Emerson in B. L. Packer's usually quite contained *Emerson's Fall*, 92–3. Quentin Anderson's *The Imperial Self* (New York, 1971) is very instructive on what might be called the cultural politics of American writing in the nineteenth century, although he too occasionally has difficulty keeping writers and their writing separate.

tasy on the kind of life the true scholar chooses. As with action, his quick summary of the "duties" of the man of intellect was impossibly abstract: The scholar is "to cheer, to raise, and to guide men by showing them facts amidst appearances." He was interested, really, not in "duties" at all, but in where his duties led the scholar. He drew two pictures of the scholar's life, reversed images, both very drastic. To fill his "office," the scholar "must relinquish display and immediate fame." His "preparation" must be long, and because of this he will "betray often an ignorance and shiftlessness in popular arts." Able men will "shoulder him aside."

> Worse yet, he must accept—how often! poverty and solitude. . . . For the ease and pleasure of treading the old road, . . . he takes the cross of making his own, and, of course, the self-accusation, the faint heart, the frequent uncertainty and loss of time, . . . and the state of virtual hostility in which he seems to stand to society, and especially to educated society.

But against this prospect of solitary impoverishment and powerlessness, Emerson had prepared an alternative fantasy of heroic "dominion" over men—a metamorphosis of poor Ichabod into Brom Bones. The scholar should "feel all confidence in himself," for there was a balancing reward that would raise him as high as his trial of "loss and scorn" could bring him low. Emerson knew he was approaching treacherous ground, and he seemed for a moment to hesitate. He warned his audience that what he was about to say "is deeper than can be fathomed,—darker than can be enlightened." To rivet their attention even more closely on what was coming, he almost dared them to agree with him. He fretted that "I might not carry with me the feeling of my audience in stating my own belief." Then he plunged on with an extremely gloomy assessment of mankind:

> Men in history, men in the world of to-day are bugs, spawn, and are called 'the mass' and 'the herd.' In a century, in a millennium, one or two men; that is to say—one or two approximations to the right state of every man.

Now he could reveal what was so deep and dark. The wretched state of mankind turned out to be the ground of the scholar's exaltation. His real calling was to an odd and curiously muscular greatness. The great man—he could be hero or poet, for in the end, the sociology of greatness was the same—was so obviously superior to the bugs and spawn that ordinary people could only delight in him and in his service:

> All the rest behold in the hero or the poet their own green and crude being—ripened; yes, and are content to be less, so *that* may attain to its full stature. What a testimony, what a pity, is borne to the demands of his own nature, by the poor clansman, the poor partisan, who rejoices in the glory of his chief. The poor and the low find some amends . . . for their acquiescence in a political and social inferiority. They are content to be brushed like flies from the path of a great person. . . . They sun themselves in the great man's light. . . . They cast the dignity of man from their downward selves upon the shoulders of a hero, and will perish to add one drop of blood to make that great heart beat, those giant sinews combat and conquer.

This notion of the hero was very much in the air on both sides of the Atlantic, of course. Emerson had plainly appropriated much of it from Carlyle. He had nursed his own hero worship of Napoleon for many years. But for him, the idea of a *poet* with "giant sinews," manly, combative, and conquering, was more than a convention. Nor was the pairing of the pictures of the lives of the scholar—powerlessness without limit transformed into limitless power—an idiosyncratic paranoid fantasy. The heroic vision, and the balancing lament about poverty and loneliness, were the joint outcome of a calculus that this lecture kept just under the surface.

In his opening remarks, Emerson had referred to "the millions that around us are rushing into life." At the end, he spoke of American scholars as the "thousands of young men . . . now crowding to the barriers for the career." The millions were the scholar's potential audience, tired of the remains of foreign reapings, ready and waiting for the appearance of a new, thoroughly American cultural harvest. The thousands were the potential artists, poets, and men of letters who might write and speak to those millions. But only a few of these thousands would make their way past the barriers and gain "the career." And of these, how many could hope to become one of the fantastic and heroic giants he had described? The arithmetic was plain enough. Emerson can hardly have been thinking, as he worked on his lecture, that the quotient of thousands and millions would just about equal the number of copies of the Phi Beta Kappa address that would be printed within six months—500 in September, and 515 the following February. But what made existential sense out of his impassioned exercise on the scholar's pathetic sufferings and heroic conquests was exactly this ratio between the millions and the thousands, between the public and the scholar. In immediate and practical terms, the stakes were not so great for Emerson. He did not really have to fear much in the way of poverty. And his fifteen-cent share of the selling price of each copy of the lecture was hardly enough to justify his lurid talk about a "great heart" and "giant sinews"— though it did bring in about half what he had earned off twelve lectures the preceding winter. But the address, both as an oration and as a published essay, was a step in his effort to prosecute his new career, and there was a definite relationship between its "abstraction of the scholar" and its function as a literary commodity.

Emerson was producing for the market, working without the sanctions of any permanent institutional role. He could plausibly think of himself as "free and brave." But there were limits to freedom and bravery, and his lecture implicitly identified those limits and accepted them. In the end, the kind of heroism he attributed to his figure of the poet-scholar was one that had more to do with "Patience—, patience" than with anything that might be classified as "Action." And this was because he had struck an implicit contract, not only with his Harvard audience but with the social order it exemplified. Despite his daring rhetorical gestures, and all his talk about bravery and "giant sinews," the actual effect of the lecture was to liberate the scholar from "the mind of the Past," then to confine him to language, to the production of poems, essays, books, and lectures—to being a figure of speech. Emerson's scholar and poet would do nothing to challenge any specific feature of existing social and political arrangements like family, church, or property. He would set himself only to converting the whole world in the long run, and not to the more demanding task of persuading particular groups of people to do specific things about concrete features of their social lives, here and now. His scholar would write and speak of "principles," but these would have much more to do with heaven than with earth. And his very long timetable would make him a perfectly acceptable presence in books and magazines and on the lecture circuit.

This implicit bargain was not just an outcome of some set of traits of Emerson's personality—a certain shyness, or a vague preference for a placid domestic life over social activism. Some version of the bargain had to be struck by every man and woman who was interested in coming to terms with the literary marketplace. In fact, the effect of the marketplace on writers was not, in the end, very different from its effect on other people. The new system of mass production for exchange—the production of books or lectures as well as shoes or stoves—tended to make everyone's experience (as Marx put it) "atomic." Any writer assumed an anonymous and tenuous relationship with the public, much more distant and uncertain than the kinds of relationships that traditional systems of patronage had imposed on artists and men of letters. Any lecturer who took the train to some new town, just to speak and then travel on again, faced an audience of strangers, not the "congregation of a hundred hearts" that Emerson had once preached to. It might be exhilarating to substitute the "whole world" for the contractual patronage of the Second Church. It might be satisfying to talk of leaving the government of the world to "clerks," and to dream instead of celebrity and giant sinews. But such choices also required a relinquishment of the hope of any measure of the kind of practical control over affairs that had always been assumed to belong to ministers, officeholders, and other sorts of "able" men who were always threatening to shoulder the scholar aside. And this was so because the logic of the literary marketplace, as Emerson understood it, required the man of intellect to renounce the social and institutional forms of identity, collaboration, and action that enabled some men to think they could actually manage the collective experience. This was the essence of the transaction that Emerson devised for himself and proposed to his readers and listeners in 1836 and 1837. It made sense of his own recent past, of his passage out of the calling of his ancestors and into his new career. It did even more. It declared an effective truce to the state of "virtual hostility" that, he had complained, too often existed between the scholar and society.

It worked. Emerson's career during the quarter of a century that followed his Phi Beta Kappa address was triumphantly successful. He became famous, even popular. He lectured everywhere and often, not just in Boston and nearby towns, but up and down the seaboard and even in rough places like Wisconsin. At his peak, he was giving as many as eighteen lectures a month, and earning as much as $1,200 a year from the performances. Out of this flood of lectures came a tide of essays. From the essays he made book after book. And they sold well. By 1860, the first printings of his books were running around 6,000—four times the size of the first printing of *Nature.* He acquired more property, and it was not the mysterious property in the horizon that the poet "has," but land in which men might dig, including some acres beside what he called Walden Water, where Henry David Thoreau could hoe beans for a couple of seasons. With the fame and the money that accompanied it also came memberships and titles, in everything from the local fire company and committee to create a cemetery to the American Association for the Advancement of Science. He joined a club in Concord, the Social Circle. He founded another, the Town and Country, in Boston, that had over a hundred members, all men of prominence. And when it was succeeded by the Saturday Club, he was a charter member. The man who had fretted about the noxious influence of the mind of the Past, especially as it was manifested in colleges, became a member of the Board of Overseers of Harvard, and was appointed to a second term.[39]

The success and fame, and the increasingly elaborate web of family, property, and membership, were things that Emerson wore lightly and with grace in his private life. But there was a nagging problem that came to light from time to time in his essays. The figure of the poet-scholar he had projected was at odds with the facts of his own life, which tended toward the complacent and the tame. He could hardly think he had converted the whole world. But he seemed to have fully mastered any "disgust" he may ever have felt at the "principles on which business is managed." Of course he could not allow that he had simply "turned drudge" in the service of the social and economic order.[40] So he fretted, during the 1840s and

---

[39] On the Town and Country and Emerson's other clubs, see Allen, *Waldo Emerson,* 524–5. Unlike his figure of the poet, Emerson was an extremely "club-able" man, as were most of his fellow Unitarian transcendentalists.

[40] There were times, especially in the 1840s, when he did seem to be a "drudge" for the system, only an apologist for capital, for expansion and economic development, and for blustering patriotism. In a lecture to a large audience, composed mostly of young merchants and manufacturers, he said, "I call upon you, young men, to obey your heart, and be the nobility of this land." He celebrated the rise of "Trade." And after fretting a little over the exploitation of immigrant labor, he said that in the end "their plight is not so grievous as it seems. . . . Perhaps they may thank these dull shovels for safe vents for peccant humors; and

1850s, very tentatively and incompletely, over the relationship between the poet and society, casting about for ways of making his
poet a fluent and effective member of a healthy society. But the task
was not an easy one, and in practice he chose to leave his initial
version of the poet more or less intact. He was more than ready to
declare, with the passing of time and the success of his own career,
that

> 'Tis worse, and tragic that no man is fit for society who has fine
> traits. . . . But there is no remedy that can reach the heart of the
> disease but either self-reliance . . . or else a religion of love. . . .
> This banishment to the rocks and echoes no metaphysics can
> make right or tolerable. . . . A man must be clothed with
> society.

But the remedies for the poet's isolation that he could call to mind
during the decades after *Nature* were not remedies at all. Self-reliance
was only another justification for privacy. And the idea of a "religion
of love" was only a utopian abstraction. The only language of community Emerson had ever mastered was the language of the pulpit,
the language of that 1827 sermon in which he had spoken of the
congregation as the cure for "savage solitude." When he quit the
ministry for the market, he surrendered that language in order to
produce a figure of the poet that was consistent with his being an
independent producer of works of art, a man with no congregation.
What he needed now, if he were to succeed in revising his picture of
the man of letters, was a new idea of what society amounted to. The
problem was not experiential and practical, for Emerson was perfectly at ease with his life and career. It was a conceptual problem and
required a conceptual solution. Ironically, the occasion for the solution was eventually to be found in the most practical thing he could
have imagined: war.

The Civil War brought a kind of climax to Emerson's success and
fame. He rushed into the fray as quickly as he could, with the only

---

this grim day's work of fifteen or sixteen hours, though deplored by all the humanity of the
neighborhood, is a better police than the sheriff and his deputies." The lecture was sponsored
by the Boston Mercantile Library Association. It is reprinted as "The Young American," in
Collected Works, 1:222–44.

means at his disposal, speech. When he heard about the attack on Fort Sumter, he was in the midst of giving one of his many series of lectures in Boston, this time on "Life and Literature." The scheduled topic for April 23, 1861, was an exercise on something called "The Doctrine of Leasts." But the news from Charleston Harbor was compelling. He quickly finished a new talk, which he called "Civilization at a Pinch." In it, he explored the meaning of the war, giving it some of the cosmic moral significance he had attributed to Nature in 1836, making it "mightier than logic, wide as light, strong as gravity." He decided—with suspicious speed—that the war had transformed the whole society, "magnetizing all discordant masses under its terrific unity." A few days after Sumter, just as the first recruits were being raised in Concord to march off to the murderous humiliation of Bull Run, he decided that "now we have a country again." The war had become the basis for a new kind of community, binding a whole people into a cohesive spiritual body prepared to act "under the best heads":[41]

> War civilizes, for it forces individuals and tribes to combine, and act with larger views, and under the best heads, and keeps the population together, producing the effect of cities; for camps are wandering cities.

This hasty enthusiasm for the war was not the result of the "impact" of a historic event on Emerson. He was not just responding or reacting. Nor was he merely being blown about by what he described as the "whirlwind of patriotism." He was seizing on the war, not as fact but as meaning, appropriating it to his purposes as an artist. What the Civil War offered him was, finally, a context in which he could subject to a new kind of scrutiny the figure of the man of letters that he had created at the beginning of his career as a writer. In the 1830s, his solution to the "state of hostility" between the poet and society had been to restrict the man of letters' role to language, to writing and lecturing on matters of "principle." In effect, he had made the poet-scholar the harmless custodian of high principles in a society that "aimed at low objects." Now, as Abraham Lincoln called for volunteers, Emerson could suddenly con-

---

[41] Cabot, *Memoir*, 2:600. The remark on the civilizing influence of war is quoted by Edward Emerson, *Works*, 7:356.

clude that society itself had finally become principled. And this solved the problem of "action" in a way that had not been workable twenty-four years earlier. Now there was no need to resort to "the hoe and the spade" as an example of action. The highest duty of poets and ordinary men had, at a stroke, become the same: the salvation of the Union, a work made into a spiritual crusade by the anticipation that if the Union prevailed slavery would end. This purpose was as "noble" as any landscape could ever have been. In such a context, the woodcutter's and the poet's tree could finally become one. Even poems could become moral timbers of the engines of battle. If laborers laid down their "dull shovels" and took up arms, then poets could find their "delight" even in public meetings, without feeling at all ridiculous:[42]

> It is the day of the populace; they are wiser than their teachers. . . . Go into the swarming town-halls, and let yourself be played upon by the stormy winds that blow there. The interlocutions from quiet-looking citizens are of an energy of which I had no knowledge.

The very speed with which Emerson discovered "energy" in a swarming Concord town meeting, and in the same quiet-looking citizens among whom he had lived for twenty-five years, was a measure of the degree to which he—and many other intellectuals, too—needed something like the war to help them create a workable vision of a society in which the life of a man of letters did not lead toward either irrelevant solitude or mere success and fame.[43] He had been ready for many years to abandon his own careful creation, the picture of the poet-scholar as a man at odds with the world of ordinary men. But he had not been able to write or speak about society in ways that made it a fit setting for the poet. For years he had been groping for usable synonyms for the term "society," but he had customarily ended with trivializing words, like "conversation," or "soiree," or "cordials." Once, as an example of the isolation of the man of genius, he had been reduced to talking about Dante's refusal of dinner invi-

[42] Cabot, Memoir, 1:600. Emerson could become quite blustery about the prospect of battle, at least before the casualty lists began to come in. On a visit to the Navy Yard at Charlestown, he apparently exclaimed that "Sometimes gunpowder smells good." Ibid., 601.
[43] In The Conduct of Life, published the year before, he had said, "Leave all this hypocritical prating about the masses. . . . I do not wish any mass at all, but honest men only." Works, 6:241.

tations. Now, with the war, he could speak or write about society in ways that made it as sublime and terrific, as full of electrifying wind and storm, as replete with wisdom, as Nature had been in the 1830s.

So Emerson was able to use the war to clarify a version of the mission of the man of letters that would finally make concrete sense out of the vocabulary of "manliness" and "courage" that he had struggled so hard with in 1836 and 1837. The idea of rushing eagerly into social experience and grasping the hands of the others in the "ring" to work and to suffer need not sound hollow to a man who was soon invited to lecture at the Smithsonian, and could hope that the most powerful leaders of the government might be in the audience to hear him plead for the emancipation of the slaves. And when he did go to Washington to give the lecture, he was taken twice in two days to see Lincoln. He was escorted everywhere by his senator, Charles Sumner. He spent hours with Secretary of State William H. Seward, discussing the intricate connection between emancipation and relations with Britain. He was invited to call on the secretary of war.

Some months later, when Lincoln did at last issue the Emancipation Proclamation, Emerson was ready to publicize it at an abolitionist rally as a grand "poetic" act, of a sort that history produced only once in a hundred years. He produced a hymn for the Jubilee rally in Boston on New Year's Day of 1863, to mark the effective date of the Proclamation. At the end of his hymn, he proposed that the old idea of "compensation" for the slaveowners (an idea he had supported for years) be inverted. Who owned the slaves? he asked. The slaves themselves. So[44]

> *Pay ransom to the owner*
> *And fill the bag to the brim.*
> *Who is the owner? The slave is the owner,*
> *And ever was. Pay him.*

He may have been surprised, and must have been gratified, when the crowd, which included a number of blacks, came to its feet and began to shout and sing. He was also led by his enthusiasm to think of soldierly "duty" as the thing that brought men closest to God and to grandeur. He responded to one report of battle deaths with some

---

[44] The hymn is in *Works*, 9:203–4. A nice brief account of the occasion is in Allen, *Waldo Emerson*, 618. The poem on Duty is in *Works*, 9:207.

lines that quickly became part of the Northern repertoire of war slogans—though the words would have fitted Confederate needs just as well:

> *So nigh is grandeur to our dust,*
> *So near is God to man,*
> *When Duty whispers low,* Thou must,
> *The youth replies,* I can.

   It was all heady stuff, and provided a very troubling context for his realization, soon after he returned from Washington to Concord, that Henry Thoreau was surely dying. More than anyone else, Thoreau had seemed ready to try to *be* Emerson's figure of the poet. He had defined his life around his disgust at public and private avarice. He had accepted the "virtual hostility" between the scholar and society. He had gone into solitude, taken up country labors, planted himself indomitably on his own instincts and waited for the huge world to come round to him. Emerson insisted that there be a formal church funeral, with singing and readings from Thoreau's own work. He also delivered a eulogy before the body was taken out to the cemetery at "Sleepy Hollow."

   Emerson's affectionate regard for Thoreau was no doubt deep and real, and it showed through almost every paragraph of his remarks in the church. And his discomfort with some of Thoreau's personal quirks also found its way into what he said. But his talk on Thoreau, and the essay he made of it, were much more than an episode in a long and sometimes tangled friendship. The occasion was as heavy with emotion and memory as the Phi Beta Kappa lecture had been weighty with ceremony and tradition. And Emerson explored its possibilities fully, producing the first piece of writing in many years that was as artful and passionate as *Nature* or "The American Scholar." He made the eulogy—and the lecture he adapted from it for a Boston audience, and the version of it he soon published—into a vehicle for doing something more than praising or burying his disciple, friend, and colleague. He engaged in a subtle evaluation of Thoreau's life that amounted to an unsparing reevaluation of the conception of the scholar-poet spelled out in 1836 and 1837.[45]

---

[45] The essay that came out of Emerson's eulogy is in *Works*, 10:449-85. Except where noted, all quotations in the next few pages are from it.

Emerson understood very well that the task of the memorialist is to transform any faults he might find in his subject into endearing foibles, and to make the ordinary good points of the deceased into imposing virtues, until talent has been transformed into genius, or mere stubbornness into courage. He did his duty. He made the requisite little jokes about Thoreau's tendency to be pigheaded and unforgiving. He even referred to him once, with affection, as "that terrible Thoreau!"—no doubt pausing for a moment while some members of the audience smiled wistfully, perhaps able now to forget how they had once winced at some sharp remark Thoreau had made to them. On the other side of the account, Emerson had more than enough good things to say about Thoreau. He called him a "genius" and "noble." He said that Thoreau had "an excellent wisdom." He made him into a figure of almost impossible fortitude, consistency, and patience. "It was," he said, "a pleasure and a privilege to walk with him." He even painted him in the patriotic colors that were everywhere so visible in 1862: "No truer American existed than Thoreau." The nation did not know yet how "great a son it has lost." Emerson did not even neglect to praise Thoreau's physique, his "wonderful fitness of body and mind." He even found the beard that Thoreau—like Lincoln—had recently grown "becoming."

But Emerson's real subject was the way Thoreau had fitted his life to the kinds of specifications set down in *Nature* and the Phi Beta Kappa address. The "cardinal fact" about Thoreau was that he belonged to "a rare class of men" who knew the "material world as means and symbol. This discovery, which sometimes yields to poets a certain casual and interrupted light, serving for the ornament of their writing, was in him an unsleeping insight." Like the poet-figure of *Nature,* Thoreau had had to relinquish many things. Emerson hammered at the point insistently:[46]

Few lives contain so many renunciations. He was bred to no profession; he never married; he lived alone; he never went to church; he never voted; he refused to pay a tax to the State; he

---

[46] The sentence beginning "He chose . . ." was probably added to the text for publication. It is in a journal entry made during June 1862, a month or more after the funeral. There Emerson continued the sentence in a way that emphasized Thoreau's chastity, writing ". . . bachelor of thought and Nature that he was—how near to the old monks in their ascetic religion!" But he dropped the comparison to "old monks" in the version he published. Edward Waldo Emerson and Waldo Emerson Forbes, eds., *The Journals of Ralph Waldo Emerson,* 10 vols. (Boston, 1910–14), 9:425.

ate no flesh, he drank no wine, he never knew the use of tobacco; and, though a naturalist, he used neither trap nor gun. He chose, wisely no doubt for himself, to be the bachelor of thought and Nature.

This listing of Thoreau's denials and refusals came near the beginning of Emerson's essay, and he meant it to serve as a kind of general framing for his sketch of Thoreau's character. The list ended with a phrase meant to be both striking and summary: Thoreau was "the bachelor of thought and Nature." But the phrase was accompanied by a reservation—"wisely no doubt for himself"—that broke the rhythm of the sentence, and gave a clear signal that Emerson had important second thoughts about all those "renunciations." The "no doubt" was ironic (in the same way that his "indubitably" had been in that sentence in *Nature* about the way the Concord landscape consisted of twenty or thirty farms). In fact, the signal had already been studiously anticipated in Emerson's opening words, a seemingly limp observation that "Henry David Thoreau was the last male descendant of a French ancestor. . . ."[47] He went on to say that Thoreau also had "a very strong Saxon genius." This beginning tapped into current popular conventions about national and ethnic "character" and promised that Emerson was going to explore oppositions in the personality of Thoreau.[48] But the words "last male" were unnecessary in this context. The point about Thoreau's mixed ancestry stood perfectly well without the phrase. But "last male" did aim directly at Emerson's characterization of Thoreau as "the bachelor" of thought and nature. Being that meant being a terminal man, a man of no genealogical consequence. Emerson was going to end the essay with the observation that Thoreau's death left his "broken task" unfinished, and that it was a task "which none else can finish."

[47] He may even have meant, by beginning on this genealogical note, to remind the members of the audience who knew it that Thoreau had been christened David Henry, and had changed his name because he thought Henry David sounded better. There is no way to know whether Emerson put the stress on the first syllable of "Thoreau," a practice Thoreau preferred because he thought it would make people think of the Norse god. In the matter of self-consciousness about words and names, there was nothing to choose between the two men.

[48] Actually, Emerson dropped the Norman-Saxon idea as soon as he had finished his first paragraph, and never returned to it. This makes it clear that the opening device of ethnicity was only a verbal prop for the telling phrase "last male." David Simpson, *The Politics of American English, 1776–1850* (New York, 1986), is a most interesting study, with a superb treatment of the way the stereotypes "Norman"and "Saxon" were invested with heavy ideological import during the first half of the nineteenth century.

Between the opening words about the "last male descendant" and the closing words about the "broken task" would come a great deal of praise. But it was clear that Emerson had the most serious doubts about the kind of life that had been made out of so much renunciation, so sleepless an insight into Nature.

He let the doubts come to the surface cautiously, and with more real artistry than he had exhibited in a long time. He told stories about Thoreau—to an audience that probably knew most of them already. But the stories he gave the most time to were those that made Thoreau seem merely eccentric—though they were explicitly intended to endear him to listeners or readers. One of the two anecdotes Emerson chose to spin out to the greatest length was the tale of Thoreau's experiment at making a pencil. Emerson took pains to point out that in this undertaking Thoreau was following his father's trade. But, he recalled, once Thoreau had been assured that there was no better pencil manufactured anywhere, he refused ever to make another, with the remark that "I would not do again what I have done once." The second longish anecdote was the story of a quarrel Thoreau had had with Harvard over the circulation policies of the college's library. The rule was that only a graduate who lived within ten miles could borrow books. Thoreau had managed to convince the president of the university that Henry Thoreau, not the librarian, was the "proper custodian" of the books. He won the argument, but Emerson pointedly observed that what Thoreau had won was not a change in the rules, but a personal "privilege, which in his hands proved unlimited thereafter."[49]

Emerson used a lot of sentences in the telling of these two stories. By comparison, he paid the briefest possible attention to the two other exploits that were at least as interesting as the stories of pencil and library books, and had yielded much richer public results: the stay at Walden Pond (which had given *Walden,* by far Thoreau's most ambitious work), and Thoreau's refusal to pay a tax that he

---

[49] Thoreau was certainly an eccentric man. But so were most of the writers who were his contemporaries. The important point for the historian—as distinct from the biographer or the gossip—is that Thoreau's formulations about solitude and society, failure and success, were just that, formulations, not mere eruptions of "personality" onto the pages of his journal or into his books and poems. He lived in history, not just (as he liked to say) in Concord, and he arrived at his formulations—just as Emerson had—as part of his own careful attempt to come to a usable (that is to say, write-able) understanding of what it meant to be an intellectual in the new setting of the marketplace. The"I" of Thoreau's journals, much less the "I" of a book like *Walden,* must not be confused with a historically real Thoreau—even if Thoreau himself sometimes got mixed up on the differences.

thought would support the Mexican War (which had led to his most significant piece of political writing, the essay on "Civil Disobedience"). It would have been unthinkable for Emerson to have omitted these two episodes entirely, but he came as close as he dared. He gave them very brief treatment, and he did not mention the writing that resulted from either. In fact, anyone who read the published version of the eulogy would not have been able to tell that Thoreau had ever published anything, or even written anything more than a journal and a few poems, or had ideas much more systematic than the sayings typified by the page of curious aphorisms that Emerson chose to "subjoin" as examples of "literary excellence": "Some circumstantial evidence is very strong, as when you find a trout in the milk." Or, "The bluebird carries the sky on his back." Or, "Fire is the most tolerable third party."

From evidence like this, a reader might have inferred that despite all his fine words about "genius" and "nobility," Emerson really was dismissing Thoreau as an eccentric failure, a man whose final destiny was to be the last of his line, and to leave only a "broken task" behind him. But Emerson did not depend on readers' inferences. Toward the end, he openly chastised Thoreau, in as tough an assessment of his life and labors as any critic has ever made:

> Had his genius[50] been only contemplative, he had been fitted to his life, but with his energy and practical ability he seemed born for great enterprise and for command; and I so much regret the loss of his rare powers of action, that I cannot help counting it a fault in him that he had no ambition. Wanting this, instead of engineering for all America, he was the captain of a huckleberry party. Pounding beans is good to the end of pounding empires one of these days; but if, at the end of years, it is still only beans!

Emerson's careful diction pointed back to two other remarks he had carefully planted earlier in his essay. Both were meant to be praiseful: that Thoreau was the truest "American," and that he was

---

[50] Emerson used "genius" in both its contemporary senses in the essay, meaning sometimes "character" or personality traits, as in "Saxon genius," and sometimes great intellectual ability, as in "I know not any genius who so swiftly inferred. . . ." His use of the word in this crucial paragraph is thus ambiguous, and perhaps purposefully so. He could intend one or the other meanings, or both at once, as a way of finding fault simultaneously with Thoreau's character *and* his mind.

"somewhat military in his stature." He knew, and knew his audience would know, that the most likely institution where a professional engineer could receive formal training was still the United States Military Academy. (As a kind of commendation for his new sense of the scholar's public duties and responsibilities, Emerson was going to be appointed to the Board of Visitors of the Academy the next year.) So now when he said that Thoreau had been born for "command," when he lamented the fact that he had not taken up "engineering for all America," when he referred to him derisively as the "captain of a huckle-berry party," when he spoke of "pounding empires," he was making an implicit but very definite reference to the war. He was saying that the life of the scholar-poet as Thoreau had lived it was socially irresponsible, and, exactly for that reason, a failure. Leaving the final sentence of the paragraph unfinished gave it great force—made it, for any reader, the climactic point of the essay, as though the consequent of that dangling antecedent were simply too awful or too pathetic to put into words.

It is beside the point to wonder whether Emerson was being cruel, and even more beside the point to try to decide if he was being fair.[51] The intellectual issue for him was not really Thoreau at all. In his journal, Emerson generalized his judgment about "command," saying that "I see many generals without a command, besides Henry." But, like most of his best writing, this piece was about himself—or about the kind of projective figure of himself that had been the subject of *Nature* and the Phi Beta Kappa address. If his words were angry, the anger was not for Thoreau, alive or dead. It was for the conceptual bargain Emerson himself had made in 1836–37. That bargain had served him well enough over the years, to be sure. But

---

[51] Scholars and critics have for a long time haggled over the relative merits of Emerson and Thoreau, sometimes descending to the kind of village gossip about them that might have gone on in Concord at the middle of the nineteenth century. The gossip goes a long way back. One early example was Henry James' 1887 judgment that Thoreau was only one of those "Concord-haunting figures which are not so much interesting in themselves as interesting because for a season Emerson thought them so." *Essays on Literature: American Writers, English Writers* (New York, 1984), 264. The most important modern contribution to this particular discussion is Perry Miller's essay in *Consciousness in Concord: The Text of Thoreau's Hitherto Lost Journal, 1840–1841* (Boston, 1958). Miller presents Thoreau as a man driven by extreme egotism and conceit to seek a failure decisive enough to satisfy his inflated vanity. What this misses, of course, is that the equation linking artistic "egotism" and the imaginary possibilities of failure was not something Thoreau patented, but was almost a commonplace among the writers of the period. For a keen but labored attempt to prove that Thoreau's was a different and better mind than Emerson's, see Sharon Cameron, *Writing Nature: Henry Thoreau's Journal* (New York, 1985).

it had been costly in exactly the terms he now chose to unleash on Thoreau. It had cost the figure of the man of letters any "ambition" for real "enterprise" or for "command," not to speak of any opportunity to "pound empires." Now it was too late to remedy the situation in ways that would make any practical difference for experience.

But there was time enough to revise the figure of the poet as a work of art. He needed only to grasp the war as an occasion that history had been generous enough to provide, and to make it into a metaphorical context for the idea of commanding participation by the poet-scholar in the making of history through action. He took up the war as a cause with such energy and urgency because it provided him at last with a functional alternative for both the idea of Nature and the reality of the marketplace. He used it to transform the "populace" from a distant, anonymous, and discordant public of "other men" into a source of electrifying wisdom and energy. What had been an audience now seemed a militant constituency, and one that the artist could both serve and lead, a noble instrument for the pounding of empires. The oddly warlike language of his 1837 discussion of the scholar and "Action" at last made some kind of sense—if only temporarily. And for Emerson that was enough. For when he finished the essay on Thoreau, he had finished his last fine work of art. He continued to be a man of enormous charm, and even managed the genuinely heroic personal task of living with a serious aphasia with extraordinary good humor—for a figure of speech like Emerson, a terrible irony, for one of the main symptoms of his disease was an inability to remember quite ordinary words. He would continue for many more years to lecture and to write. But for the rest of his life, it would be only beans he would pound. And why not? He had already produced some of the most interesting meditations on the relationship between the artist and the marketplace that any American of his century was able to make. And for the purpose of his art, it did not matter that the imaginary uses he made of the Civil War were as vague and strained as the imaginary uses he had earlier found for Universal Being.

Emily Dickinson, a daguerreotype of 1847 or 1848

V

———

EMILY DICKINSON

Only one picture that is surely of Emily Dickinson has survived, a daguerreotype made when she was a seventeen-year-old student at the Mount Holyoke Female Seminary. It has become a famous photograph; but it is only a conventional school picture, with the standardized costume and props school pictures usually have. The protocols of the sitting were laid down by the photographer, who was no doubt experienced in such matters. The dress is dark and formal. The obligatory bouquet is in the hands, and the compulsory book is on the table. Any hint of adolescent gawkiness or disorder is kept carefully in check. The hair is neatly parted in the center and held tightly to the scalp. Long arms are immobilized. One rests—but does not lean—on the table; the other is placed on the lap. Young hands that might flutter, or just dangle, are composed into a neat, ninety-degree angle, bisected precisely by the bouquet. And this careful angle is exactly plumb below the right shoulder.

The picture declares only what such portraits are meant to declare: Here is a girl from a good family, a well-brought-up ingenue. She is acquainted with books but closer to flowers. She is earnest, perhaps, but without passion. She is intelligent enough, probably; but she is more certainly decorous. The face does nothing to cast doubt on

these declarations. The expression is vacant, opaque, and imper-
sonal. The eyes are not quite focused. They might conceal a great
deal, or nothing.[1]

Fifteen years after she sat for this school picture, Emily Dickinson
was writing poems about desperation, exaltation, and pain. She was
finishing them (or at least making fair copies) at the rate of one a day,
and some of them were among the best—perhaps *the* best—poetry
written in the United States during the nineteenth century. In April
of 1862, exactly at the peak of this remarkable effort, she opened a
now-famous correspondence with Thomas Wentworth Higginson.
He was an author of considerable reputation and a man with important literary connections, and he had just published a "Letter to a
Young Contributor" in *The Atlantic Monthly,* an essay of advice and
encouragement to would-be professional writers.[2]

Dickinson responded with a letter asking Higginson for an editorial judgment of her work. She sent him several poems, apparently in the hope that he would help her launch what he had called
a "literary career." He responded with criticism, but not rejection,
and he asked her a set of questions about her life. When she gave
him impossibly gnomic replies, he asked for a picture—perhaps
hoping that a picture might not be so evasive. But Emily Dickinson was not to be cornered. She told him she had no picture, and
offered instead her most detailed description of herself, in a sentence that eventually became even better known than the schoolgirl
daguerreotype.

In this verbal self-portrait, her expressions were as wily as the
expression in the picture had been ingenuous:

[1] Dickinson's principal biographer, Richard B. Sewall, in collaboration with Martin Wand, has
used this slightly out-of-focus daguerreotype (among other things) as evidence that the eye
problem that pestered Emily Dickinson in early middle age was exotropia, popularly known
as "walleye." Sewall and Wand, "Eyes Be Blind, Heart Be Still: A New Perspective on Emily
Dickinson's Eye Problem," *New England Quarterly* 52 (1979): 400–6. There is much to be
suspicious about in this little essay, but Sewall is Dickinson's most exhaustive student. His *The
Life of Emily Dickinson,* 2 vols. (New York, 1974), will for many years be the starting point for
anyone interested in her and her poetry.

Cynthia Griffin Wolff, relying somewhat on this diagnosis, has gone further, to argue that
Emily Dickinson was "deprived" of easy and effective eye "contact" with other people. In
Wolff's view of things, this physical disability reinforced the mental and spiritual deprivations
in Dickinson's life; these deprivations, in turn, were the motive and ground of her art, which
was her "comfort." Cynthia Griffin Wolff, *Emily Dickinson* (New York, 1986), 164–5, 581n.
For another point of view, see John Cody, "Watchers upon the East: The Ocular Complaints
of Emily Dickinson," *Psychiatric Quarterly* 17 (1968): 548–76.

[2] *The Atlantic Monthly* 9 (1862): 401–11.

> I had no portrait, now, but am small, like the Wren, and my Hair
> is bold, like the Chestnut Bur — and my eyes, like the Sherry in
> the Glass, that the Guest leaves—Would this do just as well?

The sequence of similes was a mockery of Victorian clichés of sentimental description. Dickinson began gently enough, comparing herself to a very unprepossessing bird. Then she launched into a phrase
that any seasoned reader would expect to be about color: "My hair is
bold, like . . ." But she quickly punctured the promised effect by
comparing her hair not to the color of a chestnut, but to the outside
of a prickly chestnut bur. In the simplest terms, she was saying that
her hair stuck out in all directions. As for her eyes, the promising idea
that they were the color of sherry was similarly deflated. Instead of
"my eyes, like sherry," she wrote, "like the Sherry in the Glass." This
might have suggested only a lightening of the color. But then she
added "that the Guest leaves." The normal word order ("like the
sherry that the guest leaves in the glass") was broken, and the result
was one of progressively diminishing effect: from sherry, to sherry in
the glass, to sherry in the glass that the guest leaves.

One of the main purposes of school pictures like Dickinson's
seminary daguerreotype is to standardize dress, stance, and expression, so that each subject looks as much as possible like every other,
with everything that might amount to eccentricity or idiosyncrasy
obliterated in a visual ritual of effacement. In her correspondence
with Higginson, Dickinson was embarked on an opposite kind of
venture, a verbal riot of eccentricity. But the effect of the two
pictures of herself is in the end the same. In the daguerreotype, she
is hidden by the protocols of the photographer and the occasion; the
enigmatic character of the picture is the result of its predictability. In
the sentence of self-description that she worked up for Higginson,
she is hidden by the very unpredictability of her maneuvers, her
abandonment of protocols. She was hardly picturing herself at all,
but only making a wry comment on the conventional forms preten-
tious people might use to describe themselves. When Higginson
finished reading it, she was still physically invisible to him, and she
has remained so for the rest of the world ever since her death.

In nonphysical ways, though, Emily Dickinson seems to be one of the
most visible of people. She wrote thousands of poems and letters that

seem to invite readers into the most private corners of her life. They speak openly of terrors and passions. They reveal—or seem to—transports of joy and abysses of suffering. Their vocabulary is "pain," "ecstasy," "anguish," and the like. She was, for some of her life at least, a recluse. But in her writing her program appears to have been not solitude at all, but intimacy—as though she spent so much time alone just so people could eventually get to know everything about her. She told many riddles in her poems and in her letters. But they are not impossible riddles. And when they are solved, we seem to have gained direct access to Emily Dickinson's inner life. If we cannot know what she looked like, we can apparently know an astonishing amount about how she felt. She seems almost to reverse the ordinary state of affairs, to display a visible soul in an invisible body.

One of the effects of Emily Dickinson's apparent determination to explore every depth of her own experience, and to set down the results of her explorations in letters and poems, has been that her writing has been read as a kind of confessional testimony. And the fact that she did not publish her poems, but left them in handwritten packets, neatly folded and sewn, has given her testimony great weight. Her decision not to publish has helped to give her work a privileged status—not as art, only, but as evidence about her life.

A writer like Franklin, with a powerful and habitual concern for what his readers would think, might be tempted to toy with the truth, to conceal and even to deceive. A writer like Washington Irving might be driven by professional ambition to invent all sorts of personal myths, and even to allow those myths to find their way into his fiction. Someone as deeply dependent as William Lloyd Garrison on his reputation as a man of unyielding conscience might be tempted to distort the figure he presented to his public. A man as anxious as Emerson to justify the writing career in elevated spiritual terms had every motive for describing the life of the poet in ways dictated by a concern less for candor than for effect. And so it would be for any writer who treated authorship as a profession. But a poet who chose emphatically not to enter the literary marketplace—who said with scorn that publication was the "auction" of the mind—surely had no need to distort or polish the figure she presented in her poetry.

So Emily Dickinson's writing has been treated as a very special kind of documentary evidence, a sort of deathbed statement made with no other motive than to speak the truth, to leave a straight record of a very private life. And since she wrote with such evident passion about so many things, her readers have been able to find evidence in her poems and letters for a striking variety of different ways of looking at both her art and her life. She has been dressed out as a "Puritan," a residue of some sort of elusive "New England Mind" that hovered about Massachusetts from the seventeenth century on. She has been analyzed as a woman who suffered all her life from a profound "Electra" complex, almost broken by a powerful father and a retiring, even incompetent mother. Or her poetry has been treated as a function of a psychosis that resulted from her mother's incapacity to love her during her infancy (so that the intensity of her seeming preoccupation with her father was really only a side effect of a painful, unsatisfied need for maternal affection). Or she was a woman whose controlling wish was to be a man. Or her life and work were the result of a desperate love, a love that either could never be declared or that met cruel rejection when it was confessed. (The candidates for the might-have-been lover are many: Higginson; a girlhood friend—male or female; her sister-in-law, Susan Gilbert Dickinson; Charles Wadsworth, a minister she first met in Philadelphia; Samuel Bowles, a Springfield newspaper editor and publisher; and still others.) Or she was a woman whose life was essentially religious, whose deepest quest was for God, and who was able to translate her exquisite religious yearnings into verse.[3]

Curiously, all these different ways of looking at Emily Dickinson— and others too bizarre to mention—have found persuasive support in the evidence of her own testimony. If the poems and letters are a record of her uncompromising attempt to tell the truth about herself, and if they are not tainted by the ordinary professional confidence games that make us wary of most writers' statements about themselves, then once her writing is understood, Emily Dickinson is understood. On such assumptions, the task becomes only to decipher the messages she left behind, messages that seem clearly to be about herself, that seem even more clearly to be serious, and that seem most clearly of all to speak the truth. So different ways of decoding the poems and different ways of reading her letters have yielded drastically different versions of Emily Dickinson. But all the versions have one thing in common: They all suppose that the evi-

---

[3] There is little point in giving particular examples of such interpretations of Dickinson's life. Anyone who makes even a small dent in the literature will encounter them soon enough. A number of recent books on Dickinson have been brilliantly analyzed by David Porter, in "Dickinson's Readers," *New England Quarterly* 32 (March 1984): 106–17.

dence is *there,* that Emily Dickinson invested herself in her writing directly, passionately, and truthfully; that she wrote of anguish because she felt it; of ecstasy and terror because she felt them, too; of death because she feared it or yearned for it; of beauty because she loved it; and of love because she had it, or was afraid she never would.

The notion that Emily Dickinson's writing—or anyone else's—is a testimonial record of her experience, a kind of unmediated jaculation of the mind, is very dubious. Artists are no more able than ordinary people to make transcripts of their lives. No novel or story is autobiographical in a simple and direct way. No poem is a mere upshot of something the poet undergoes. To be sure, the lived experience of the writer is there, always. It determines whether the essay or book or poem will be written at all. It helps to shape choices of form, tone, and manner. But the outcomes—the actual words on the pages—are never merely dictated by experience. They are the result of artistry and effort, and of choices that can be either deliberate or made for reasons that the writer may be at most half-conscious of. The result can be as much invention as fact. Poets can write of anguish who never felt it, or of intimacy whose lives are solitary, or of solitude whose lives are dense with intimacy. And these things are just as true of unpublished writing as of work that is done expressly for the public and the marketplace. No piece of writing—not even in letters or diaries—is a plane mirror of the writer's mind or personality.[4]

[4] Cynthia Griffin Wolff's *Emily Dickinson* takes quite seriously John Cody's intricate psychoanalytic study of Dickinson, *After Great Pain: The Inner Life of Emily Dickinson* (Cambridge, Mass., 1971), a study whose point of departure is that Dickinson was actually made ill by a profound disruption of a normal mother–child relationship during infancy, and whose conclusion is that her poetry was a symptomatic upshot of that "great pain."

Wolff's point of departure on this question is her suggestion that there is a profound difference between treating Dickinson as a patient and the poetry as a symptom, and (as she proposes to do) seeing Dickinson as an artist and the poetry as something we ought to "understand and appreciate." Wolff suggests that Cody's program was to use the poems as a means to understand or diagnose the life, as though the poems were a kind of presentation of affect. Wolff suggests that the life ought to be used as a means to grapple with the poems as productions that were highly mediated, and characterized by a supremely canny use of poetic devices and strategies.

In practice, of course, such distinctions are difficult to maintain. Cody often writes of the poems as though they were, in the end, the appropriate focus of attention. And Wolff often does use the poems (and Dickinson's other art form, the letters) to diagnose the life. In the end, whatever her theoretical disputes with Cody may be, Wolff proposes a psychological view of Dickinson not very different from his. (See note 12, page 233.)

Sewall discusses the Cody "diagnosis" warily, and somewhat inconclusively, in *The Life of Emily Dickinson,* particularly at 1:75n. Cody's work distressed a great many Dickinson buffs

Of course, certain kinds of writing do make a formal claim to exactly this kind of privilege. Autobiographies claim, by convention, to be accurate renderings of the self. So do letters and diaries, especially if they are about "private" things like sex or religious conversion, or if they confess failings and wrongdoings. And lyric poems, by an old and powerful set of conventions, make a similar claim to be not only recordings of the inner life, but almost manifestations of it—as though they somehow *escaped* from the poet, unscreened by calculations of advantage or of marketability.

Emily Dickinson chose two of these forms, intimate letters and lyric poetry, for her life's work. She insisted that she had no thought of publication, and that she wrote her verses just to get "relief" from the "terrors" of her life. Higginson, who was the only really important literary man to know her and her work during her lifetime, promoted this same picture of her. She was, he said, one of those poets who wrote "for the relief of their own mind and without thought of publication." He even suggested that she had no control over what she wrote, and that the poems were like the speech efforts of a child. But, despite her choice of the lyric as her form, despite her own insistence that she wanted her poems to be "true," and that she had no wish to publish them, there is no compelling reason to suppose that her writing had any different relationship to her actual experience than Franklin's autobiography did to his, or Garrison's abolitionist writing to his. Washington Irving may have invested as much of himself in the fantastic story of Rip Van Winkle as Dickinson invested in poems that began with stunning testimonial statements like "I felt a Funeral, in my Brain," or "I felt a Cleaving in my Mind." The implicit claims that such lines make to being the truth about the writer herself are, in the end, only conventional claims. They are part of the set of tacit and provisional assumptions on which lyric poetry is written and read.[5]

---

and admirers. For an example of the kind of initial reception his book received, see Cynthia Chaliff's review essay in *Literature and Psychology* 22 (1972): 45–7, and S. A. Grolnil, "Emily and the Psychobiographer," ibid., 23 (1973): 68–91.

[5] "I Felt a Funeral" and "I Felt a Cleaving" are numbered 280 and 937 in the modern collection, Thomas H. Johnson, ed., *The Poems of Emily Dickinson*, 3 vols. (Cambridge, Mass., 1955). Johnson's ordering and numbering of the poems, no matter how carefully he went about it, has given Dickinson scholars a sense of precision that is probably excessive. But neither this nor anything else detracts much from his invaluable efforts. All poems quoted here will be taken from this edition of the poetry, and his numbering system will be followed. The poems will be cited simply as *Poems*, followed by Johnson's number.

Whether Emily Dickinson, in real life, ever felt a funeral in her brain or a cleaving in her mind, or anything that could be appropriately signaled by such metaphors, is an extraordinarily difficult question. It cannot be settled by invoking other examples of similar sentences from other poems or letters. A dozen instances, in verse or prose, of Dickinson's saying she felt anguish, dread, or love count for no more than a single one. For each new example is subject to the same doubt. The problem is to make some sort of estimate of what the letters and poems—especially the poems— meant to Dickinson when she wrote them and revised them, or copied them into the carefully kept little packets she tucked away, or sent them to Bowles, to Higginson, or across the lawn to Sue next door.

For literary critics (and for people who simply like to read poetry) the question is of no real importance. The poems are there, just as fine and moving, or just as poor and tedious, as if they were found objects, author and date unknown. But for anyone who is interested in *why* people write the things they write, the question is perplexing and important. It is also simple. Did Emily Dickinson write lines like[6]

> *It would have starved a Gnat —*
> *To live so small as I —*
> *And yet I was a living Child —*
> *With Food's necessity*

because she actually felt that she had been somehow starved, and wanted or needed to give voice to an unsatisfied "necessity"? Or was she doing something else in such poems, something that did not have a straightforward origin in her own experience—either in childhood, in her thirty-second year (when these lines probably were written), or in any of the years between?

The question has nothing to do with sincerity or with truthfulness in any ordinary sense. Poems like "It would have starved a Gnat" could have been written by a woman who really felt she had been starved. The poem would then have a certain kind of truth about it. But it could just as well be a gifted poet's attempt to find a telling formula for saying how it would be if some person were wretchedly deprived—were, say, some poor character

[6] *Poems*, 612.

she had run across in Dickens, the Brownings, Burns, or some other of the sentimental writers she was fond of. And there would be a certain kind of truth to the poem in this case, too. Either way, sincerity is not the issue. Instead, the problem is to find some way of deciding on the epistemological *mood* of the poems: Are they in the indicative or the subjunctive? Do they say something directly about Emily Dickinson's own life, or do they speak only for her capacity to invent and imagine experience? Do they testify to the things she actually thought and felt, or are they a record primarily of her poetic practice?

Sometimes the answer to such questions is obvious and unambiguous. Some of Dickinson's poems were about shipwrecks or other disasters she heard about, or read about in newspapers and magazines. "Glee," she could write, "the great storm is over/Four have recovered the Land/Forty gone down together/Into the boiling Sand." Or about a man trapped in a mine or construction disaster: "In falling Timbers buried/ There breathed a Man/Outside—the spades—were plying—/The Lungs—within." Such poems were obviously not about her own life. They were in an old ballad-and-broadside tradition (a tradition already gone too sweet with age and soon to become the object of Mark Twain's famous ridicule in the ode to Stephen Dowling Botts: "And did young Stephen sicken?/And did young Stephen die?") Or she could write a childlike poem about a train, a sort of choo-choo-pufferbelly exercise: "I love to see it lap the miles—/And lick the Valleys up." The narrative and descriptive content of poems like these plainly had little if anything to do with Dickinson's own experience, much less with any sort of spiritual crisis. (And such poems are by custom ignored, as though they are not part of a perfected and serious Dickinson canon.)

A large number of other Dickinson poems were written for special occasions—poems for the graveside or the anniversary of a death, poems of congratulation or sympathy, poems to be sent with the gift of a wildflower to her sister-in-law, or to Samuel Bowles or his wife, or to some other neighbor or friend. Such poems usually seem innocent and not about very much. A poem like "Tho' my destiny be Fustian," written about 1860, near the onset of her most creative years, was probably no more than a verse message she wrote Samuel

Bowles, to accompany a gift of a dried late-summer wildflower pinned to the paper, perhaps with a rose:[7]

> *Tho' my destiny be Fustian —*
> *Her's [sic] be damask fine —*
> *Tho' she wear a silver apron —*
> *I, a less divine —*
>
> *Still, my little Gipsey being*
> *I would far prefer,*
> *Still, my little sunburnt bosom*
> *To her Rosier,*
>
> *For, when Frosts their punctual fingers*
> *On her forehead lay,*
> *You and I, and Dr Holland*
> *Bloom Eternally!*
>
> *Roses of a steadfast summer*
> *In a steadfast land,*
> *Where no Autumn lifts her pencil —*
> *And no Reapers stand!*

This poem—and dozens of others like it—was a greeting-card exercise. (J. G. Holland was a friend of Bowles and the Dickinsons, and Emily Dickinson often wrote poems and letters for him and his wife, just as she did for Bowles, and she often pinned a flower or two to the paper.) But a strong tradition has grown up among Dickinson critics of "deciphering" such poems as this, on the theory that they are not really about such things as flowers, birthdays, and funerals, but are about some inner turmoil, or about her profound commitment to her own radical experiments in poetry—as though she were insisting that her "Fustian" and "Gipsey" poetic tactics were superior to the genteel silver-and-damask verses written by most of the women whose simpering poems she read in Bowles' newspaper or *The Atlantic Monthly*. On such a reading, her untamable "sunburnt bosom" would be the source of a spiritual and esthetic "summer,"

[7] Ibid., 163.

which will outlast the "Frosts" that will eventually waste all conventionally "fine" and "divine" art.[8]

The difficulty with such interpretations is obvious. They suppose that Dickinson's poetry—at least the poems that deserve to be taken seriously—is really about herself. And when the superficial subject is roses, the reader's task is to see through them to the thornier "meanings" that are the real burden of the verses—and reveal the real burden, too, of Emily Dickinson's life. What is assumed is precisely what ought to be explored: the very *status* of the poems as evidence about Emily Dickinson's life.

The question is not what such poetry reveals, but whether it reveals anything about Emily Dickinson. No decipherment of a Dickinson poem—at least no decoding that goes beyond the solution to some explicit linguistic or symbolic riddle—can avoid the issue. It is a straightforward question of historical fact: When she wrote poems about flowers or funerals, did she have some other intention or purpose, some other subject and meaning that she wanted her readers to spy out? (It makes little difference whether these intentions or purposes were conscious or not, for there are unconscious purposes, and they do generate meanings just as indelible as those generated by the deliberate manipulation of symbols, ironies, metaphors, and other literary devices.)

The material for an answer could lie in a third type of poem, in which her intention seems to have been both conscious and plain. In a number of poems, Dickinson does appear to have been making testimonial statements about love, death, salvation, or the like. On the face of things, at least, there is no compelling reason to doubt that she sometimes was talking about herself, saying what she meant and meaning what she said. These poems need no elaborate "deciphering." This is particularly true of the poems in which she talked about poetry and poets. She appears to have been asserting a conception of the poet's exalted calling, and so giving voice to the deepest

---

[8] Ruth Miller, in *The Poetry of Emily Dickinson* (Middletown, Conn., 1978), argues that Dickinson's principal effort was to define herself as a poet with an original and free voice of her own. The most serious poetry (and the poetry that deserves to be taken most seriously), she suggests, was about poetry as a vocation. "Tho' my destiny be Fustian," for example, should be read as a declaration of spiritual and artistic independence of Bowles' (or anyone else's) authority. Miller's work probably is the most strained modern attempt to make Emily Dickinson out to be a poet with a definite architectonic program, centered on a transcendentally heroic ideal of the poetic undertaking itself. And Miller's reading of this particular poem is one of the more strained of her explications.

motives for her own determined striving, to "dwell" where only
poets—and God, perhaps—dwell: "in Possibility." In this kind of
poem, she does seem to have been giving the most direct kind of
accounting she could make of the ways she valued the things of the
world.[9]

> *I dwell in Possibility —*
> *A fairer House than Prose —*
> *More numerous of Windows —*
> *Superior — for Doors —*
>
> *Of Chambers as the Cedars —*
> *Impregnable of Eye —*
> *And for an Everlasting Roof*
> *The Gambrels of the Sky —*
>
> *Of Visiters — the fairest —*
> *For Occupation — This —*
> *The spreading wide my narrow Hands*
> *To gather Paradise —*

When Emily Dickinson claimed the title of poet for herself, she
seems to have been fastening on a vocation she thought of as one of
supreme, infinite, and transcendent worth:[10]

> *I reckon — when I count at all —*
> *First — Poets — Then the Sun —*
> *Then Summer — Then the Heaven of God —*
> *And then — the List is done —*
>
> *But, looking back — the First so seems*
> *To Comprehend the Whole —*
> *The Others look a needless Show —*
> *So I write — Poets—All*
>
> *Their Summer — lasts a Solid Year —*
> *They can afford a Sun*
> *The East — would deem extravagant —*
> *And if the Further Heaven —*

[9] *Poems,* 657.
[10] Ibid., 569.

> *Be Beautiful as they prepare*
> *For Those who worship Them —*
> *It is too difficult a Grace —*
> *To justify the Dream —*

What the poem means to say is obvious: Poets have a power to constitute objects—the sun, or heaven—that are at least as sublime as "real" ones. So prizing poets makes it unnecessary to prize the "real" versions of the objects they can create. The world's loveliest things are "a needless Show" once poets have managed to "Comprehend the Whole." And in a clever commentary on theological notions of preparation for salvation and justification by grace, she makes the heaven that poets "prepare" for their worshippers as perfect as anything God could conceivably make: No grace *can* justify a faith in a heaven more beautiful.

Similarly, a poem like "This was a Poet —" seems to be an equally unproblematic celebration of the transcendent worth of the makers of verse:[11]

> *This was a Poet — It is That*
> *Distills amazing sense*
> *From ordinary Meanings —*
> *And Attar so immense*
>
> *From the familiar species*
> *That perished by the Door —*
> *We wonder it was not Ourselves*
> *Arrested it — before —*
>
> *Of Pictures, the Discloser —*
> *The Poet — it is He —*
> *Entitles Us — by Contrast —*
> *To ceaseless Poverty —*
>
> *Of Portion — so unconscious —*
> *The Robbing — could not harm —*
> *Himself — to Him — a Fortune —*
> *Exterior — to Time —*

---

[11] Ibid., 448.

The terms of the evaluation are plain enough: The poet is able to distill, arrest, and disclose "amazing sense" from the world of "ordinary Meanings." And this makes him the possessor of a treasure that cannot be lost. Like the poet of Emerson's *Nature,* whose eye "integrates the whole," he *has* no fortune; he *is* his own Fortune. And this makes him—again like Emerson's poet—able to transcend even time. Indeed the poet has some of God's own essential attributes. He is infinite, not divided into "portions," immediately identified with himself, and outside time.

In such celebrations of the vocation of the poet, Dickinson seems to speak most directly and clearly about herself and her own choices. There is no immediately obvious need for elaborate decoding. There are no wildflowers and roses that could be tokens of something "deeper." There is no need to wonder what nameless lovers, sexual perplexities, or family nightmares might lie "behind" the poems. In one small body of poems at least—poems about poetry itself—Dickinson does seem to speak in an uncomplicated way, and to be her own subject. It is tempting to read these poems about the poet's calling as her ultimate and indubitable testimony about what mattered most to her: a notion of her own art that was so grand and so demanding that she could never have compromised it for any ambition so low as publication, let alone for any concern for success in the literary marketplace.

This version of the vocational equation Emily Dickinson formulated to help her make sense out of her idiosyncratic life is quite simple. She elevated Art—as a "spiritual" activity—to a plane on which it became, simply, incompatible with ordinary experience. In fact, experience itself—what she called "prose"—became the antithesis and even the enemy of poetry. Her conception of the poetic career denied the relevance of any concern with economy, society, or politics. But she went further. In practice as well as theory, she eventually repudiated many of the routine realities of ordinary life: tending property, getting married and raising children, going to church, supervising servants, entertaining visitors, and all the rest of the daily round of women of her social class in mid-nineteenth-century New England. During a period of about ten years, from the mid-1850s to the mid-1860s, Emily Dickinson did transform herself from an ordinary-seeming woman in her middle twenties into an increasingly reclusive spinster. And it was in these same years that she wrote most intently, as though art could displace experience.

What drove her at last into solitude was surely complicated and perhaps even inexplicable. Like most people, she was no doubt a tangle of class anxiety, the exigencies of gender, sexual confusion and deprivation, unresolved struggles with parents or siblings, problems with her eyes—or maybe even some kind of unknowable problem of brain chemistry. But whatever was happening to her, she did not merely undergo it. She made a determined attempt to define it as an uncompromising choice between the low tedium and frustration of ordinary life on one side, and her art on the other, with all its intimations of "Possibility," "Circumference," "Mind," "Paradise," and "Infinity."[12]

Of course Emily Dickinson did not invent this formulation. By the 1850s, it had become a cliché. But what she did do that most writers did not was to act out the formula consistently. Other nineteenth-century writers became famous by warning against fame, rich by railing against money, influential by complaining about the fickleness of the public, or celebrated by speaking to large audiences in crowded halls about the virtues of solitude in the woods. Emerson's generation of American writers formulated, then lived out, a contradiction between their notions of art and their actual practice as professional artists. But Dickinson—so it seems—lacked either the capacity or the need for such a contradiction. She not only said that art was above experience, and that publication was an auction of mind. She ratified that belief in action—and doubly so—by guarding herself from the world, and refusing to publish her poems. And it is this that makes her commentaries on the writer's vocation seem more authentic than most of her contemporaries'. She really did seem to believe that she dwelt in Possibility, had Circumference as

---

[12] Wolff, in *Emily Dickinson,* 45–57, 64, 136, argues that Dickinson as an adult exhibited an extreme preoccupation with the superiority of "seeing" as against "words," and that this was the result of the fact that Emily Norcross Dickinson failed to provide her daughter with crucial "pre-verbal" communication. This caused Emily Dickinson to experience the accession of language as a compensatory "fall" from non-verbal and superior forms of communication into mere words. This infant experience informed and shaped her life. Her preoccupation with language was a symptom of the failure of mother-daughter exchanges in infancy, but so was her intense desire to elevate language to a plane of perfect "sight." "Thus the obsessive preoccupation with communication by seeing, and the conviction that language is a 'fallen' form of discourse combine to exhibit the traces of the problems that had afflicted her earliest relationship with her mother." To "raise language to its highest capacity," then, can "begin to recompense the loss—as visual and verbal become one." "The child who had experienced a 'Fall' into language as the only way to repair the earliest failures of unspoken communication also construed language as a force that could combat the various dangers of separation."

her business, and spread her narrow hands to gather Paradise. Her poems about poetry itself do seem to be straightforward declarations about herself. And they do seem to deserve a special place at the center of any Dickinson canon, in fact to serve as the standard against which other poems are weighed and measured. In these poems about her life's work, surely, Emily Dickinson made perfectly plain the relationship between her art and her experience, made it plain, in fact, that her art *was* her experience.

But there are several problems with taking Emily Dickinson's poems about being a poet as privileged declarations about herself, her life, and her art. First, it is not altogether clear that some of the most important of them are about herself and her poetry after all—at least not simply and decisively so. A poem like "This was a Poet" could perfectly well have been an obituary poem for one of her favorite poets, and not a summary of her own program for her work.[13] It is quite possible that "I dwell in Possibility" is really just another of her many poems about death and immortality, about what it might be like to be free of life (Prose), and in one of the numerous "Chambers" of the heavenly mansion. Similarly, a poem like "I reckon—when I count at all" may be just as much about salvation and eternity as about poets. The key words in the poem could, in the end, be the theological terms of the final verse: "prepare," "worship," "Grace," and "Justify."

Taken by itself, this difficulty would not be serious. If Emily Dickinson wanted to write about what it meant to be a poet, and to claim that it was the highest calling, then it surely made sense for her to make her case in language that her neighbors and family would quickly recognize. How better to do this than to lace her discussion with the language of the Gospels and the pulpit? She was much more sophisticated than the young William Lloyd Garrison or his mother. But the case she was making was, in effect, a response to the kinds of complaints Frances Maria Garrison had made about her son's "turning author," and seeking fame and fortune. If the author dwelt in Possibility and took Circumference as her business, then this

---

[13] In any case, "This was a Poet" was Emily Dickinson's rendering not so much of her own private thoughts as of another's published ones. It is one of the many poems identified by John Evangelist Walsh, in *The Hidden Life of Emily Dickinson: A Biography* (New York, 1971), 258, as borrowings and reworkings of sections of Elizabeth Barrett Browning's *Aurora Leigh*. Of all the modern books on Emily Dickinson, Walsh's is still the most pleasant read.

world counted for nothing. Turning author need not mean forsaking the things of God for the things of this world. The poet in fact became not a fortune seeker, pursuing what Frances Maria Garrison had called the "applause of mortals," but immortal and divine: "Himself—to Him—a Fortune— / Exterior—to Time—."

A somewhat more serious problem with Emily Dickinson's poems about being a poet is that she did not really lay out a coherent argument about what poetry is, and what poets are finally all about. Instead, she struck attitudes, and the attitudes were at bottom conventional—however quirky her manner of proposing them. From the time of Keats, at least, numbers of poets and critics had promoted the idea that true art was a traffic in matters that transcended the ordinary and the quotidian. The Poet was necessarily a person of such insight and genius that he—or, increasingly with the passage of time, she—could only be thought of as a locus of creativity so burning and keen as to make routine commerce with the world a matter of pain and alarm. For such an artist, life was inescapably an affair of "terror" or "palsy," and writing only a kind of "relief" from the insoluble contradictions between sublime moments of insight and realization on one side of experience, and the tawdry demands of the "world" or "society" on the other side. A decade before Emily Dickinson was born, Washington Irving had worked this conception of the artist into his mythic version of his own life as a writer. By the time she was ready for school, Emerson was making the same notion of the poet his stock in trade. When she began to write poetry, it had become a somewhat sodden cliché that even Emerson was becoming weary of.

Clichés can be transformed into great art, of course. And Emily Dickinson's genius may have been her ability to take the most conventional kinds of ideas, fuse them with the equally conventional poetic forms of the standard Protestant hymnals of the day, and to turn these ideas into extraordinary poetry. The issue is not whether her ideas were original. (Indeed, any attempt to reconstruct the "thought" or "mind" of Emily Dickinson—to uncover formal philosophical themes in her writing—is likely to reveal only confusion or triviality.)[14] The issue is rather to discover what the convention of

[14] The attempt to make Emily Dickinson a philosophically serious and sophisticated poet has gone on for a long time now. One interesting way to follow it is to track various scholars' attempts to lend a precise, technical, and sophisticated meaning to her concept of "Circum-

the poet meant to her. How did she understand its terms? What bearing did it have on the simple question of whether she ought to try to publish her work? Was she really a woman whose final commitment was to her art, and does this make her poems—taken as a body of work—a telling, confessional revelation of her inner life?[15]

The poems about being a poet cannot answer such questions. They only help *set* the questions. If there are answers, they have to lie instead in her decision not to publish her work, for it was in this choice, more than any other, that she gave a concrete and existential import to what she thought it meant to dwell in Possibility. It was this choice that seems to elevate her conception of the poet above convention and cliché. This decision not to engage in the auction of mind is what makes her into a figure of mystery with a somewhat cultish following, and makes her poems seem more than mere art, seem in fact to be her exquisitely private and anguished "letter to the world."

It happens that the years in which she was hardest at work were precisely the years when she made her nearest approach to trying to become a publishing author. It was in 1862, the year in which she wrote or copied out more than three hundred poems, that she began her correspondence with Higginson, responding to his *Atlantic* essay, the "Letter to a Young Contributor." If there are answers to questions about the relationship between Emily Dickinson's art and her experience, they probably lie in that correspondence, in the things she told him, the mysteries she dangled before him, and the resolute silences she maintained. And some of the answers have to be looked for in Higginson's "Letter" itself. For she read it with great care, and devised her letters to him very much on its terms. Whatever pro-

---

ference." See Thomas H. Johnson, *Emily Dickinson: An Interpretive Biography* (Cambridge, Mass., 1955), 134–54; Charles R. Anderson, *Emily Dickinson's Poetry: Stairway of Surprise* (New York, 1966), 53–70; Albert J. Gelpi, *Emily Dickinson: The Mind of the Poet* (Cambridge, Mass., 1966), 94–127; William Robert Sherwood, *Circumference and Circumstance: Stages in the Mind and Art of Emily Dickinson* (New York and London, 1968), especially 216–27; Scott Donaldson, "Minding Emily Dickinson's Business," *New England Quarterly* 16 (1968): 574–82. Wolff, *Emily Dickinson,* argues that Dickinson's claim that circumference was her business was a "blasphemous" move in her lifelong religious struggle—first to "wrestle" with God, and to wrest from Him what orthodoxy reserved to Him, a struggle occurring within what Wolff calls (for some reason) "the semiotic system of latter-day American Puritanism."
[15] A skillful discussion of hymnal forms is M. W. England's "Emily Dickinson and Isaac Watts: Puritan Hymnodists," *Bulletin of the New York Public Library* 690 (1965): 83–116. This superbly learned and convincing essay is marred only by the invocation of the irrelevant category of "Puritan," which does not have any real bearing on either Watts or Dickinson.

nouncements she might make to him about being a poet, she would make them in the context Higginson had established.

The Dickinsons, like most cultivated New England families, had a subscription to *The Atlantic*. In fact, they were charter subscribers. And Emily Dickinson was an admirer of Higginson's essays on nature—in which he managed to combine occasional strokes of concreteness reminiscent of Thoreau with complacent assurances that a genial Unitarian rightness saturated the world. Also, the April 1862 issue of *The Atlantic* had been singled out for particular praise in the *Springfield Republican,* in a comment that was signed by her friend Samuel Bowles. It was practically inevitable that Emily Dickinson would read Higginson's "Letter."[16]

When she did, she found one particular passage that echoed some of her own exclamations about language and art. In this passage, Higginson rehearsed a bit of intellectual history, and proposed a theory of writing that was bound to catch Dickinson's eye. Higginson's theory valued language above content, words above thought. A generation ago, he said, William Ellery Channing had created a New England "standard" of style that had put exclusive emphasis on controlled clarity of thought. To be sure, this disciplined manner of writing had exercised a beneficial influence "in a raw and crude nation." And if a writer had great ideas, even this "pure and polite" style could be "uplifted into expression by the high thoughts it utters." But, Higginson argued, there is another way of writing, in which language—in itself "powerless"—becomes "saturated with warm life and delicious association." When this happens, ideas become irrelevant. Words themselves "palpitate and thrill with the mere fascination of the syllables." Higginson then reeled off a few sentences that made him sound like a man who could regard poetry as an elevated spiritual calling: "A phrase may outweigh a library," he said.[17]

Keats has left behind him winged wonders of expression which are not surpassed by Shakespeare, or by any one else who ever dared touch the English tongue. There may be phrases which

---

[16] Sewall, *Life,* 2:540–1. Sue had asked Bowles to see whether he could find in New York a picture of Higginson. Jay Leyda, *The Years and Hours of Emily Dickinson,* 2 vols. (New Haven, 1960), 2:32, 46, 51 ff.

[17] All of the quotations here and on the next several pages are from Higginson's "Letter."

shall be palaces to dwell in; a single word may be a window from which one may perceive all the kingdoms of the earth. . . . there may be years of crowded passion in a word, and half a life in a sentence.

This suggestion that there is a loveliness of "expression" that has nothing to do with the ideas that are being expressed might have prompted Emily Dickinson to believe that Higginson could read her verses with sympathy and approval. And it was surely this passage about language becoming "saturated with warm life" to which she would peg her first question to Higginson, when she asked him to "tell me if my verse is alive."

But Higginson proposed his theory of "expression" almost in passing. And no one who had read as much Emerson as Emily Dickinson could have been intrigued by it anyway. (Not long before Higginson published his letter, Emerson himself had come to Amherst and had stayed next door, with Sue and Austin Dickinson. If theories of art and language had been the issue for Emily Dickinson, she could easily have sent a few poems to Emerson—or just slipped them anonymously under the door to his room, as Franklin or Garrison had done with their first efforts.)

Besides, there was much in Higginson's "Letter" to repel a young woman who had recently finished a poem characterizing any attempt to "be somebody" as making froggish noises to an "admiring bog."[18] For Higginson's real agenda was not to celebrate palpitating sentences and thrilling phrases. His purpose was exactly to justify every writer's attempt to be somebody, and to argue that the public was anything but an admiring bog.

In truth, Higginson's "Letter to a Young Contributor" was a sort of confidence game. It was presented, explicitly, as a manual of advice to would-be authors. But the essay was the lead article, and no magazine like *The Atlantic* could have given such precious space to a piece that was really aimed at a few dozen young contributors. What Higginson and the other editors had in mind was much more than a set of instructions for aspiring authors. His "Letter" was meant to be read as an essay on modern literary practice, and was meant for all the subscribers, not just for would-be writers. His real subject was both writers and readers, and the moral and economic relationships between them.

---

[18] "I'm Nobody!" is in *Poems,* 288.

The argument that gave shape and direction to Higginson's "Letter" was that the two sides of the literary marketplace—writers and readers, sellers and buyers—had mistaken estimates of each other. Writers—those at least who aspired to be fine artists—conventionally supposed that the literary public was a fickle mass that always demanded to be written down to. On the other hand, the public might suppose that since "the profits of true literature are rising," authors write only for money and fame, and not for "noble" ends. On one side, Higginson set out to persuade authors of the validity of the judgments of a new and "formidable" literary public. On the other side—a side probably much closer to Higginson's own professional heart—he wanted to convince the public that literature was as legitimate a "pursuit" as any other kind of commerce, and that writing for money only heightened the "nobility" of the author's calling.

Like many writers working from a covert agenda, Higginson wavered among voices, and he deployed several that Emily Dickinson can hardly have found attractive. In some passages of his "Letter," he spoke like an amiable uncle, who might occasionally make a bit of innocent fun at the expense of a young niece—though always with affection. (This voice could not have appealed much to a retiring woman whose favorite subject was death and who was entering middle age.) Then Higginson would take up the raspy voice of a tough professional, a man of practical sense hammering out imperatives like "Use good pens, black ink, nice white paper and plenty of it." (Not a very likable voice, either, for a woman who was never plainspoken, and who copied poems into her packets with an eye, mainly, for finding spaces where they would fit on a page, as intent on saving paper as on ordering her work.) Suddenly, though, Higginson would shift into the rounded intonations of what he called the "New England mind": mannered, genteel, uplifting, and above all cultivated. In this voice, he larded his essay generously with references and citations. In a few pages, he managed to mention Keats, Coleridge, Gray, Ariosto, Addison, Pope, Marvell, Shakespeare, Wordsworth, Milton, Hazlitt, Ctesiphon, Carlyle, Tiberius, Euclid, Goethe, Byron, Plato, *I Quatro Poeti*, Louis XIV, Johnson, Homer, Tennyson, the Brownings, Balzac, Ruskin, Emerson, and a dozen others—none of them very much to the point, all displayed like literary credentials. (This kind of thing can hardly have been attractive to Dickinson, whose modest habit was rarely to name other writers, even in letters where it might have been appropriate.)

Higginson's inability to settle into a consistent tone was not a result of lack of skill. His problem lay in a certain reluctance to be plain about the argument he was setting out to make. Instead, he sandwiched his case between a beginning that verged dangerously close to avuncular triviality, and an ending that nearly dissolved into pious divinations of eternity.

His opening was all innocence: "My dear young gentleman or young lady,—for many are the Cecil Dreemes of literature who superscribe their offered manuscript with very masculine names in a very feminine handwriting." And in the first paragraph, he resorted to such obviously overblown words as "superscribe," "epistle," and "perusal," as a signal that he was not a man taking himself *too* seriously. To seal the casual effect, in his second paragraph he compared an author whose manuscript had been rejected to a young lady who had not been asked to dance at a ball. Then he said that an editor who had been lucky enough to discover a new author was like the apocryphal physician who had boasted that he was the first man to discover cholera and communicate it to the public.

At the end of his essay, though, Higginson gained a very different prospect. Suddenly, eternity seemed close at hand, and the "temporary distinction" of a Shakespeare or a Milton seemed negligible and irrelevant:

> Who cannot bear a few disappointments, if the vista be so wide that the mute inglorious Miltons of this sphere may in some other sing their Paradise as Found? . . . I fancy that in some other realm of existence we may look back with some kind of interest on this scene of our earlier life, and say to one another,—"Do you remember yonder planet, where once we went to school?" And whether our elective study here lay chiefly in the fields of action or of thought will matter little to us then, when other schools shall have led us through other disciplines.

Between his beginning, bland and straining for humor, and his ending, just as bland but straining toward piety, Higginson's tone was neither joshing nor unctuous, but serious and even a little urgent. The questions he was addressing were important ones, not just for him but for any nineteenth-century writer. What was the new reading public like, after all? What did it really want from authors, editors, and publishers? What kind of "pursuit" was writing for the marketplace? Was there a fundamental contradiction between grand claims that art was the disinterested service of truth and beauty, and an acknowledgment that writers were actually selling truth and beauty on the open market? Then there was the question that Emerson had fretted so much over, from his 1837 Phi Beta Kappa lecture to his eulogy for Thoreau in this same year of Civil War: What was the relationship between thought and action, between the writings and sayings of intellectuals and the sometimes deadly undertakings of "practical" men?—a question that had considerable point for Higginson, who was about to become a colonel in the Union army.

Higginson's strategy for dealing with such questions was to introduce, early in his essay, a temporary protagonist, the editor to whom the young contributor might send an article. This editor's task was to mediate between the "interests" of the writer and the "interests" of the public. But Higginson was planning a neat bit of moral arithmetic. It would turn out that the interests of the editor and the author were identical. And it turned out, as well, that the true interests of the editor and the public were also the same. And this meant, on Higginson's logic, that there was an identity of interests all around. So he would be able to drop the editor from his formula about halfway through the essay. Simultaneously, the young author that Higginson was supposedly addressing was going to be quietly redefined as one who had passed beyond the "opening of your literary career" and was already "fairly in print."

So, in the end, the professional writer and the public would be the only actors in Higginson's version of the literary marketplace. Each could be confident that the truest interests of both were the same. With this knowledge, authors and their public could live happily together, not just in Higginson's vague Unitarian everafter, but in the here and now. They could be confident that in the last analysis all was harmony, between writers and publics, between thought and action, and even between the literary pursuits of peace and the struggles of armies in the field.

Higginson pursued this ambitious program with a certain amount of stealth. He began by saying that "the real interests of the editor and writer are absolutely the same, and any antagonism is merely traditional. . . . No editor can ever afford the rejection of a good thing, and no author the publication of a bad one." Then he introduced his temporary protagonist by pointing out that "Of course no editor is infallible." He sometimes "lets in" a bad piece of writing, an "ungainly intruder." Then he has to "meditate and groan . . . in the night-watches." But this only proves that the editor is "human." He is not a "despot," but a "bland and virtuous man," whose only purpose in life is to "secure plenty of good subscribers and contributors." So authors ought not to treat the editor as an "enemy" but should "draw near him with soft approaches" and "honest propitiation."

Such a rhetorical strategy was important to Higginson because his next step was to tick off an utterly obvious list of injunctions to writers, about pens, ink, and paper, and about sending in carefully edited and proofread drafts of their work. But he had set the stage carefully, so that this advice would not seem trivial. Within the frame he had set up, good pens and ink were not just tactics in a contest between author and editor. Careful writing and copying on good paper were transformed into important ways of signaling a writer's understanding of the vital collaboration between writer and publisher.

After establishing this harmony, Higginson introduced "the reading public." He gave it concrete form as the "two hundred thousand, more or less," who read *The Atlantic*. But he characterized it in much grander terms as "this vast, unimpassioned, unconscious tribunal, this average judgment of intelligent minds." Writing for such a public did not compromise the values of art, for the new and increasingly tasteful public "rapidly cancels all transitory reputations, and at last becomes the organ of eternal justice and infallibly awards posthumous fame." Any writer who thought that such a public needed to be written down to was misguided—and probably had nothing worth saying anyway. The intelligent receptivity—even infallibility—of the "popular mind" made it possible for any author to succeed without compromising either elegance of style or difficulty of thought.

Higginson was sure that this was a new phenomenon, a nineteenth-century transformation that was particularly advanced in America, where the modern forces of "democracy" and "industry" had had their strongest influences.

> Political freedom makes every man an individual; a vast industrial activity makes every man an inventor, not merely of labor-saving machines, but of labor-saving words; universal schooling popularizes all thought and sharpens the edge of all language.

This brought Higginson to a crucial point in his strategy. If the public was infallible, then writers ought to be willing to make important changes in literary practice. A public shaped by mass education, mass politics, and mass production would inevitably expect its authors to write in ways consistent with those social and economic realities. For a moment, Higginson shifted person, and the public became not "it" or "they" but "we"—a grammatical signal that he was not only about to endorse but also to identify himself with a new public taste. And for his analogy, he chose the two sectors of the economy that everyone knew were at the cutting edge of industrialization—railroads and textiles: "We unconsciously demand of our writers the same dash and the same accuracy which we demand in railroading or dry-goods-jobbing."

In the same way that the identity of interest between writer and editor gave moral dignity to the use of good ink and paper, the legitimate demands of the new public ought to be met by writers who were willing to write efficiently—with "dash and accuracy." And this lent moral weight to a second list of elementary injunctions to the writer that Higginson now introduced: to avoid italics and exclamation points, parentheses, and dashes; to refrain from pedantic citations and Latin, German, or French phrases. Like the earlier injunctions about pens and handwriting, these rules had been lifted above the tactical and made part of the implicit new contract between authors and readers.

Now Higginson could propose the bargain he had been working toward from the beginning of his "Letter." Authors in America, he said, were being constantly tempted away from art by the prestige and money their intelligence could command elsewhere: "if one can learn languages, he must go to Congress; if he can argue a case, he must become agent of a factory." The remedy was higher rewards for the artist. If the public was going to insist on writers who worked with the dash of dry-goods jobbers, then it would have to accept the fact that they wrote for money. The public's demand for a new kind of writing, consistent with the "efficiency" of the new economic and social order, was legitimate. But so was the author's desire for new levels of profit.

Higginson had brought his case to a point where he could make an unembarrassed linkage between two crucial terms of his argument, "profit" and "true literature":

Because the profits of true literature are rising,—trivial as they still are beside those of commerce or the professions,—its merits do not necessarily decrease, but the contrary is more likely to happen; for in this pursuit, as in all others, cheap work is usually poor work.

The profits of true literature were well deserved. For writing was as important as any other pursuit, even war. Both a "column of newspaper" and a "column of attack," both Wordsworth's "Lines on Immortality" and Wellington's lines of battle in Spain were "noble, if nobly done." And the nineteenth century was deciding the case between art and action in favor of art: "Once the poets and sages were held to be pleasing triflers, fit for hours of relaxation in the lulls of war. Now the pursuits of peace are recognized as the real, and war as the accidental." And if war was accidental, so was politics. The "notoriety" of a Calhoun or a Webster was going to fade quickly, and what would endure would be the works of writers.

From this point a seasoned minister like Higginson could pass to his closing, to the prospect of "immortality," and to the idea that everyone—writers, editors, readers, and even generals and politicians—would understand in eternity that all earthly striving and distinctions had been trivial anyway, only preparations for the "other schools" and "other disciplines" of the cosmos. As for this world, where Higginson's own strivings still lay, he had managed to fuse two ethics that his contemporaries worried might be contradictory, the ethic of "noble" art and the ethic of large profits. He had also managed to celebrate an esthetic of industry and trade, and to justify the artist's pursuit of "gain." He had sketched a world where literary "jobbing" was not tawdry but a rich source of new linguistic "coinage" and "exchange." And in such a world, writing for publication, for the literary marketplace, was not only an acceptable thing to do; it was the *only* acceptable thing for a writer to do, the only thing that put the artist truly in touch with the "average judgment of intelligent minds."

On April 15, two weeks after Higginson's "Letter" was published, Emily Dickinson wrote him, sending four poems and asking her question: Was her verse alive? The question was carefully keyed to Higginson's talk about the "warm life" that saturated fine writing.

What was not at all clear was what she wanted. Encouragement, merely, for a poet who was casting herself as one of Higginson's "young contributors" on the threshold of a career? Or something more, some recognition for a writer who had already passed that threshold and was already "fairly in print"? Or even more? A sympathetic hand to help support her through some emotional trial for which her writing was a consolation and a remedy? Or was she doing the most obvious and simple thing of all, asking him to help her get her poems published in *The Atlantic,* to become a Young Contributor?[19]

At this point, Emily Dickinson had already published four poems in the *Springfield Republican.* Within the next four years, she would publish six more, three in a newspaper raising funds for wartime philanthropic work, one in a New York literary magazine, another in the *Brooklyn Daily Union,* and a sixth in the *Republican.* (All of them would be reprinted by the *Republican,* as well, and one by the *Boston Post.*) She did not really make an irrevocable decision not to publish her work until 1866, after which she let only one poem be printed before she died. For the moment, though, she was willing to see her verses published, and even to take the risk that an editor might tamper with her lines and correct her studiedly vagrant grammar and punctuation. The most likely thing Higginson might suppose was that she was asking for help toward publication. He was well placed. *The Atlantic* was an admirable vehicle for a poet. He had just encouraged young men and women to become contributors. Above all, he had assured them that the literary marketplace was a place of honor, a place for "noble" undertakings.[20]

The only certainty is that whatever she wanted from Higginson, Emily Dickinson did not ask for it openly. In her first letter, she fussed with the idea of verse being "alive" until it became a conceit, hoping that hers "breathed," and promising to feel "quick" gratitude whether his answer was yes or no. He would realize, with a moment's thought, that her "quick" did not mean prompt but live gratitude if the answer was yes, and perhaps even that she would feel a negative reply to the quick. She did not tell him anything about

[19] Her first letter to Higginson is in Thomas H. Johnson and Theodora Ward, eds., *The Letters of Emily Dickinson,* 3 vols. (Cambridge, Mass., 1958), 2:260. These volumes will be cited here simply as *Letters.* The quotations in the next few paragraphs are from this first letter.

[20] CF. Karen Dandurand, "Publication of Emily Dickinson's Poems in Her Lifetime," *Legacy* (Spring 1984): #7, and "New Dickinson Civil War Publications," *American Literature* 56 (March 1984): 17–28.

herself—especially not the crucial fact that she had already written enough poetry to fill a very substantial volume, and had published some of it. She did not even sign her letter, but enclosed a card with her name on it. And she asked for secrecy, as though she were doing something that might trouble or disgrace someone if they found out she was writing poetry. She addressed him, too, the way someone ten years younger might have: "if you please — Sir." She was casting herself very much as an inexperienced beginner, asking him to make a life-or-death judgment.

But if she was straining a little, being coy, and kneading Higginson's own metaphor into a conceit, she was also meeting him directly on his own ground. It was, after all, his metaphor of living language that she chose to play with. And she carefully noticed other things, too. He had put considerable emphasis on the fact that an editor is a very busy man, whose time should not be wasted. So she asked if he was "too deeply occupied" to read her work, and a few words later wondered whether he would have the "leisure" to do it. One of the four poems she chose to send him, "Safe in their Alabaster Chambers," had not only been recently printed, it had been put through major revisions of exactly the type Higginson had asked for in his "Letter."

Higginson answered within a week. He was guarded, but he did not discourage her. He asked her to send some more poems if she had them. And he asked her to tell him something about herself: How old was she? Whom did she read? Did she have companions and family? He mentioned Whitman in some connection—probably as someone she might want to read. And he recommended "Circumstance," by Harriet Prescott Spofford (a silly, forest-Gothic tale about a monster of the Maine woods, the "Indian Devil," who attacks a pious frontierswoman with the intent of either raping or eating her, perhaps both). He also seems to have asked her whether she had published any of her work before.[21]

Dickinson took a little time to study her reply. She may have been ill. At least she told him she was. But that may have been an effect, to heighten the dramatic convention she chose as the opening for her second letter. His "kindness," she said, deserved "earlier" gratitude—

---

[21] Harriet Prescott Spofford, "Circumstance," *The Atlantic Monthly* 7 (1860): 558–65. Almost all of the letters from Higginson's side of this correspondence have been lost. It is a simple matter, however, to reconstitute many of his questions and observations from Dickinson's replies.

a reference to her own play on "quick." But she was sick, writing even now from her bed. Then she thanked him for the "surgery" he had done on her poems, fixing a doctor-patient relationship between one whose "life" is in danger, and another who had the power to preserve it.[22]

His surgery had been "not so painful as I supposed," so she was glad to send him three more pieces. She admitted that she had some difficulty choosing them—hinting now that there were many to choose among. But this difficulty was one that Higginson would surely understand, for he had talked in his "Letter" about writing as giving ideas a "clothing of words." Again she took up his metaphor. She had "thoughts," she said, and could tell the good ones from the bad as long as they were "undressed." But when she put them into words—"in the Gown"—they all "look alike, and numb." Her method at this point was cautious, but its direction was plain: She was gradually piecing together a picture of herself as a poet who was serious, had written much, and had thought deeply about her work— and in the very terms Higginson had proposed.

When she turned to Higginson's specific questions, though, she was elusive, passionate, comic, and childlike by turns, and sometimes all at once. She began with the simplest question, her age. But she transformed it into another question, and she answered it with a lie that concealed another truth: "You asked how old I was? I made no verse — but one or two — until this Winter — Sir." Higginson may never have noticed that this answer was given in iambic feet, the line made perfect by the final "Sir." But he could hardly fail to notice that she was once again equating being alive with writing poetry, saying that she was only as old as her first verses. And the point became inescapable when she went on, still in meter. "I had a terror— since September — I could tell to none." The sentences added up to a perfect stanza, in what the hymnals called "common meter," four lines alternating between four and three iambic feet, with rests at the ends of the second and fourth lines:

> *I made no verse — but one or two —*
> *Until this Winter — Sir —*
> *I had a terror since September —*
> *I could tell to none —*

---

[22] Her second letter, dated April 25, 1862, is in *Letters*, 2:404–5.

She was equating the writing of poetry with life itself. That much was plain. (She may even have meant to suggest that she had been pregnant with verse for almost nine months—since September—and terrified that it might not "be alive.")[23]

Whatever she may have meant by "terror," she was certainly not giving Higginson the information he had asked her for. And the rest of her letter was just as crafty and evasive. She did make a concession by listing a few of the people she had read—but most were writers he had named in his "Letter." Instead of telling him what her education had been, she said "I went to school — but in your manner of the phrase — had no education." She did admit she had had a companion when she was "a little girl," a man who had "taught me Immortality." But he had died, she said in words meant more to mystify than inform: He had "ventured too near, himself," to immortality. Another "companion" had refused to let her "be his scholar — so he left the land." The first was no doubt her girlhood friend Benjamin Franklin Newton. The second could have been Bowles or Wadsworth. But it made no difference at all whom she was talking about, since Higginson could never had guessed anyway. She was not giving him the brief curriculum vitae he wanted, but was striking a stance whose purpose was to intrigue, not to inform.

The central message she was trying to get into her second letter is that she was isolated, with no one whose judgment of her work she could trust, and with no teacher but "my Lexicon." (Higginson, in his "Letter," had said that an unabridged dictionary was the origin of all the writer's art.) And so she framed her account of her family in a way that made introducing them at all into a tedious courtesy that ought to fatigue Higginson as much as it did her. To make sure the point would not be lost, she prefaced it with an insistence that her true companions were not people at all, but superior "natural" things: "You ask of my Companions Hills — Sir — and the Sundown — and a Dog — large as myself, that my Father bought me — They are better than Beings — because they know — but do not tell." This

---

[23] Wolff, *Emily Dickinson,* supposes that this "terror since September" was quite specific—a terror she might go blind. It is true that years later Dickinson wrote at least one letter describing this fear. It is equally true, however, that she was treated in Boston for problems with her eyes in 1864 and 1865, not in the relevant years of 1861 and 1862. And no matter what the biographical sources of the supposed terror may have been, there is no blinking the facts that she gave Higginson no clue at all to what it was, and that she carefully joined the months of terror she had felt to the question of whether her verse was alive or "numb."

brought the family into the picture in a way that said plainly that they were at best of no consequence to her, and at worst an impediment to her learning "how to grow":

> I have a Brother and Sister — My mother does not care for thought — and Father, too busy with his [lawyer's] Briefs — to notice what we do — He buys me many books — but begs me not to read them — because he fears they joggle the Mind. They are religious — except me — and address an Eclipse, every morning — whom they call their "Father." But I fear my story fatigues you.

Susan Gilbert Dickinson, who had been giving Emily Dickinson intelligent criticism and encouragement for years from the house next door, was not mentioned. And the stifling picture of Dickinson family life was far from true. But truth and accuracy were beside the point. Her goal was to get Higginson to help her. The poems she was sending were to convince him that she deserved the help. The letters were to convince him that she needed it. It was a delicate strategy. If she went too far, or became too baffling, Higginson might turn away, convinced that she was just another "hysterical" young writer. And so she worked her way through his questions quickly, pausing for only a sentence or two on each. And she left the most difficult question of all for the last.

Higginson had asked her about publishing. The exact form of this question is impossible to reconstruct from her reply. He may have asked, simply, whether she had ever had contact with an editor before. Or he may have asked more directly whether she had published any of her poems—a perfectly appropriate question in the circumstances. He may even have asked whether she wanted to publish. But whatever Higginson asked her, she couched her answer in a way that was meant to explain—in her riddlesome fashion—why she had written to him, and what she wanted from him:

> Two Editors of Journals came to my Father's House, this winter — and asked me for my Mind — and when I asked them "Why," they said I was penurious — and they, would use it for the World —
> I could not weigh myself — Myself —

> My size felt small — to me — I read your Chapters in the
> Atlantic — and experienced honor for you — I was sure you
> would not reject a confiding question —
>   Is this — Sir — what you asked me to tell you?

No doubt the two editors she was talking about were Bowles and
Holland. But, again, it makes no difference: Higginson could never
have guessed, and it would not have mattered if he had. Her point
was that she would not give her "Mind" unless she were sure it had
"weight" and "size" enough. To signal the importance of the point
she had lapsed again into meter: "I could not weigh myself —
Myself — / My size felt small — to me." There was only one sensible reading Higginson could give this: Would he weigh and
measure the poems? And the immediate invocation of his *Atlantic*
piece, coupled with what might strike him as a bit of editorial
terminology—the word "reject"—must have convinced him that
what she had in mind was publication. But she was very reticent. All
she was sure of was that he would not "reject" her "confiding
question." But he still had not answered it definitely enough, so she
was reformulating it even as she explained why she had asked it in
the first place: Were the poems big enough and heavy enough? To
help him with his answer she sent three more sample pieces with this
second letter.

Higginson could hardly have understood the intricate and deliberate game Emily Dickinson was playing out. She had given Bowles'
Republican more than one piece of her "Mind" already, and had sent
him other poems that he had decided not to print—though there can
be no doubt that she would have let Bowles publish them if he
wished. She seemed ready enough to stop being "penurious" with
her work. She probably was thinking hard about Higginson's infallible public, and about submitting her work to his "average judgment of intelligent minds." What she was not willing to do was to
say, simply and directly, that she wanted to begin to publish her
work. In effect she was asking him to make the commitment first, to
tell her that her poems ought to be published. Then, and only then,
would she declare herself.

This time, she had to wait several weeks. But when Higginson did
reply, he told her she really was a poet, and that he wanted to stretch

out his hand "in the dark" to her. This, she said, did not exactly make her drunk, since she had tasted "Rum"—praise—before. But it did make her so grateful that if she tried to thank him, "my tears would block my tongue." His judgment had surprised her, she said, and had even for a moment "swung" her. He had "bled" her with his first letter, but now had sent a saving "balm." True, her "dying tutor"—Newton—had told her he would like to live to see her become a poet. But in those early years, he was the only public she could conquer: "Death was much of Mob as I could master — then." Later, she had been troubled by "a sudden light on Orchards, or a new fashion in the wind." These had brought on a kind of "palsy," which her verses barely "relieved." But she had not been certain, until Higginson told her so, that she was really a poet.[24]

Higginson must have puzzled mightily over these maneuvers. Her implicit narrative of her career was plain enough. She had once been a beginner, whose tutor thought her promising. Then she had assumed the conventional stance of the poet driven to write by a troubled heart—"a palsy, here"—for whom art was only a remedy for pain. Now Higginson's assessment—that she was a serious poet after all—had brought her to a new stage. But if all this was clear, Higginson could only have struggled as she went on. What did she mean by saying next that after she had gotten his first letter she had recognized the "justice" of his criticisms, but could not "drop the Bells whose jingling cooled my Tramp"?

No matter how much he puzzled, though, Higginson could hardly have understood what was happening on the apparently erratic pages of this third letter. An enormously talented poet was making a declaration about the nature of her calling, and was using his judgment that she really could be a poet as a rhetorical occasion for a cryptic soliloquy on herself, her work, and—most urgently—her relationship to the literary marketplace. But it would have taken a reader much more attentive than Higginson could plausibly have been (and a reader who knew Emily Dickinson much better) to have deciphered her pronouncements.

She went about her task with even more than her usual craftiness. The first step was to make it clear to Higginson that his was not the only judgment of her worth as a poet she had had. This was the real point of the little exercise on the fact that she had tasted "Rum"

[24] This third letter, dated June 7, 1862, is in *Letters,* 2:408–9.

before. And to drive the point home, she said archly that, after all, "Domingo" could come but once. "Domingo" was obviously a synonym for rum. But it alluded also to the Lord's Day, and it was meant to suggest that she already had had the Sabbath assurance of being told by someone she could invoke as a deathbed authority, her dying tutor, that she could truly be a poet. This was also her way of revealing to Higginson that she had been writing poetry for years, and not just "since September." This in turn was meant to claim an artistic center of gravity of her own, a method and a manner that were hers by dint of effort and "trouble," and one that she could not—or would not—surrender. This was the meaning of her odd remark that despite his earlier criticisms of her poems, she could not drop the bells whose jingling cooled her tramp. The horse's "Tramp" was her work, and the harness bells were the idiosyncratic poetic effects she employed, effects Higginson had from the start found too irregular.

These initial moves laid the groundwork for a gesture that made this letter just as artful as any poem she ever wrote. She told Higginson that she valued his praise to the point of weeping. But then she told him that she would not follow either of the two pieces of advice he had given her. One was that she try to smooth the syntactical and metrical bumps and snags out of her poems. He found her "gait spasmodic" (the prompt for the horse metaphor she used in her reply). Her answer was a sarcastic "I am in danger — Sir." Higginson's second bit of advice had followed from the first. Until she learned to write better-regulated verses, she ought to postpone publishing. Her response to this was to spring a trap she had carefully built into their correspondence. She "smiled" that he could suggest such a thing, insisting—in iambic feet and with much alliteration—"that being foreign to my thought, as Firmament to Fin."

It was important to Emily Dickinson that Higginson understand that she was rejecting both kinds of advice he had given her, and for reasons that were connected. Since she would feel like a fish out of water if she published her poems, she would have no public. This meant that her poems would not be judged by Higginson's "infallible" mass of readers. But neither would his criticisms. This set her at liberty to dismiss his statement that her work was "uncontrolled" by saying tersely "I have no Tribunal." The implication was plain enough: If she had no tribunal—Higginson's own term for the public—then he also had no court of appeals to sustain his school-masterly complaints.

This was a curious outcome for a correspondence that had begun with Higginson's advice to young contributors who *did* want to publish, and with a letter from Emily Dickinson submitting poems to his editorial judgment. The moment she had created was, in fact, perverse. And she knew perfectly well that she had to give some sort of justification for her sudden lateral maneuvers, her insistence that publishing had never crossed her mind, and her near-ridicule of the very editorial help she had asked for. The justification she chose amounted to a little meditation on the relationship between publication and "fame." She made an important but unspoken assumption that the deepest meaning of publication was that it was the pursuit of fame. But "If fame belonged to me, I could not escape her — if she did not, the longest day would pass me on the chase." The desire for fame was ruinous. If she had it, it would define and confine her; if she did not get it, she would never rest from her pursuit of it. And either way, she would lose the hills, the sundown, and her dog—those "Companions" so superior to human "Beings." Better, she said, to keep her insignificant "Barefoot-Rank."[25]

However spasmodic the gait she chose for putting it, her point was quite conventional. Generations of artists on both sides of the Atlantic had learned to assume a modest posture, a barefoot rank, a relinquishment of fame—all as a way of establishing credentials that gave them a claim on the moral and esthetic high ground. But this claim was precisely what promised to lift them out of modesty, shoe their bare feet, and bring them fame—and to do all this without making them seem to be either the captives or the pursuers of success in the marketplace. With variations of detail, this was precisely the strategy that had been deployed by Irving, Garrison, and Emerson. It was, in fact, the conventional way most serious professional writers in the first half of the nineteenth century justified their struggles in the literary marketplace. Confronted with this strategy, a wily man of letters like Higginson would have to choose between smiling

---

[25] Wolff, *Emily Dickinson,* has some interesting comments on Dickinson's use of terms like "feet" and "gait" as a way of talking about poetry itself. The observations are somewhat marred, however, by a supposition that every reference to feet, and even toes, must refer to poets and poems. One of the strongest temptations Dickinson's poetry holds out to its readers is the notion that the poems are systematically encoded, with certain words like "circuit," or "circumference" serving as master cryptological keys. See, for a quite intelligent example, 214–16.

at a familiar maneuver, or dismissing this mysterious poet as a waste of time, a true amateur who simply did not understand the way the game was played. If she stopped here, he could either write back assuring her that there was no real contradiction between fame and a barefoot rank, or he could politely end the correspondence, sure that she had not gotten the point of his "Letter."

Shrewdly enough, though, Emily Dickinson did not stop here, with her dismissal of fame (and of Higginson's criticisms of her work). Instead she swiftly proposed that Higginson think of her *neither* as a would-be professional nor as a misguided amateur. She proposed, instead, that she become his apprentice. She had just turned ironically on his criticisms, saying archly that she was in danger and had no tribunal. Now, without missing a beat, she suddenly asked him to be her "friend" and her "Preceptor." And she did more. She promised to be a docile, pliable student who would be no bother to him. She had already said that her size "felt small." Now she insisted that she had "a little shape" and would not crowd his desk or make more noise than a tiny mouse in his bookshelves. She wrote these lines across the page as prose; but in fact they were a jingle, in her customary meter:[26]

> *I have a little shape —*
> *It would not crowd your Desk —*
> *Nor make much Racket as the Mouse,*
> *That dents your Galleries —*

She had begun this third letter addressing Higginson as "Dear friend." She ended it by addressing him more formally: "But will you be my Preceptor, Mr. Higginson?" Then she signed it as "Your friend, E. Dickinson." This was not a sign of wavering or uncertainty, though. It was only the final gesture in a letter in which she had run an astonishing course, taking up successive stances with bewildering speed. She had made herself, in the space of a few paragraphs, a child prodigy whose first Tutor had promised she would someday be a poet; a stock romantic figure who wrote to relieve the "palsy" that troubled her heart; a toughened eccentric, scorning to publish and determined to keep her own spasmodic gait

---

[26] The idea of the poet as a mouse was no doubt adapted from Browning's *Aurora Leigh*. Cf. Walsh, *The Hidden Life*, 260.

no matter what Higginson might say; and, finally, a docile apprentice, looking to him for "control" as the sailor who "cannot see the North" looks to "the Needle." This exercise must have astounded Higginson (though in the end it probably flattered him, too). But the postures and stances all had one thing in common: They all were alternatives to precisely the thing he had invited the "Young Contributor" to be, a publishing author pursuing a career in the literary marketplace with dash and efficiency.

After a variety of feints, Emily Dickinson had finally defined her relationship to Higginson as one of student and apprentice. She submitted more poems in July and August—along with her verbal portrait of herself, with the eyes like sherry in the glass the guest leaves. She asked for more "surgery," and promised to repay him with "Obedience — the Blossom from my Garden — and every gratitude I know." She asked him if her work was becoming "more orderly." She confessed "ignorance" of large things, and promised to follow his "precept," even when she did not "understand it, always." If he called her "wayward," she would ask him to help her improve. If he fell silent for more than a month, she would ask, "Did I displease you, Mr. Higginson. But won't you tell me how?"[27]

It was in this unlikely context that she made her famous claim that "My Business is Circumference," as though signing herself "Your Scholar" and assuming the role of the student-apprentice gave her title to "Infinity" and all of "Possibility." She understood the logic that lay behind the seeming contradiction between being an unobtrusive "mouse" and making such extravagant claims. The capitalized "My" in "My Business" referred not to herself—a lower-case me—at all, but to the figure of the poet. "When I state myself, as the Representative of Verse — it does not mean — me — but a supposed person." She was relinquishing the possibility of becoming a publishing poet, a writer of substantial size—something between a mouselike "student" and the master of "Circumference." And her reasoning was much the same as Emerson's had been in *Nature*. The figure of the poet had to become diminished, in worldly terms, in order to know the "horizon." In order to see all, her "supposed person"—like his—had to become "nothing."[28]

It all lasted only a few months, really—though the correspondence

---

[27] July, August, October 6, 1862, *Letters*, 2:411–12, 414–15, 417.
[28] The comments about "Circumference" and the "Representative of Verse" are in a letter of July 1862, *Letters*, 2:411–12.

generated an intermittent afterglow that lasted for many years. By November of 1862, when Higginson went south to take command of his regiment, it was clear that in practice his actual role as her preceptor had ended as soon as she proposed it. He did not even trouble to tell his "student" that he was going off to war, but left her to find out from an article in the *Republican*. On her part, when she wrote him in South Carolina, she could only wonder how she would find out if he died: "Should you, before this reaches you, experience immortality, who will inform me of the Exchange?" Higginson did not answer, so she asked him for a second time whether she had somehow offended him. After he was wounded and came home to Massachusetts, their correspondence was scattered, warm enough on both sides, but without any of the urgency of the 1862 letters. She refused at least three times to go to Boston to meet him—even though one of these invitations was to attend an intimate reading by Emerson at an afternoon salon. Higginson finally came to Amherst for a brief, baffling call on her. She continued to write poems, but at nothing like the pace of the late 1850s and early 1860s. From time to time, she asked him again to be her teacher, but whatever potential that notion ever had had was plainly gone. In 1869, and again ten years later, she thanked him for having saved her life—bursts of gratitude that must have confused Higginson more than any of her other remarks.[29]

Taken in itself, Emily Dickinson's brief attempt to apprentice herself to Higginson was unimportant. It was even a bit of a sham—perhaps on both sides. But she was playing out a personal drama that is extremely important to an understanding of the ways that nineteenth-century writers adapted to the literary marketplace. Her idea that she might become Higginson's "scholar," and submit her work to the judgment of a "preceptor," was her way out of the same kind of tangle that Irving, Garrison, and Emerson had struggled with. Like their solutions, hers was idiosyncratic. But its idiosyncrasy does not mask the fact that her solution was, like theirs, a response to the one fact that no writer of her generation could ignore: the market and the writing career it defined. For her—as for Hawthorne or Melville, Thoreau or Whitman, Poe or Longfellow, or any other writer or would-be writer—the marketplace was the most important existen-

[29] The remarks about Higginson's saving her life are in letters of June 1869 and c. 1879, *Letters*, 2:460, 649.

tial reality. Its enticing possibilities, its demands, and its potential for humiliation set the boundaries within which she, no less than any other writer of the nineteenth century, defined her work.

Higginson has taken a good deal of criticism, sometimes rather harsh criticism, for his supposed failure to see that Emily Dickinson was a great poet. The truth of the matter is that he did see her as much more than a curiosity (which she also was, of course). In 1869, he wrote her that she sent out "rare sparkles of light" from a "fiery mist." He acknowledged the "strange power" of her letters and verses. And he even struggled to understand her isolation on the exact terms she had proposed to him. It "isolates one anywhere to think beyond a certain point," he said, "or have such luminous flashes as come to you." Perhaps no nineteenth-century reader could have been more intrigued by Dickinson's poetry than Higginson was, or have understood it better.[30]

Higginson's problem was not esthetic or literary at all, but professional. He could hardly imagine thinking without writing, or writing without lecturing, or lecturing without publishing—all as steps in "the career." If he was confused or put off, it was not by her poetry but by her insistence that what mattered was not career at all, and even less his infallible public tribunal. What mattered to her was the "luminous flashes" themselves. Even turning the flashes into written poems, putting them "in the gown" (much less seeing them in print), made them seem "numb." Little wonder that Higginson told her that he thought often that he should write to her, but was always afraid he might say the wrong thing, and "miss that fine edge of thought which you bear." If the two of them ran skew to each other, it was not because he failed to appreciate her great talent as a poet. It was because they had two different notions of what the writing enterprise was all about.

The real point, though, was that they could have these opposing notions precisely because they shared some common understandings. She had made a number of crucial choices—choices that actually accepted Higginson's conception of the authorial career—which made dialogue between the two of them possible at all. Her first choice was to write to a man who had published an essay of advice

[30] Higginson's letter of May 11, 1869, is in *Letters*, 2:461–2.

for authors who wanted to publish their work, an essay designed to put to rest delicate fears of the cheapening effects of the marketplace. She then chose, as Higginson had carefully prompted his readers to do, to set aside the question of sex. Her letters to Higginson—like most of her poems—took no explicit notice of the fact that she was female. She also accepted the conventional (though still quite new) relationship between a writer and an editor. She submitted work. She asked for criticism and evaluation. She used good ink and good paper. She promised not to waste his time. In all these important ways, she stepped fully into Higginson's professional world.[31]

So Emily Dickinson's notion of apprenticeship was not made out of whole cloth. It was contrived on a set of assumptions that Higginson and other professional writers understood. There was a reading public, a literary marketplace, whose dimensions everyone described as "vast" or "infinite." The existence of this well-defined marketplace was what now gave practical meaning to the notion of a literary career and to fame. In this context, the decision to be always a student-apprentice had implications it would not otherwise have had. In a market economy with little place for masters and apprentices in any industry (and no place at all for them in the industry of literature) the notion of apprenticeship was plainly archaic. In Higginson's version of the world, there were no masters or patrons, no apprentices or clients, but only authors and the public—with editors between, playing their amiable role of brokerage. And exactly because it was archaic, an apprenticeship could be permanent. The time never need come, in a world where professional writers could imitate dry-goods jobbers, when the apprentice had to stand forth a journeyman, actually producing goods for sale. On this

[31] In an essay written a few years before his "Letter," Higginson had taken a rather strong position in favor of treating women as the intellectual equals of men. "Ought Women to Learn the Alphabet," *The Atlantic Monthly* 6 (1859): 137–50. It is highly probable that Dickinson had read this essay, too. No doubt Emily Dickinson's complicated, masked minuet with Higginson was determined by many things of a purely individual and psychological nature, things peculiar only to her. The odd combination of overweening modesty and halting pride, the impossible dangling of riddles whose answers he could not have understood, the pronounced rhetorical flirting, the quick flights from intimacy to distance and back again—all these may have been symptomatic of something even she did not understand. But individual "psychology"—the set of deeply private determinants that no doubt contend for the control of every individual's consciousness, language, and deeds—is only a facet of experience, not its key. Emily Dickinson, like everyone else, had her own secret burden of "terror." But she, again like everyone else, had to translate mere psychology into the quite public terms and categories that her time and place made available. She made conceptual choices among those terms and categories, and in the process she came to a definition of herself and her art.

logic—and precisely this logic was dictated by Higginson's characterization of the writing career—the notion of the apprentice poet was an explicit repudiation of the marketplace, with its "average judgment of intelligent minds."

But it was more. In its specific historical setting in mid-nineteenth-century New England, the idea of being always a student or an apprentice poet was liberating. It made every poem an exercise. Every possible theme, every possible point of view, every experience, real or imagined, posed a disciplining task: to write an exemplary poem on that theme, about that kind of experience, or from that point of view. The tools were ready to hand: the highly ordered, commonplace poetic forms of the Protestant hymnal tradition. The materials were equally plentiful and convenient: her beloved unabridged dictionary, her "Lexicon." She had models enough in the poets she loved to read. As for subject matter and point of view, she could range easily among the conventional attitudes of her time, place, and social class. She had easy access to a great variety of stock and even sentimental concerns—anything from trains and shipwrecks to flowers and the passing of the seasons; from birth, love, and marriage to the paradoxes of Scripture, conversion, and the problem of faith. Even death and the afterlife, and particularly the question of the relationship between the living and those already "gone," were not a peculiar preoccupation of Emily Dickinson. In her social class, at least, death and the afterlife were probably the topics that writers were most certainly expected to master.[32]

Of course every writer of the time—and especially every poet—worked with these same tools and materials, and took up these same subjects. What made Emily Dickinson unusual—aside from her talent—was that she elaborated a conception of her work that made it always a preparation. In principle, she was always learning how to write. What mattered was technique, the workings of the art and craft of poetry itself. What mattered in fact was exactly what Higginson had called "expression," language with a "warm life" of its own. Every poem could be, in effect, a kind of practice piece, a study. And each study could be thought out and completed with little or no concern for *what* was being said. The sewn packets

---

[32] An interesting discussion of the sentimentalization of death in the middle part of the nineteenth century is Ann Douglas, "The Domestication of Death," in *The Feminization of American Culture* (New York, 1977). See also Arien Mack, ed., *Death in the American Experience* (New York, 1973).

into which she copied her poems were not her urgent statement about the world, or even about herself. They were a kind of portfolio, a display collection of the best work the apprentice could do.[33]

Emily Dickinson's portfolio was large, and it included a bewildering variety of poems. Scores—perhaps even hundreds—were written to accompany a gift—a sprig of evergreen or some garters she had knitted; to console or to congratulate or to patch up a quarrel. Such poems were quite literally occasional pieces. A great many other poems (probably more than we will ever be able to say with any certainty) were first written to be included in letters. Another large body of poems was prompted by something someone had said to her, or that she had heard about in the town, seen in her garden, or read in some magazine, novel, or newspaper. It might be something personal, like the religious conversion of someone she knew. It might be something as trivial as watching a caterpillar make a cocoon. It could be a civic occurrence, like the opening of a new railroad line into Amherst. It could be one of those events, like a ship's sinking, that showed up in mid-nineteenth-century newspapers under formulaic headlines such as "Pathetic Tragedy."

There were many things Emily Dickinson did not know about, of course. Also, there were constraints on the kinds of things members of the upper middle class—male or female—were supposed to discuss, and by and large Emily Dickinson respected the decorum of her social class. But within the boundaries set by ignorance or decorum, she could take up anything, however casually, as a fit subject for a poem. And when she did, she had little trouble adjusting her tone, her point of view, her selection of metaphors, and even a poem's intellectual content to the occasion or to the person she was writing for.

She could write in the voice of a child—fretful, innocent, or pathetic. She could speak with the voice of an old woman, too weak to sew straight seams anymore. Or she could deploy a voice that belonged to no particular time of life. She could speak as a woman; more often, she could write as a poet whose sex was irrelevant. Occasionally, she even used an explicitly male voice. And she had an

---

[33] Higginson described Dickinson's poetry in 1890 as "The Poetry of the Portfolio," of the type people write "for the relief of their own minds, and without thought of publication." In "An Open Portfolio," reprinted in Caesar R. Blake and Carlton F. Wells, eds., *The Recognition of Emily Dickinson* (Ann Arbor, Mich., 1968), 3.

astonishing repertoire of tones and manners for use with any of these voices. With equal ease, she could be naive, as she admired a flower; plaintive, as she mourned the loss of a friend; sarcastic, as she mocked the "dimity convictions" of some churchgoing ladies; cute, as she put a riddle whose answer might be something as simple as the name of a plant; piously ministerial, offering assurances that a host of battle dead would be raised because their names were on God's "Repealless — List"; or petulant, complaining that Moses was treated unfairly when he was not allowed to enter the Promised Land. All these and a dozen more tones and stances came readily to her—perhaps not in her daily life, but certainly in her poetry.

Of course, it would be absurd to doubt that Emily Dickinson invested a great deal—perhaps most of what she *had* to invest—in her poetry. But the investment was in writing the poems, in the activity itself. And she could make this sort of investment without committing herself at all to what the poems actually said about any particular subject, or even to the tone and manner in which it was said.

Her flexibility is most apparent in the many poems that deal with religious questions—probably the most urgent set of questions for her social class at midcentury. She could—and often did—hold out the possibility of an afterlife of the cheerful sort many of her neighbors seem to have believed in. "Tie the Strings to my life, My Lord, / Then I am ready to go!" she could write:[34]

> Goodbye to the Life I used to live —
> And the World I used to know —
> And kiss the Hills, for me, just once —
> Then — I am ready to go!

On the other hand, in "I felt a Funeral, in my Brain," she could picture dying as a limitless fall into mere nothing, and the terminal consciousness of the dead as no more than a chilling realization of that intolerable truth:[35]

> And then a Plank in Reason, broke,
> And I dropped down, and down —
> And hit a World, at every plunge,
> And finished knowing — then —

---

[34] *Poems*, 279.
[35] Ibid., 280.

She could comfortably copy these two poems into the same sewn packet. Even more: She could use the same quirky metaphor in both these poems to define the community to which the dead would belong. In "Tie the Strings to my life, My Lord," the "Everlasting Race" is the traditional community of the saints elect, persevering forever, even unto eternity; dying is a kind of joining, and the dead one is "Held fast in Everlasting Race — / By my own Choice, and Thee." In "I felt a Funeral, in my Brain," the "Race" has only two members, for the dead one is joined only to emptiness: "And I, and Silence, some strange Race/ Wrecked, solitary, here."

In the voice of a fretful child, she could take up a pair of related questions about eternity that were much agitated in the popular religious literature of the day. Would the soul lose its particular human identity in paradise? Would the family circle be restored in heaven?[36]

> What is — "Paradise" —
> Who live there —
> Are they "Farmers" —
> Do they "hoe" —
> Do they know that this is "Amherst" —
> And that I — am coming — too —

But, probably in the same year, she could also describe death's aftermath in a voice that was not only mature, but bitter and older than death itself. Some of her most famous lines were meant to say, unambiguously, that there was no resurrection ("Morning") and no eternal life ("Noon"). The meek may inherit the earth, but no more than the earth; for them there is only the grave.[37]

> Safe in their Alabaster Chambers —
> Untouched by Morning
> And untouched by Noon —
> Sleep the meek members of the Resurrection —
> Rafter of stain,
> And Roof of stone.

[36] *Poems*, 215. On this theme in Dickinson's work, see Joan Burbick, "'One Unbroken Company': Religion and Emily Dickinson," *New England Quarterly* 53 (1980): 62–75.
[37] *Poems*, 216.

This verse and the poem about the child's hopeful questioning—"Do they know that this is "Amherst"/ And that I—am coming — too?"—were written within a few months of each other. During these months, nothing changed in Emily Dickinson's ideas about death. In these and dozens of other poems on immortality and faith, she was exercising her talents, experimenting with different poetic solutions to the standard religious problems of her day, making verses that bespoke by turns confidence, hope, doubt, or bitter surrender. The choice was dictated by the poem she happened to be writing, not by a determination to make an enduring record of her ideas.

Immortality was, as Emily Dickinson told Higginson, the "flood" subject. But she could fluently adopt, for the sake of her poems, openly contradictory positions on it. And on the closely related subjects of faith, grace, and election, Dickinson wrote dozens of poems proposing drastically differing solutions. Her views not only ran the gamut of available doctrinal positions in the Protestant discussions of her time and place, but toyed as well with doubt and even atheism. Sometimes she appeared simply to endorse the old notion of God's lordly power to choose whomever he wished for a "Title" to a place in the "Kingdom":[38]

> *He put the Belt around my life —*
> *I heard the Buckle snap —*
> *And turned away, imperial,*
> *My Lifetime folding up —*
> *Deliberate as a Duke would do*
> *A Kingdom's Title Deed —*
> *Henceforth a Dedicated sort —*
> *A Member of the Cloud.*

She understood the religious language of her day perfectly well, and could speak it as well as anyone alive. So she knew that this conception of salvation as an unbreakable contract between the Sovereign and the chosen placed the elected person in a chaste relationship to the world: bound still to the chores that made up everyone else's daily round but equally bound to treat every human intimacy as secondary to the exclusive covenant with God. So she went on to

[38] Ibid., 273.

describe, in a highly condensed way, that "Dedicated" life that would "henceforth" be in the world but not of it, declining its "invitations" on God's behalf:

> *Yet not too far to come at call —*
> *And do the little Toils*
> *That make the Circuit of the Rest —*
> *And deal occasional smiles*
> *To lives that stoop to notice mine —*
> *And kindly ask it in —*
> *Whose invitation, know you not*
> *For whom I must decline?*

But with equal skill—and perhaps an equal lack of conviction—she could turn completely away from traditional notions of covenanted election. She could write of the human capacity for unending hope in the somewhat childlike fashion of the sentimental revivalism that was gradually subverting New England's older religious orthodoxy:[39]

> *"Hope" is the thing with feathers —*
> *That perches in the soul —*
> *And sings the tune without the words —*
> *And never stops — at all —*

But it cost her nothing to shift into the conventions of Victorian doubt, and to suggest wryly that if we must live in the world, seeing through a glass darkly, a scientific apparatus is probably more useful than the tunes of a feathered hope:[40]

> *"Faith" is a fine invention*
> *When Gentlemen can see —*
> *But Microscopes are prudent*
> *In an Emergency*

Emily Dickinson's capacity to write poems from disparate and even contradictory points of view was not limited to poems about

[39] Ibid., 254.
[40] Ibid., 185.

religious matters. She could do it at will (and do it brilliantly) on any subject whatever. She could write love poems without being in love. (She could also be in love—whatever that might have meant to her—*without* writing poems about it, surely.) She could write pieces about marriage without thinking of marrying anyone, ever. "I'm wife," she could write, and then go on to make an analogy that equated marriage to heaven, and the single state to earthly life:[41]

> *I'm "wife" — I've finished that —*
> *That other state —*
> *I'm Czar — I'm "Woman" now —*
> *It's safer so —*
>
> *How odd the Girl's life looks*
> *Behind this soft Eclipse —*
> *I think that Earth feels so*
> *To folks in Heaven — now —*
>
> *This being comfort — then*
> *That other kind — was pain —*
> *But why compare?*
> *I'm "Wife"! Stop there!*

But she could also produce a fine working of a delicate conundrum on the impossibility of life together on earth for any two devout lovers, laying out all the options and rejecting each in turn. The poem begins simply enough: "I cannot live with you." But it leads through four logical steps to a final "Despair." Her first step is to say that she could not live with her love, because "real" life lay beyond the grave—the "shelf" the sexton kept the key to:[42]

> *I cannot live with you —*
> *It would be Life —*
> *And Life is over there —*
> *Behind the Shelf*

---

[41] Ibid., 199.

[42] Ibid., 640. There is nothing at all in this poem to suggest that the speaker is female. For the sake of simplicity, "she" is a workable term to use in a discussion of it; "he" would do just as well.

> *The Sexton keeps the Key to —*
> *Putting up*
> *Our life—His Porcelain —*
> *Like a cup —*
>
> *Discarded of the Housewife —*
> *Quaint — or Broke —*
> *A newer Sevres pleases —*
> *Old Ones crack —*

Second, she could not die with her love, since in the nature of things one had to die first, and she could not bear to go either before or after:

> *I could not die — with You —*
> *For One must wait*
> *To shut the Other's Gaze down —*
> *You — could not —*
>
> *And I — could I stand by*
> *And see You — freeze —*
> *Without my Right of Frost —*
> *Death's privilege?*

But, she could not "rise" with her love, since the glory of "Your Face" would outshine Jesus' and make heaven seem trivial. While her lover might have tried to serve God, she had been blinded by love to anything as "sordid" as paradise:

> *Nor could I rise — with You —*
> *Because Your Face*
> *Would put out Jesus' —*
> *That New Grace*
>
> *Glow plain — and foreign*
> *On my homesick Eye —*
> *Except that You than He*
> *Shone closer by —*
>
> *They'd judge Us — How —*
> *For You — served Heaven — You know,*
> *Or sought to —*
> *I could not —*

> *Because You saturated Sight —*
> *And I had no more Eyes*
> *For sordid excellence*
> *As Paradise*

Fourth, it would be equally unthinkable to suppose that one of the lovers might be saved and the other damned. Either way, she would be lost:

> *And were You lost, I would be —*
> *Though My Name*
> *Rang loudest*
> *On the Heavenly fame —*
>
> *And you were You — saved —*
> *And I — condemned to be*
> *Where You were not —*
> *That self— were Hell to Me —*

Of course there was a fifth possibility: The lovers might live together and both be damned. This possibility is not explicitly explored. Instead, the poem treats it implicitly as the deductive *outcome* of the reasoning. The lovers must suffer a kind of damnation. Exactly because they do love, they must undergo an infinite suffering, which begins not after death but here, and now:

> *So We must meet apart —*
> *You there — I — here —*
> *With just the Door ajar*
> *That Oceans are — and Prayer —*
> *And that White Sustenance —*
> *Despair —*

It posed no intellectual problem, on the other hand, for Emily Dickinson to write gently of the sentimental idea that a husband and wife were joined for earthly life as "One Being." She could easily, and without irony, celebrate marriage in the terms set forth in the conventional ceremony, in which the couple was united as bone of bone and flesh of flesh, for better or for worse. In this life, the wife vows to take the greater part of any grief that comes; if joy comes instead, she will lay up her share of it for him; he can taste his cake and have hers, too:[43]

> *Forever at His side to walk —*
> *The smaller of the two!*
> *Brain of His Brain —*
> *Blood of His Blood —*
> *Two lives — One Being — now —*
>
> *Forever of His fate to taste —*
> *If grief— the largest part —*
> *If joy — to put my piece away*
> *For that beloved Heart —*

All their lives this couple will "know" each other. But there will be something else that neither will "learn" about the other until they die and the great "Change" of heaven comes. They will join the neighborhood of the rapt, made "Just" by grace. Then their knowledge of each other will be completed; they will know what no book—not even the best of books—could teach them on earth:

> *All life — to know each other —*
> *Whom we can never learn —*
> *And bye and bye — a Change —*
> *Called Heaven —*
> *Rapt Neighborhoods of Men —*
> *Just finding out — what puzzled us —*
> *Without the lexicon!*

Perhaps the simplest fact of all about the body of poetry that Emily Dickinson produced and hid away is that it is intellectually disjointed. Within any given poem, she might drive relentlessly along very visible and very straight lines; indeed many of her poems strike an argumentative stance, and read like syllogisms laid neatly end on end. But taken as a whole, her work is a tangle of conflicting ideas. To be sure, there are stylistic habits aplenty; and because of this, it is usually quite easy to recognize a poem as one of hers. But the poetry

---

[43] Ibid., 246.

does not provide consistent answers to the rather ordinary kinds of questions she characteristically chose to address. And even the emotional attitudes she struck in the poems varied enormously. On paper, at least, she was as deft at being cute as she was at grieving; she was as apt a cynic as she was a believer. Tokens of affection came easily to her, but so did poetic despair. If they are innocently read, the poems do not yield up a coherent and consistent way of understanding the world.

But Emily Dickinson has been studied mainly by people who have admired both her work and the person they thought did the writing. And Dickinson scholars and critics have been almost unanimous in their hope that the poetry could somehow be read as a coherent and consistent manifestation of that person. They have used a variety of tactics for dealing with the obvious contradictions, disparities, and discontinuities of her surviving poems. But the tactics all fall within one of two main critical strategies. One is canonical. The other is interpretive.

The canonical strategy is a simple one (and one that poets, more than most writers, are frequently subjected to). The whole corpus of poems is submitted to a process of selection. Poems that do not fit a particular view of what Emily Dickinson really thought are dismissed as "cloying" or "sentimental," and so outside a proper Dickinson canon. The remaining poems are described as "urgent," "tense," "embittered," or "gentle"—depending on what version of Emily Dickinson is being generated.

The interpretive strategy normally comes into play when canonical maneuverings threaten to exclude too *many* poems or to exclude poems that seem fine on some set of esthetic criteria. Such poems can always be "read" and "deciphered" in a way that makes them consistent with a particular version of what Emily Dickinson was really up to, and what the poems are really about. They might seem to be trivial, merely sweet, or tediously conventional. But once they have been "understood," they can be fitted into a given scheme, a specific view of the poet's work and experience.[44]

---

[44] Obviously, all writers—and particularly poets—are fair game for both processes, canonization and interpretation. Indeed, these two processes are the very life of literary criticism as "appreciation." But writers who publish their work have somewhat more to say about the matter than writers who do not; they at least participate in making initial decisions about what they want to have counted among their "works." And this fact can have some restraining effect on the ways later generations go about deciding not only what to take seriously, but how to "read" a given text.

Emily Dickinson's poetry has been peculiarly vulnerable to the effects of both canonical selection and excessively imaginative deciphering. She participated very little in initial decisions about what parts of her work should be published, when and where, and in what order. Her own selective editing, which consisted mainly of making fair copies in her hand-sewn packets in the early 1860s, has not helped much. She has been extremely susceptible to being made over in the image of her readers, who—like readers of Poe, Blake, Whitman, and other idiosyncratic poets—have become something of a cult. And nothing has been more important for her admirers than the simple fact that she did not publish her work, that she scorned the corrosive effects of the literary marketplace, where anxious vanity, deception, and trimming were the rule.

Sometime after the climax of her correspondence with Higginson, Dickinson wrote the familiar poem that has become almost an anthem for some of those admirers:[45]

> *Publication — is the Auction*
> *Of the Mind — of Man —*
> *Poverty — be justifying*
> *For so foul a thing*
>
> *Possibly — but We — would rather*
> *From Our Garret go*
> *White — Unto the White Creator —*
> *Than invest — Our Snow —*
>
> *Thought belong to Him who gave it —*
> *Then — to Him Who bear*
> *It's [sic] Corporeal illustration — Sell*
> *The Royal Air —*
>
> *In the Parcel — Be the Merchant*
> *Of the Heavenly Grace —*
> *But reduce no Human Spirit*
> *To Disgrace of Price —*

What the poem was meant to say seems perfectly obvious. Publication is a foul thing to do. It might be justified by poverty. But "We"

---

[45] *Poems,* 709.

would rather preserve our white innocence unto death than "invest" our poems and our innocence ("Our Snow" serves as a convenient metaphor for both). Thought is the property of God, who gives it. Its true heir ("The Royal Air") is Jesus, God's Thought become corporeal, the Word become flesh. If you must, sell Christ, and in the bargain—"In the Parcel"—you might as well merchandise God's grace, too. But do not deprive any human spirit of grace—that is, do not dis-grace it—by putting a price on it.

It is difficult to imagine a more uncompromising rejection of the practices of the literary marketplace. But there are oddities in the poem, oddities that may cut against the grain of its explicit argument. To start with, Dickinson chose a word—"auction"—that she must have known derives from the same Greek and Latin words that also give "author," "authentic," and "augment." Etymologically, the first lines suggest that by publishing, authors "give increase" to the mind of man. This lends an ironic ring to the line describing publishing as "so foul a thing." Whatever irony may be present is reinforced by the remainder of the poem, which says that publishing is worse even than the very worst crime the Christian imagination could contemplate, the selling of Christ by Judas. And Dickinson went directly on to a second, slightly less obvious blasphemy when she substituted the Human Spirit for the Holy Spirit that ought to complete the Trinity.

If there is a potential for irony—even for plain sarcasm—here, there may be even more in the clichéd picture of a poet in a garret, demurely preserving a white innocence until she meets her spotless Maker. Decades earlier, the notion that an author probably will "starve in some garret" was already conventional, so conventional that a woman like Frances Maria Lloyd Garrison could use it to mock her own son's literary ambitions. Dickinson's use of the cliché gives point to her observation that this poet—whose "We" may be editorial, but might also be comically regal—is straining after a purity so perfect that it will not allow her to "invest" her poems. In the context established by the poem, the primary sense of "invest" is certainly economic. But there is a plausible second sense, too. Higginson had talked of writing as a way of giving thoughts a "clothing of words." In her letters to him, Dickinson had spoken of writing poems as putting them "in the Gown." The garret poet's conscience is so severe that she will not deign even to write poetry, much less to publish it.

It is certainly true that Dickinson scorned the marketplace. She did repudiate fame, and say that she preferred to be "nobody." She did insist that she had no business but "Circumference." But all these scornings and repudiations did not really free her from the effects of authorship by profession. On the contrary, they made her in the end even more the creature of the literary marketplace than many of her contemporaries were. "Success," she once wrote, "is counted sweetest — /By those who ne'er succeed." In the same paradoxical way, the literary marketplace shaped her experience as a poet at least as definitely as it did the experience of any professional writer. She chose to be a permanent apprentice, to be always *learning* to be a poet. This choice, in the abstract, implied nothing. But choices are not made in the abstract. She defined herself against a historically specific conception of a career in "letters" as a "profession." She understood perfectly well what this meant. In the nineteenth-century world of market capitalism, literary productions had become commodities, valued like other commodities not for their use but for what they might yield in the system of exchange. She also understood that no amount of pretending by professional writers that they were serving "expression," "spirit," "art," or some other higher end could finally wipe away the insistent realities of their trade. For her these realities had little practical bearing. Her father lived almost as long as she did, and left her very well off. This made her independent of the market, economically free of Higginson's "average judgment of intelligent minds."

But Emily Dickinson had, in the end, no way of appraising art that could replace the weights and measures of the literary marketplace. The idea that a writer ought to serve a church or a political party, taking its values and needs as the measure of the worth of his work, was almost dead, in the United States at least. It had certainly become unthinkable for a writer to serve an individual patron. But parties and governments, churches and patrons, had always been disciplines, allowing writers to serve purposes, and giving their work a measurable instrumental import. Now, in the world of the market, there was only publication and the approval of some sort of reading and buying public. To repudiate publication was to repudiate the only discipline, the only available conception of art as an instrument with any purpose that lay outside itself. And so what Emily Dickinson chose when she chose to be always the student-apprentice was freedom.

But it was a peculiar sort of freedom, that "white Election."
Within the boundless circumference she claimed for her work, every
verse counted for as much or as little as any other. The play of words
might be stunningly brilliant—as it often was. But it was only the
play of words, only "expression," only the poetic moments, that
counted. She really was a creature of the literary marketplace, perhaps its ultimate creature. She deplored it, but she always accepted its
terms and defined herself against its criteria rather than on positive
criteria of her own, so that her most vigorous statements about
herself were renunciations, statements about what she would not be,
rather than about what she would be. So the marketplace used her,
perhaps even more completely than it used those many men and
women who did submit their work to Higginson's public "tribunal." It may be that "Publication — is the Auction" was really her
balance sheet, a way of counting the costs; and not the costs of
publishing, only, but the cruel price of not fully "investing" her own
work.

Walt Whitman, frontispiece of Leaves of Grass, *1855*

Epilogue

THE ESSENCE OF RETAIL

On the first left-hand page of the 1855 edition of *Leaves of Grass* was a superb engraving, made from a daguerreoetype. Readers were left to suppose that it must be a picture of the author, a visual token for the name, Walt Whitman, that was mysteriously missing from the title page at the right. The picture is of a man watching. It is a smallish picture, at least in relation to the trim size of the book. In part, this was necessary because engraving needed to be condensed enough so that the lines and hatchings did not show too plainly. But the requirements of technology were perfectly consistent with the writer's esthetic purpose. Situating the picture on a much larger blank page was obviously meant to heighten an effect of solitude and separation, as though this figure of a man were self-imposed on elemental space.

The parabola—defined only by a careful arc in the shading around the legs—is an implicit peephole, and was part of a very skillful attempt to control the effect of looking in such a way that the line of sight is unidirectional, and travels from the figure, through the page, to the reader, as if the viewer is not so much seeing the man as being watched by him. One of the poet's eyes is nearly hidden in the shadow, but this only calls attention the more strongly to the other eye. There is also a rather emphatic suggestion that this figure cannot do anything *but* look. His dress—the open shirt, the rumpled trousers, the soft hat—is vaguely like a workingman's, an artisan's perhaps—or, more accurately, a bohemian version of artisanal garb. But his stance argues, plainly, that work is the remotest of possibilities. Hands and fingers, which might do something, are kept sedulously out of sight, touching only his own body. Legs and feet, which might have suggested that he had come from somewhere to stand behind this aperture, and at some point would surely leave it, are cropped. He is not just a man watching; he is a man whose nature is to watch. The following year, in a prose sketch, Whitman would describe the figure himself, and rather well, as a "rough-looking man," with a "careless, lounging gait. Walt Whitman, the sturdy, self-conscious, microcosmic prose-poetical author of that incongruous hash of mud and gold—'Leaves of Grass.' "[1]

Five years later, in 1860, in the little New York magazine *Vanity Fair,* there appeared one of the earliest parodies of Whitman. Its premise was that the poet is a clerk, or "counter-jumper," in a dry-goods shop, and was conflated, in his "essence," with the cloths he sold and the coins he took in:[2]

I am the Counter-jumper, weak and effeminate.
I love to loaf and lie about dry-goods.
I loaf and invite the Buyer.
I am the essence of retail. The sum and result of small profits and quick
*   returns.*
The Picayune is part of me, and so is the half cent, and the mill only
*   arithmetically appreciable.*
The shining, cheap-woven sarsnet is of me, and I am of it.
And the white bobinet,
And the moire antique, thickly webbed and strewn with impossible
*   flowers. . . .*
All these things are of me, and many more also,
For I am the shop, and the counter, and the till.

Considered only as a piece of literature, *Leaves of Grass* is probably a great poem. At least there is a long critical tradition that says so.

[1] Walt Whitman, "Street Yarn," in *New York Dissected,* Emory Holloway and Ralph Adimari, eds. (New York, 1936), 130.
[2] Quoted in Eugene T. Lalor, "The Literary Bohemians of New York City in the Mid-Nineteenth Century" (Ph.D. diss., St. John's University, 1977), 318.

Indeed, it has always invited parody exactly because it has a peculiar "essence" that is distinctive and perhaps even fine. And so it may be a grievous lapse of taste even to quote an insulting parody written by an obscure man like Fitz-James O'Brien, who was part of an equally obscure literary bohemia that flourished only briefly in New York during the decade just before the Civil War. But *Leaves of Grass,* like every piece of literature, was something else, too. It was a *work* of art, a made thing, a product of human action. And more, still. It was an object produced for sale, a commodity. And O'Brien's parody captured *this* "essence" of the poem perfectly. Perhaps more than any other American writer of his age, Whitman was the manufacturer and retailer of his own goods. He not only wrote *Leaves of Grass,* he designed the book and its cover, set some of the type, and sold the product by mail order for a number of years before he gave it to a bookseller to market for him. And if his fine and distinctive lines were "part of him," like the sarsnet, bobinet, and moire of the parody, so was the simple existential fact that he was producing those lines for the marketplace. The picayunes (nickles), half-cents, and mills that it brought him were "part of him" as well.

Of course, the figure of the poet in *Leaves of Grass*—that "I, Walt" who is its dramatic speaker and the rhetorical locus of whatever lyrical force or narrative continuity the poem has—stands quite apart from such pecuniary purposes. He loafs and lies, not about the grass, but in it. He makes his observations at an appropriate distance from the hot struggles of men and women, standing "apart from the pulling and hauling." And as the "Song of Myself" that begins *Leaves of Grass* unfolds, it becomes very clear that this figure has not the slightest interest in half-cents and mills. What makes the parody shocking is not just that it mocks the poet as well as the poem, but that it mocks the poet in a particular way: by charging him with a shopkeeper's materialism that lies about material goods, pretending that they have some kind of elevated spiritual significance when all they are in truth is his means of livelihood and profit. The parodist had a canny eye for the most urgent pretension of Whitman's poem. The figure of the poet was willing to take on the burden of every human shortcoming and frailty but one: the desire to produce something that could bring him a material reward. The figure of "I, Walt," the figure of the engraving, was capable of anything and everything *but* writing for money.

Indeed, Whitman defined the essence of his figure of the speaker of

Leaves of Grass precisely by substituting the capacity to see for the ability to *do* anything, until finally, when the poet has at last learned to see everything, there is nothing left for him but to die—as he does in the last lines of "Song of Myself." So, in the quaint and curious sexual stereotyping of the period, the figure of the poet really was "weak and effeminate," as the parody said. He is given to looking and to talking, rather than to more "manly," practical things like action, invention, and production. But for Walter Whitman, writing—in countless newspaper pieces, in hackney-writer short stories and novels, and in his poems, too—had also been an activity, and a distinctly entrepreneurial activity at that. Whatever else writing was for him, it was the career that he hoped would bring him both fame and a livelihood. He had known perfectly well what it meant to be, at the end of the day, "the sum and result of small profits and quick returns." Walter Whitman was as much a creature of the literary marketplace as his "I, Walt" was a renunciation of it.

But if Whitman's figure of the poet had no capacity for action, he still was avowedly heroic, as though he were the principal character in an epic struggle in which Homer—not Ajax or Achilles—would do the battle. The task Whitman gave him could hardly have been more demanding. He was to give voice to a poetic vision of the world that would capture and reveal the essential "spirit" of his nation and his age. Such a thing could be the achievement, according to the theory of the poem, of only one man and only one work of art. And so the poet-figure confronted a terrific alternative. Either he would be uniquely successful, would be that triumphant seer for all America, or, if he failed, his suffering would be equally heroic, even like that of Christ crucified.

At an important juncture in "Song of Myself," Whitman had his poet say he has been "stunned" by his own efforts, that he needs a moment to get his bearings: "O Christ!" he says, "My fit is mastering me!" He has come, in more than one sense, to a crux. He realizes that all his looking and talking, all that seeing and chanting the lives of the multitudes, has made him into a type of Messiah, taking onto himself the burden of sin for mankind. His tour de force of insight has become a staggering burden, a fit of possession. He feels the hammer blows and the bludgeon, and the "bloody crown." He hears the mockers and the insults. It is almost too much for him. But he realizes, suddenly, that he is "on a verge of the usual mistake." The mistake is to suppose that he is alone in his effort, that he "could look with separate look on my own crucifixion and bloody crowning." He realizes that the limitless human multitude he has been observing and chanting is not only an object of sight and a subject for poetry, but that it is his audience and constituency as well. This gives him the courage to go on, to be "confided" to the "grave of rock," knowing that he will rise again and this time "troop forth replenished with supreme power," exactly because he has become one with the "average, unending procession."

A good deal of pathos has been attached to this exalted vision of the poet and his constituency, the poet "replenished," filled again with "power" because of his intimate relationship with an "unending procession" of people. The plain historical fact is that the earliest editions of *Leaves of Grass* did not reach the multitudes at all, but only a small body of readers, many of them manifestly eccentric in one way or another. But the pathos is misplaced, for the vision belonged properly not to Walter Whitman himself but to the figure he created in the poem. That figure was, in the end, a linguistic figment, a figure of speech. And for that figure of speech, the vision worked admirably. His nexus with the multitude, who served not just as a subject matter but as audience and constituency, too, was realized perfectly well within the poem and on its terms. There was, in other words, an inherently ironic relationship between Whitman and his figure of the poet—ironic in the root sense that Walter Whitman knew about something that was concealed from the poet-figure, and concealed as a dramatic necessity.

But what begins as irony can end in simple belief. In the long run, Whitman himself became more than a little confused about the fact that his figure of the poet was only his own work of art. For Whitman, "Song of Myself" seemed to become a kind of script for real life. In the process, he appeared to forget that he had written a poem whose dramatic action turned on a certain relationship between the poet and his public, but had done so in a way that was pointedly silent about one significant element of that relationship: The real poet, the man who created the figure of the poet, was also a seller, and his readers were not just an audience and certainly not a constituency, but a body of consumers. And, ever since, we have read Whitman more or less on his own terms, accepting his contention that the motives that produced his poetry had nothing to do with the fact that he lived in a society that was above all capitalist, a society in which poets, no less than other people, had become habituated to the production of goods for exchange in the marketplace.

The primary conceptual undertaking of *Leaves of Grass* was to generate the figure of the poet and to define his relations with the world around him. Those relations were quite noninstrumental and unprofitable, and in a practical sense inconsequential. They rested entirely on the poet's capacity to see and to speak, rather than to do. And he derived nothing from them but suffering, solitary exaltation, and the final release of death. But this set of dramatic choices was to a considerable extent an outcome of Whitman's own acute consciousness of the conditions that anyone who wrote for the market—instead of for patrons, governments, political parties, or churches—labored under. Whitman's figure of the poet realized the seductive promises of the marketplace completely: He insistently claimed nothing less than the whole world as his audience, and he presented himself as the perfection of autonomy, a man bound to the world only by his words. Whitman's figure of the poet also realized perfectly the negative implications of the literary marketplace. He was as vulnerable and frail as he was imperious and brash. And his travail was most acute when he realized that he "could look with separate look," cut off from the "unending procession," isolated from the multitude he so much needed, not only to write about but to be read by.

Whitman's figure of the poet—his principal artistic creation—was in these important ways a reflex of his consciousness of the literary marketplace. He was, finally, the "essence of retail." Of course, the poet-figure may have been other things as well. He may have been a product of the influence of various models of the poet created by other writers (of Emerson's idea of the poet, perhaps most particularly). Or Whitman's conception of the poet may have been an upshot of a set of personal, "psychological" traits that Walter Whitman had, perhaps even a symptom of some kind of personality "disorder." Alternatively, a case could be made that Whitman's poet expressed the mentality of a social class—of artisans, shopkeepers, and small entrepreneurs perhaps—and that *Leaves of Grass* was only Whitman's effort to find an appropriate voice and manner for an art that would be the class-property of a petite bourgeoisie in its hour of most alert self-consciousness. Or, the figure of the poet could be seen as a conception that was related somehow to the emergence of certain vague and ultimately silly myths about "national character" that were taking shape at the time—a growing conviction that

Americans were somehow more "democratic" and "individualistic" than other people.

These and a variety of other ways of getting at the meaning of Whitman's manner of figuring the poet are certainly plausible. But whatever else Whitman was—the subject of literary influences, an idiosyncratic, perhaps half-mad man, the son of a carpenter and the partisan of independent producers, or, more simply, a peculiarly "American" voice—he was a writer by calling. And it may be that writers' individual "psychological" characteristics, the "influences" they choose to be under, the popular mythologies they decide to tap and use, all must finally be accommodated to the way they conceive the nature of the writing career. And that conception, which lies behind their ways of figuring the writer, must necessarily come to terms, one way or another, with the relations of production, the set of arrangements that make writing and reading possible as social acts in given historical situations.

If Whitman chose to be influenced by other writers' ideas about the poetic calling, it was because he found those ideas could be adapted to the ways he defined the relationship between his figure of the artist and the "average unending procession." Whatever personal or psychological dispositions he had, he could only translate them into art in ways that comported somehow with the fact that he was an author by profession. If he chose to work with some of the language and manners of the hard-handed artisan, impatient of elite pretensions and refinements and given to some of the boastful "yawping" of a self-made man, it was because he intended to force his poet rhetorically into a constituency-relationship with a large, ungainly, and ill-mannered public. If he chose to toy with myths about national character and destiny, he did so only to claim them as the proper subject matter for a figure of the poet who could "sing" the myths only because he could present himself as the supremely independent voice of an entire society, not subject to any patron or party, church or institution that had any prior claim on his words. And this was, ultimately, the essence of retail.

INDEX

A NOTE ON THE TYPE

The text of this book was set in a digitized version of Bembo, a well-known Monotype face. Named for Pietro Bembo, the celebrated Renaissance writer and humanist scholar who was made a cardinal and served as secretary to Pope Leo X, the original cutting of Bembo was made by Francesco Griffo of Bologna only a few years after Columbus discovered America.

Sturdy, well-balanced, and finely proportioned, Bembo is a face of rare beauty, extremely legible in all of its sizes.